THE GAME IS AFOOT

THE GAME IS AFOOT

The Enduring World of Sherlock Holmes

Jeremy Black

ROWMAN & LITTLEFIELD
Lanham • Boulder • New York • London

Published by Rowman & Littlefield
An imprint of The Rowman & Littlefield Publishing Group, Inc.
4501 Forbes Boulevard, Suite 200, Lanham, Maryland 20706
https://rowman.com

86-90 Paul Street, London EC2A 4NE

Distributed by NATIONAL BOOK NETWORK

British Library Cataloguing in Publication Information Available

Library of Congress Cataloging-in-Publication Data

Names: Black, Jeremy, 1955– author.
Title: The game is afoot : the enduring world of Sherlock Holmes / Jeremy Black.
Description: Lanham : Rowman & Littlefield, [2022] | Includes bibliographical references and index.
Identifiers: LCCN 2021030044 (print) | LCCN 2021030045 (ebook) | ISBN 9781538161463 (cloth) | ISBN 9781538161470 (epub)
Subjects: LCSH: Doyle, Arthur Conan, 1859–1930—Characters—Sherlock Holmes. | Detective and mystery stories, English—History and criticism. | Holmes, Sherlock.
Classification: LCC PR4624 .B48 2022 (print) | LCC PR4624 (ebook) | DDC 823/.8—dc23
LC record available at https://lccn.loc.gov/2021030044
LC ebook record available at https://lccn.loc.gov/2021030045

™ The paper used in this publication meets the minimum requirements of American National Standard for Information Sciences Permanence of Paper for Printed Library Materials, ANSI/NISO Z39.48-1992.

For
Dan Hannan

CONTENTS

PREFACE

> The old stories of Conan Doyle had a wit and fairytale poetry of hansom cabs, gloomy London lodgings and lonely country estates.
>
> – Edmund Wilson, 'Who Cares Who Killed Roger Ackroyd?' (1944)

'Ageless, invincible and unchanging', the rolling caption at the start of *Sherlock Holmes and the Voice of Terror* (1942), and of the subsequent Universal Studios films that appeared until 1946, captured a potent approach to the most famous detective in history, one memorably depicted in these films by Basil Rathbone, who plays Sherlock Holmes as a brave and successful warrior for truth.

But Holmes was also rather a man of his time. The master-detective of his age, and a lasting presence, he enlivened late Victorian Britain. Introduced in that society, with the stories written from 1887 to 1927 (although largely dealing with the period 1887 to 1914), Holmes throws light on that society but, for us in the twenty-first century, needs to be explained in terms of his age and his readers. The role of the readers means that we will go back to include late Victorian society as a whole from about 1870, for the Holmes stories were not, of course, written for those born in 1887.

This book is designed to provide a history of England from the perspective of the Holmes stories, so as to help in their elucidation. For Holmes, we will discuss the changing England, the ways in which his problems relate to these changes and, in particular, London as the world city. We will reach out with Holmes to show how London is the place to which foreigners come, and thus presents the setting in which people identify and disguise themselves, often for criminal purposes. The problem of false identity is seen as integral to a very much speeded-up world in which the constraints of censuses and other forms of regulation are evaded. Holmes battles people passing themselves off as others, and this disguise is significant in political, family and business terms. Moreover, he is presented as the most successful and important detective in the world. In and from London, Holmes is able to consult in order to settle problems for all, including the pope.

So, let us step forth into Baker Street and accompany our assailant on crime.

ACKNOWLEDGEMENTS

Publishers, bookshops and libraries are to the fore for keeping Holmes in print and in readily available and inexpensive copies. I first encountered Holmes not in a swirling fog on Baker Street—for that was ten miles away, and fog was being banned—but as a small boy in the very impressive Edgware Public Library, a then-modern work of much glass but also, crucially, of many books. I preceded Constable Twitten, the star of Lynne Truss's hilarious series of murder stories, in reading the stories 'at an impressionable age'. The books should always come first, and those by Doyle, rather than the great many that have riffed (or ripped) off them. Doyle's books should also come before watching cinema or television versions, although they also offer us much in firing up the interest of readers and listeners.

I am most grateful to Benedict Cadbury, Bruce Coleman, Eileen Cox, Grayson Ditchfield, Alan Downie, Crawford Gribben, Mike Moore, Murray Pittock, George Robb, Peter Spear, and Philip Waller, who have kindly commented on earlier drafts. I know how much work that entails. They are not responsible for any errors that remain. It is a great pleasure to thank Susan McEachern, again, for being such a superb publisher. This book is dedicated to Dan Hannan, a friend of wit and wisdom.

1

INTRODUCTION

The Age of Holmes

One summer night, a few months after my marriage, I was seated by my own hearth smoking a last pipe and nodding over a novel, for my day's work had been an exhausting one.

– Dr John Watson in 'The Crooked Man' (1893)

Maître. . . . It is the author, Sir Arthur Conan Doyle, that I salute. These tales of Sherlock Holmes are in reality far-fetched, full of fallacies and most artfully contrived. But the art of the writing – ah, that is entirely different. The pleasure of the language, the creation above all of that magnificent character, Dr Watson. Ah, that was indeed a triumph.

– Hercule Poirot in Agatha Christie, *The Clocks* (1963)

Although Holmes in the 1940s was 'solving significant problems of the present day' in the twelve Universal Studios Basil Rathbone films of 1942–46, he was very much produced for his age and in the specific moments and opportunities of a career and a publishing world. Having written short stories without him, short stories that richly repay reading, Arthur Ignatius Conan Doyle (1859–1930) created Sherlock Holmes in 1887 for his novel *A Study in Scarlet*, which initially appeared in *Beeton's Christmas*

Annual. Of Irish Catholic stock, Doyle's Edinburgh childhood was blighted by his father's alcoholism and psychiatric illness. Dividing the family, these afflictions also caused hardship from which Doyle was rescued by wealthy uncles and given a Jesuit education before studying at the University of Edinburgh Medical School from 1876 to 1881, during which time he began to write short stories.

A ship's doctor in the Arctic and off West Africa, Doyle set up an independent medical practice in Portsmouth in 1882 but found it difficult to establish himself, subsequently also failing as an ophthalmologist – for want of patients, not talent. An Edinburgh medical teacher, Joseph Bell, however, provided Doyle with the model for Holmes; given his travails in finding work in the profession, he had the time to write. And write he could. In *A Study in Scarlet*, Holmes tells Watson: 'There's the scarlet thread of murder running through the colourless skein of life, and our duty is to unravel it'. Not Shakespeare's 'primrose way to the everlasting bonfire' from his brilliant murder story *Macbeth*, but the writing is easily good enough to accompany the adventure. Characters were rapidly defined, and the plot of *A Study in Scarlet* moved forward with both suspense and economy.

A Study in Scarlet was an impressive debut for Holmes, but, although *The Hound of the Baskervilles* (1901) is an undoubted masterpiece, Doyle generally did better with the great detective in short stories, which, indeed, was the form for most detective stories of the period. It was a form that lent itself to the magazine, which was so important a publishing outlet. Moreover, short stories fitted well into developing leisure and work patterns, the latter most clearly the case with the rise of daily commuting, particularly into London.

Highly successful, Doyle, however, found Holmes an encumbrance to his many other interests, not least writing across a range of genres. As a result, in December 1893, in 'The Final Problem', Doyle had Holmes and his apparent nemesis, Professor Moriarty, die together in a fight at the Reichenbach Falls in Switzerland. Doyle wanted to be free of this particular creation in order to better focus on others. He wrote widely for the remainder of the decade, including *Round the Red Lamp* (1894), *The Exploits of Brigadier Gerard* (1896), a successful historical novel, *Tragedy of the Korosko* (1898) and *The Green Flag* (1900), both the latter dealing with imperial struggle.

Nevertheless, in 1901, in large part in response to strong public demand, the great detective returned in the gripping *The Hound of the Baskervilles*. Its presentation was such that it could have been set before 'The Final Problem'. However, the *Hound* was followed in October 1903 with 'The Adventure of the Empty House', a short story in which the episode at the Reichenbach Falls is fully explained. Continuity was demonstrated with its appearance in *The Strand Magazine*, which was then selling four hundred thousand copies monthly.

Thereafter, there followed a series of stories that, according to their sales numbers and years of publication, to the surprise of many, rendered Holmes as more of a post-Victorian hero than a Victorian one. Yet, at the same time, many of these stories were still set at precise moments in Victoria's reign, while the character is Victorian. Indeed, Holmes's world is very much that of Victorian London, not least with its murky streets and its drug use. The stories also offer a world of order and meaning that predate the shocks of World War One (1914–18) and its aftermath. There is a different way of approaching reality to that which was to become fashionable after World War One, although Doyle's long-standing interest in Spiritualism might also be seen as an aspect of the flux of the 1920s. At any rate, Holmes was a way of remembering the Victorian age. After a period of mixed writing in the 1920s, much of which lacked the intensity of the earlier short stories, Holmes last appeared in 1927, bringing to a close his fifty-six short stories and four novels.

Two years later, Doyle reviewed Holmes in the John Murray introduction to the four 'long stories'. In the preface, written just over a year before he died, Doyle shaped his experience, writing of *A Study in Scarlet*:

> It represented a reaction against the too facile way in which the detective of the old school, so far as he was depicted in literature, gained his results. Having endured a severe course of training in medical diagnosis, I felt that if the same austere methods of observation and reasoning were applied to the problems of crime some more scientific system could be constructed. On the whole, taking the series of books, my view has been justified.

Indeed, Holmes is very much a detective of method. He is both the forerunner of crime scene investigators with his forensic approach, and yet also able to deduce drives and causes from his strong understanding of psychology and willingness to engage with the unexpected.

The range of Doyle's writing also deserves attention. This includes character creation, as with Mr Sherman, the Lambeth animal keeper in *The Sign of Four*, a brilliantly realised Dickensian grotesque, and one delivered with more economy than Dickens, who had only been dead for two decades. In the same novel, Jack Smith, the 'prodigy' child who prefers two shillings to one, is another brief Dickensian flurry, as likewise is the idea of the 'Baker Street irregulars'. The irony in that book operates on many levels, as when Watson calls on Mary Morstan and Mrs Forrester at Camberwell and tells them about developments:

> 'It is a romance!' cried Mrs Forrester. 'An injured lady, half a million in treasure, a black cannibal, and a wooden-legged ruffian. They take the place of the conventional dragon or wicked earl'.
>
> 'And two knight-errants to the rescue', added Miss Morstan, with a bright glance at me.

Doyle's other writings were wide ranging; the first novel, *The Mystery of Cloomber* (1888), related to the eventual punishment in Britain by Buddhist *chelas* (priests) of two British officers for a war crime during the First Anglo-Afghan War (1839–42). This was an echo of an important theme in Wilkie Collins's successful detective novel *The Moonstone* (1868). Indicating variety and energy, Doyle also produced many historical novels, as well as the science fiction classic *The Lost World* (1912), and several plays. His protagonists varied greatly. Thus, Dr Challenger of *The Lost World* was very different to Holmes.

A keen amateur sportsman, the impressive Doyle played in goal for Portsmouth Amateur Football Club, and he also played in ten first-class cricket matches between 1900 and 1907, taking the wicket of W. G. Grace on one occasion. Doyle's *Wisden* obituary remarked: 'he could hit hard and bowl slows with a puzzling flight'.

Doyle was also a protagonist of Empire, serving as a volunteer doctor in 1900 during the Boer War (1899–1902) and writing in defence of British participation in both that war and World War One. Subsequently, one of his sons was seriously wounded in the Battle of the Somme in 1916. Living life to the full, Doyle twice stood for Parliament as a Liberal Unionist (1900, 1906), but without success, and campaigned against miscarriages of justice. A lapsed Catholic who was president of the Divorce Reform Union from 1909 until 1919, Doyle was very interested in Spiritualism and a prominent supporter of it.[1] Short or long, any and every account and biography of Doyle captures his energy, his ability and the opportunities presented him by a meritocratic, commercial and hugely energetic society.

So also with Holmes, introduced from the outset as the 'consulting detective', whose biography can be reconstructed in part through the Doyle stories, although less so than with many other characters in fiction. Born in 1854, with ancestors who were country squires, although his ancestry receives scant attention, Holmes is a talented but somewhat reclusive undergraduate. His university is not identified, but an East Anglian contemporary possibly implies Cambridge, while the science pursued at Holmes's university suggests that he may have gone to Sidney Sussex College, which, unusual among Cambridge colleges, had a laboratory.[2]

Holmes then finds London a basis for his fame and fortune. He literally stars there as if in a play, as captured in 'The Six Napoleons' (1904), when he reveals to Inspector Lestrade and Dr Watson the famous black pearl of the Borgias concealed in the bust of Napoleon that has driven the destruction of a sequence of busts:

> Lestrade and I sat silent for a moment, and then, with a spontaneous impulse, we both broke out clapping as at the well-wrought crisis of a play. A flush of colour sprang to Holmes's pale cheeks, and he bowed to us like the master dramatist who receives the homage of his audience. It was at such moments that for an instant he ceased to be a reasoning machine, and betrayed his human love for admiration and applause.

Many of the stories were inherently theatrical, which explains why they subsequently worked well on film and television. Holmes craves adventure, and that is his compulsion. It leads him, in *The Sign of Four* (1890) and thereafter, to cocaine when there is no adventure:

> 'I cannot live without brain-work. What else is there to live for? Stand at the window here. Was there ever such a dreary, dismal, unprofitable world? See how the yellow fog swirls down the street and drifts across the dun-coloured houses. What could be more hopelessly prosaic and material? What is the use of having powers, doctor, when one has no field upon which to exert them?'

Reflecting the strong nineteenth-century fascination in the potential of machines, including the development of calculating machines, Holmes is presented as sublimating his personality accordingly. In *The Sign of Four*, Holmes claims not to note the attractiveness of Mary Morstan, leading Watson to remark: 'You really are an automaton – a calculating machine. There is something positively inhuman in you at times'. Holmes responds in a critique of Victorian sentimentality, one that rests on the clinical observation of Doyle, a doctor:

> 'It is of the first importance . . . not to allow your judgment to be biased by personal qualities. A client is to me a mere unit, a factor in a problem. The emotional qualities are antagonistic to clear reasoning. I assure you that the most winning woman I ever knew was hanged for poisoning three little children for their insurance-money, and the most repellent man of my acquaintance is a philanthropist who has spent nearly a quarter of a million upon the London poor. . . . I never make exceptions'.

This theme is developed later in the novel when Holmes underlines to Watson that 'with all these data you should be able to draw some just inference'. In turn, Athelney Jones, the Scotland Yard detective, refers to Holmes as the 'theorist. I'll never forget how you lectured us all on causes and inferences and effects in the Bishopsgate jewel case. . . . Stern facts here – no room for theories'. Thus, fact and theory are treated by Jones as opposed, while Holmes, in contrast, emphasises 'very simple reasoning'.

We turn to London in the next chapter, but, first, it is the market that is of note. Like other novelists, Doyle wrote for money. He needed it, both for himself and to support and establish his family. He had five children from two wives: the first, Louisa Hawkins, died in 1906, and he married Jean Leckie the following year. The first two Holmes novels, *A Study in Scarlet* (1887) and *The Sign of Four* (1890), brought him money, the former £25, the amount Agatha Christie received for *The Mysterious Affair at Styles*. However, it was the short stories published in *The Strand Magazine* that were crucial to his success. This was a new monthly appearing in Britain and the United States from January 1891, with early sales of about three hundred thousand an issue in Britain – sales that subsequently rose.

These sales were an aspect of the interaction between entrepreneurs and the triumphant marketplace, an interaction that was to be so important to the Holmes novels and to Doyle's activity as a whole. The triumph of the market was that of the mass market as opposed to the socially more limited cultural market of the eighteenth century. Anonymous patronage was crucial to both, rather than that by individuals or institutions. Producing works for sale to individuals unknown to authors or artists led to an emphasis on the roles of intermediaries in encouraging, focusing and satisfying demand, with publishers being highly significant. The market had greatly changed during the nineteenth century, with a perfect combination of a rising population, a more affluent population and a population with greater literacy. The last owed much to the 1870, 1876, 1880, 1891, 1893, 1897, 1899 and 1902 Education Acts. Whereas the middling orders had previously provided the bulk of the public for culture and were still very important to readership – not least the short stories that were an ideal length for commuters – much of the working class, especially skilled artisans, having gained time and money for leisure during the reign of Queen Victoria (1837–1901), were added to the fold.

Much attention was devoted to sport, but a range of cultural activities encouraged interest and expenditure. Reading was particularly significant. The nineteenth century was less 'visual' than the modern age. There was no equivalent to the stimulus and excitement of cinema, television and electronic media, all of which have made visual appeal normative in modern culture. The more than 350 illustrations by Sidney Paget (1860–1908) that accompanied the Holmes stories were highly significant in fixing a visual impression, not least for providing the deerstalker cap and Inverness cape not mentioned in the stories. Moreover, the stories were rapidly adapted for stage and screen. Nevertheless, it was the written word that took precedence, which reflected the traditional prestige of print – the medium of the Bible and the classics – as well as its power as the language of authority. Thanks to rising literacy, far more people were able to enjoy the printed word than ever before, and print culture became more established. The writers of the age sought a wide readership, not only for personal profit but also because they thought it important to write for a mass readership. This wide readership was not seen as incompatible with literary excellence, and these attitudes reflected the distance between the literary world of the period and that of two centuries earlier, although Thomas Hardy (1840–1928) was very cynical about his serial publications even when they were issued as novels.

In the Holmes stories, there are frequent references to characters, including even quite humble ones, reading novels. Being followed in London, Sir Henry Baskerville feels he has 'walked right into the thick of a dime novel', and Birdy Edwards also refers to such a novel in *The Valley of Fear* (1914–15). In 'The Copper Beeches', Violet Hunter is handed by Jephro Rucastle 'a yellow-backed novel' from which to read aloud. In 'The Blanched Soldier', James Dodd tries to distract himself 'with a novel'. In 'The Abbey Grange', Lady Brackenstall claims to have been 'absorbed in a book' prior to the break-in. In *A Study in Scarlet*, Joseph Strangerson is found with his 'novel, with which he had read himself to sleep' lying on the bed.

The novelists of the mid-nineteenth century focussed much attention on the 'condition of England'. This was notably so with Elizabeth Gaskell (1810–65), Charles Dickens (1812–70), George Eliot (1819–80) and Wilkie Collins (1824–89). Collins's *Man and Wife* (1870) criticised the marriage laws, which was a theme Doyle developed in his strong critique of those on divorce.[3] This novelistic practice continued with Thomas Hardy and George Gissing (1857–1903). The harsh binds of heredity, a Doyle theme, was found with Gissing in *Workers in the Dawn* (1880), while Hardy provided insight on the corrosive pressure of urban mores on rural ways, another Doyle theme. Doyle himself told Robert Barr during an interview in 1894 for *McClure's Magazine*: 'the age of fiction is coming – the age when religious and social and political changes will all be effected by means of the novelist'.

Major novelists at the end of the century were in the shadow of Hall Caine (1853–1931), the most highly paid novelist of his day, whose *The Eternal City* (1901) was the first to sell more than a million copies worldwide. He was also a playwright and, like Doyle, wrote in favour of the British cause in World War One. Religion, social issues, sex and politics all played a role in his oeuvre. Like Doyle, Caine attacked the divorce laws, notably in *The Woman Thou Gavest Me: Being the Story of Mary O'Neill*

(1913). Doyle's contemporary reputation echoes that of Caine, but the latter was more successful in his lifetime. So also was Marie Corelli (1855–1924) – a novelist fascinated by exotericism, notably in the Faustian *The Sorrows of Satan* (1895) – and Charles Garvice (1850–1920); a writer of very many heart-tug melodramas, Garvice had sold more than seven million copies worldwide by 1914.

The world of novels ranged widely. Lurid tales included Bram Stoker's *Dracula* (1897) which Doyle mocks in 'The Sussex Vampire' (1924). Doyle refers to the reports of vampirism in Hungary and Transylvania, from the latter of which Count Dracula comes to England, but is totally unconvinced and provides a rational account of the apparent vampirism in Sussex.

In the Holmes stories, Doyle offered accessible, interesting and exciting plots with well, or at least adequately, delineated characters. He also rose to consider meaning-of-life questions, notably so in 'The Cardboard Box'. Published in *The Strand Magazine* in January 1893, it did not appear in the first British edition of *The Memoirs of Sherlock Holmes* because of its subject: female lust. At the close of the story, Jim Browner confesses to the murder of his wife and her lover, and the strong and haunting remorse he feels. Holmes, reflecting, says:

> 'What is the meaning of it Watson? What object is served by this circle of misery and violence and fear? It must tend to some end, or else our universe is ruled by chance, which is unthinkable. But what end? There is the great standing perennial problem to which human reason is as far from an answer as ever'.

That is the close. There is no throwaway line or episode to provide a lightening of the tone or a diversion, as is frequently the case in the Holmes stories.

Doyle looked to the existing world of novels, not least in his historical fiction, which, in some respects, was more accomplished than that of Dickens and was certainly far more extensive. His historical novels appeared from 1889, with *Micah Clarke* set in the Monmouth Rebellion of 1685, to 1905–6 with *Sir Nigel*, which was set in 1350–56 and described the background to the earlier *The White Company* (1891), which was set in 1366–67 during the conflict in Castile that was part of the Anglo-French Hundred Years' War.[4] There was a strand from Doyle back to Sir Walter Scott (1771–1832) in this historical fiction. Doyle also published 'The Last of the Legions. And Other Tales of Long Ago' (1910) about the ancient world, a collection that has received insufficient attention.

The drama of Doyle's works also drew on the stage of the age. There were parallels, not least with an emphasis on setting: the lavish scenery of the London stage and the dramatic setting of Holmes's adventures, most obviously Dartmoor, and most dramatically in *The Hound of the Baskervilles*. The star system was also seen, with Henry Irving (1838–1905) and Ellen Terry (1847–1928) on stage, and Holmes on the page. Augustus Harris, manager of the Theatre Royal at Drury Lane, London, from 1879 until 1896, set the tone with spectaculars featuring avalanches, earthquakes, horse-races and snowstorms. The profit from plays such as Brandon Thomas's wildly successful farce *Charley's Aunt* (1892) encouraged investment in new theatres such as the Lyric Theatre (1888) and Her Majesty's Theatre (1897), both in London.

The range of plays was considerable, but the audience for Holmes's interactions with women also saw social dramas (written by men) that focussed more profoundly on the difficult position of women. Arthur Wing Pinero (1855–1934) dealt with seduction in *The Profligate* (1889) and *The Second Mrs Tanqueray* (1893). His *The Notorious Mrs Ebbsmith* (1895) and *The Benefit of the Doubt* confronted issues that Oscar Wilde touched on in his plays of social respectability, notably *Lady Windermere's Fan* (1892) and *An Ideal Husband* (1895), but George Bernard Shaw's *Mrs Warren's Profession* (1893) and *The Philanderer* (1893) were performed only privately as they were thought unlikely to obtain a licence. Doyle himself produced plays that were staged from 1893 to 1921, starting with *Jane Annie; or, The Good Conduct Prize* and ending with *The Crown Diamond*.

The Holmes stories appeared when Britain had a buoyant cultural world. It rested on mass literacy, a highly urbanised society, and the wealth of one of the leading economies in the world. The metropolitan settings of culture were lavish and expanding in number. From the 1890s, theatre syndicates from existing music hall managements built new venues such as the 'palaces' for more respectable customers. Day's Music-Hall in Birmingham, in which Hall Pycroft is recommended to spend time by his fraudulent employer in 'The Stockbroker's Clerk', had opened in 1862 but was closed in September 1893, six months after the story's appearance. Yet that was so it could be demolished to be replaced by the far larger Empire Theatre, which opened in May 1894.

London saw extensive investment in cultural settings. For example, Bechstein Hall, a concert hall now known as Wigmore Hall, was built in 1901 at a cost of £100,000. Doyle has Holmes go frequently to hear great musical performances. Other characters were also sent to join similar audiences. In 'The Retired Colourman', for example, Josiah Amberley seeks to take his wife to the Haymarket Theatre, and the course of the outing provides a significant clue.

Facilities could be lavish. The London Coliseum, which opened in 1904, included tea rooms, a cigar bar and an American bar. The London Palladium, which followed in 1910, included facilities for gentlemen changing into evening dress.

The press, which greatly interested Doyle, was also dynamic. Unlike Dickens, G. A. Henty and many other writers, Doyle was not a newspaper man, but he had Holmes systematically read the press. Thus, in 'The Blue Carbuncle' (1892), Watson finds Holmes with 'a pile of crumpled morning papers'. This is a frequent description. Holmes also often uses the press in his cases. In *The Hound of the Baskervilles*, he establishes that the message sent to Sir Henry had been cut from *The Times* and offers an encomium on its 'leaded bourgeois type'. He also provides a social categorisation: 'The *Times* is a paper which is seldom found in any hands but those of the highly educated'. This paper would have been the foremost for the members of the Diogenes Club in Pall Mall where 'the men were sitting about and reading papers'. 'The Six Napoleons' reveals that one of the 'lumber-rooms' at Holmes's apartment in Baker Street is packed with files of the old daily papers, which in part are the sources of Holmes's prodigious knowledge.

Yet, in the same story, Holmes chuckles over a misleading as well as highly sensational account he has planted on Horace Harker and the subscribers of the Central Press Syndicate, before telling Watson 'The Press is a most valuable institution, if you only know how to use it'. In Doyle's depiction, the accuracy of the press varied. In 'The Golden Pince-Nez', the detective Stanley Hopkins, a perceptive figure, notes that the early press reports of the 'Yoxley case' are 'all wrong'.

In the Holmes stories, London newspapers circulate beyond the city's borders. In 'The Stockbroker's Clerk', for example, the Birmingham-based character 'Pinner' buys the latest edition of an 'evening paper' from a newsboy. The paper in question turns out to be an early Saturday edition of London's *Evening Standard*, which brings news of the attempted robbery at Mawson and Williams's on Lombard Street, London. Newspapers are also depicted as producing several editions each day, as reflected by Stanley Hopkins's reference to 'the Yoxley case in the latest editions' in 'The Golden Pince-Nez'. Correspondingly, in 'Silver Blaze', Watson comments: 'Fresh editions of every paper had been sent up by our newsagent'. The following day, Holmes gets a 'bundle of fresh papers' at Paddington Station en route to Exeter so that he can read them on the lengthy train journey, and he refers to the *Telegraph* and the *Chronicle*.

Holmes is particularly interested in the personal advertisements in the press and assumes that others will read them as much as he does. Thus, in 'The Blue Carbuncle', he instructs a commissionaire to:

'Run down to the advertising agency, and have this put in the evening papers'.

'In which, Sir?'

'Oh, in the *Globe*, *Star*, *Pall Mall*, *St James's Gazette*, *Evening News*, *Standard*, *Echo*, and any others that occur to you'.

Similarly, in 'The Beetle-Hunter', a non-Holmes Doyle story published in *The Strand Magazine* in June 1898, Dr Hamilton finds no news in the *Standard* but responds to an advertisement there for a resolute and strong entomologist.

Holmes regards rumour as important. In 'The Priory School', a rumour in the *Globe* is mentioned in which an attempt has been made to keep the Holdernesse abduction out of the press. Moreover, 'The Three Gables' (1926) makes reference to Langdale Pike, who is described as Holmes's

> human book of reference upon all matters of social scandal. This strange, languid creature spent his waking hours in the bow window of a St James's Street club, and was the receiving-station, as well as the transmitter, for all the gossip of the Metropolis. He made, it was said, a four-figure income by the paragraphs which he contributed every week to the garbage papers which cater for an inquisitive public. If ever, far down in the turbid depths of London life, there was some strange swirl or eddy, it was marked with automatic exactness by this human dial upon the surface. Holmes discreetly helped Langdale to knowledge, and on occasion was helped in turn.

Newspaper reports also provide opportunities to offer plot details, as with the *Daily Telegraph* account of murder printed at length in 'The Norwood Builder'. With reference to the case of the murdered Eduardo Lucas, this paper is also cited in 'The Second Stain'. Doing so is part of the process by which the stories are grounded in reality. Newspaper reports in the Holmes stories can serve a number of ends, including those of other criminals, as Holmes observes in 'The Abbey Grange':

> 'These burglars made a considerable haul at Sydenham a fortnight ago. Some account of them and their appearance was in the papers, and would naturally occur to anyone who wished to invent a story in which imaginary robbers should play a part'.

While the Holmes stories, in general, lack the sarcasm directed at the press by Agatha Christie, Doyle could be very hostile. This is expressed at greatest length in *A Study in Scarlet* and in one of the Holmes stories' wittiest passages, in which Doyle develops the technique of providing distinctly different press accounts of the same event – a technique also used by Christie. This relates to Watson's 'condensation' of newspaper accounts and leaders (editorials) about the murder in Lauriston Gardens, Brixton. He presents the conservative *Daily Telegraph*, which had a circulation of three hundred thousand by 1888, as xenophobic and rabble-rousing:

> The German name of the victim, the absence of all other motive, and the sinister inscription on the wall, all pointed to its perpetration by political refugees and revolutionists. The Socialists had many branches in America, and the deceased had, no doubt, infringed their unwritten laws, and been tracked down by them. After alluding airily to the Vehmgericht, aqua tofana, Carbonari, the Marchioness de Brinvilliers, the Darwinian theory, the principles of Malthus, and the Ratfliff Highway murders, the article concluded by admonishing the Government and advocating a closer watch over foreigners in England.
>
> The *Standard* commented upon the fact that lawless outrages of the sort usually occurred under a Liberal Administration. They arose from the unsettling of the minds of the masses, and the consequent weakening of all authority.
>
> The *Daily News* observed that there was no doubt as to the crime being a political one. The despotism and hatred of Liberalism which animated the Continental Governments had had

> the effect of driving to our shores a number of men who might have made excellent citizens were they not soured by the recollection of all that they had undergone. Among these men there was a stringent code of honour, any infringement of which was punished by death.

There was no uniformity among the newspapers, whether in content, style or political allegiance. This situation reflected the dynamic nature of British society. The press profited from it and, in turn, fostered and propagated the dynamism and variety.

The press had expanded greatly with the end of the 'taxes on knowledge': the Advertisement Duties in 1853; the Newspaper Stamp Duty in 1855; and the Paper Duties in 1861. The opportunity for a far larger press sector was exploited by means of a technology centred on new printing presses and the continuous rolls or 'webs' of paper that fed them. Aside from an increase in newspaper titles and a decrease in prices, a range of serial publications emerged, including inexpensive, mass-produced magazines and monthly serials that concentrated on fiction.[5]

The world of print, both factual and fictional, was the prime source, outside the family, of ideas and comparisons through which people could understand and structure their experience, and, alongside providing excitement, detective stories were a means to do so. This process was accentuated by the tremendous mobility of society as massive urbanisation drew on extensive migration within the country. This transformation challenged – indeed, frequently broke down – earlier patterns of communal control or, at least, influence. Indeed, the tension between longstanding and new values was frequently seen in the Holmes stories. A newly expanded urban world that owed little to traditional social discipline, and that was able to reach widely, provided a mass reading public.[6] Serial publication offered this public both news and commentary. Much of the public sought the entertainment and human interest that was offered them, rather than campaigning commitment to any specific cause. The resulting situation was criticised by Matthew Arnold, a prominent literary figure, for its focus on sensation and its lack of accuracy, in the May 1887 issue of the magazine *The Nineteenth Century*.

Arnold's critique and term, 'New Journalism', reflected an unease with some of the leading press figures of the age, such as W. (William) T. Stead, who ran *The Pall Mall Gazette* from 1883 to 1889. A prominent press campaigner, notably against the prostitution of minors, Stead was a muckraker with confidence in his own rectitude and the consequent justification for twisting facts. Stead also wrote about Jack the Ripper. Highly talented and understandably frustrated by the condescension that he experienced, often on social grounds,[7] Stead died when the *Titanic* went down in 1912.

Sensationalism in newspapers and novels bridged fact and fiction. As George Orwell noted in 1946, many famous murders had 'some dramatic coincidence, in which the finger of Providence could be clearly seen, or one of those episodes that no novelist would dare to make up, such as Crippen's flight across the Atlantic with his mistress dressed as a boy, or George Joseph Smith playing "Nearer, My God, to Thee" on the harmonium while one of his wives was drowning in the next room'.[8]

So also was such bridging offered by short stories in magazines. Popular journalists employed novelistic features[9] and vice versa. The congruence of fiction and fact, or, rather, novelistic styles and newspaper methods, was particularly evident in the reporting of crime, as in the *Illustrated Police News*, which was issued weekly from February 1864.[10] It was also demonstrated in the reporting of imperial expansion. Paralleling the focus on detectives so prominent in fiction, 'special correspondents' proved a key means, driving dramatic narratives for readers who wanted them in part-work forms, either newspapers or novels. These correspondents created the realities that were experienced by readers, not least by explicitly focussing on their first-person roles and experiences.[11]

In a world of shifting categories and complex interactions, many writers moved between journalism and fiction.[12] Thus, Doyle both wrote detective fiction and energetically sought to engage with miscarriages of knowledge. His sense of the novelist as recording historian is brilliantly captured with the device of the decent, solid and reliable Watson. Much occurs in this respect in the interplay between Holmes and Watson, through which the stories largely develop, but near the close in 'The Veiled Lodger' – a mystery supposedly of 1896, published in *The Strand Magazine* in February 1927 – Watson separately presents his yearbooks and documents as

> a perfect quarry for the student, not only of crime, but of the social and official scandals of the late Victorian era. Concerning these latter, I may say that the writers of agonised letters, who beg that the honour of their families or the reputation of famous forbears may not be touched, have nothing to fear. The discretion and high sense of professional honour which have always distinguished my friend are still at work in the choice of these memoirs, and no confidence will be abused. I deprecate, however, in the strongest way the attempts which have been made lately to get at and to destroy these papers. The source of these outrages is known, and if they are repeated I have Mr Holmes' authority for saying that the whole story concerning the politician, the lighthouse and the trained cormorant will be given to the public. There is at least one reader who will understand.

This is both a brilliant joke and a careful separation of Holmes from blackmailers like Charles Augustus Milverton, against whose injustice Holmes had committed an illegal break-in. This is but one of the more dramatic instances of Holmes breaking the law.

As with fiction, the reporting of crime in the press served to shape what were presented as social problems as well as to create moral panics, with the two often different sides of the same coin. Posters thrust forward the most alarming news, as in 'The Illustrious Client' (1924), with 'the terrible news-sheet' seen by Watson near Charing Cross Station: 'Murderous Attack Upon Sherlock Holmes'.

Crimes that were not solved, or not solved rapidly, encouraged alarm and reflection as newspapers struggled to find new and distinctive angles. Readers responded by buying more copies, as in

1888 when five young women were murdered in Whitechapel in the Jack the Ripper killings. Politics played a role in the Jack the Ripper news coverage, with the Liberal press accusing the Tory government of failing to act sufficiently, only for Tory newspapers to be more sympathetic to the government.[13] *The Times* devoted six editorials and much column space – including charts and plans – to the killing, not least a report, on 10 November, of five thousand words on another of the murderer's 'revolting and fiendish acts'. (The same issue carried a mere three paragraphs on a Parisian murder trial.) The *Daily Telegraph* of 4 October published facsimiles of a letter and a postcard allegedly from the Ripper. The East End, the Ripper's hunting ground, resonates in the Holmes stories, as with 'Black Peter' (1904), set in 1895, in which there is reference to 'his arrest of Wilson, the notorious canary-trainer, which removed a plague-spot from the East End of London'.

Crime as a cause and a reflection of political contention was an aspect of the far broader degree to which attention to criminality, however presented, drew on wider concerns. The key setting was London, and Holmes notes in 'The Red-Headed League': 'It is a hobby of mine to have an exact knowledge of London'.

2

THE SITE FOR HOLMES

London

> . . . the red brick tentacles of the London octopus.
>
> – Doyle, 'The Sealed Room',
>
> *The Strand Magazine*, September 1898

Imperial city,[1] world city, London dominated the imagination of the anglophone sphere. A phenomenon of scale, energy, power and authority unmatched by the other major cities of the world, London was the direct experience of millions, but the experience had been taken far further by those who had read their Dickens or their Trollope, their Thackeray or their Gissing. Even a rural novelist like Thomas Hardy preferred London. As brilliantly realised by Dickens in his account in *Dombey and Son* (1846–48) of the devastation brought by railway builders, part of the fascination of London was that it was constantly developing and a potent force for transformation.

The Holmes stories reflect Doyle's view of London as a Scot in the heart of Empire and the resulting outsider/insider tensions. In the Holmes stories, London is a place of extremes. There is deadly crime but also normality, as captured by Watson in *The Sign of*

Four (1890) when leaving Mary Morstan at Mrs Cecil Forrester's in Camberwell:

> I still seem to see that little group on the step – the two graceful, clinging figures, the half-opened door, the hall-light shining through stained glass, the barometer, and the bright stair-rods. It was soothing to catch even that passing glimpse of a tranquil English home in the midst of the wild, dark business which had absorbed us.

In his Holmes stories, Doyle repeatedly presents London as the focal point of change for his characters. Change indeed was speeding up in Doyle's world. Much of the technology predated him, but locomotives, steamships and telegraphs became more significant and comprehensive, and for Britain they focused on London. So also with the post, a domestic and international system in which Britain led, providing a more frequent service than that today. New technologies followed, notably radio and aircraft, but also for detection fingerprinting. Life by timetable was life in, by, and from, London.

As with Dickens, Doyle was excellent at capturing both London itself and the many worlds of the city. The censuses of 1891, 1901 and 1911 revealed 5,572,000, 6,586,000 and 7,160,000 inhabitants respectively. This was major growth. Much was due to net immigration, although natural increase was 85 per cent of all growth by the end of the nineteenth century. London was both transformed internally and also expanding, the two linked by the pressure from a rising population, and the opportunities created by the growing aggregate demand. This growth was matched by the poverty recorded by Charles Booth in his *Life and Labour of the People of London* (1889–1903). Booth estimated that 30.7 per cent of the working population lived in poverty, which he attributed particularly to the role of seasonal and casual labour. Booth was troubled by the threat of poverty to civil society:

> 'The lowest class, which consists of some occasional labourers, street sellers, loafers, criminals and semi-criminals. . . . Their

> life is the life of savages, with vicissitudes of extreme hardship and occasional excesses . . . their only luxury is drink. . . . From these come the battered figures who slouch through the streets, and play the beggar or the bully'.[2]

Holmes's most amazing characteristic, indeed, is not his prodigious intellect but, instead, his ability to bridge social groups in appearance and behaviour. This is an ability not really shared by his brother Mycroft. Sherlock Holmes's disguises, and his activities when disguised, repeatedly provide key plot elements and some of the more amusing passages, as well as varying the tone of the stories. There was also an almost anthropological quality to the writing as Holmes tours London.

Charles Booth's view of the poor, conflating social and moral classifications, highlighted a sense of menace that can be glimpsed more widely in the remarks of commentators. In part, this stance by commentators was reflected not only in fear but also in a pressure for change. Indeed, middle-class views and wealth stimulated a demand for, and process of, improvement, civic and moral, which was central to the movement for reform. Slum clearances were the geographical counterpart of this reform, although Doyle does not address their harshness and impact.

The long-standing reputation of London as being corrupt and corrupting was reiterated in Victorian melodrama. In William Travers's *London by Night* (1868), for example, a wicked French madam inveigles unsuspecting British virgins into her brothel; the plot combines xenophobia with the frisson of London as the centre for debauchery. There were certainly many brothels there, as well as much street prostitution. Xenophobia and a different form of debauchery were to be taken forward in literature about Chinese opium dens in Limehouse, including the relevant story by Doyle, 'The Man with the Twisted Lip' (1891).[3] The sins of London revealed by press and police were far more wide ranging in terms of the city's topography and behaviour, as with the West End scandals of 1889–90 involving the clients and staff of a male brothel on Cleveland Street. In 'The Abbey Grange' (1904),

Theresa, the Australian nurse, a positive force for truth, a role given in this story, and many others, to a woman, refers to the 'false London ways' of Sir Eustace Brackenstall. Nothing more needed to be said.

Mayfair provided Oscar Wilde, in his brilliantly satirical *The Importance of Being Earnest* (1895), with the opportunity to deploy the snobbish, but acute, Augusta, Lady Bracknell, who was ready to change the fashionability of the sides of London squares. Her sense of place matched that of Holmes. Like Doyle, that play also captured the economic centrality of London, for, as Lady Bracknell notes, land was an encumbrance, made necessary by social position; and, instead, the true bastions of prosperity were financial holdings.

This wealth was seen in the rebuilding of the city. The banks, a focus of criminal attacks in Holmes stories, required substantial premises, notably the big, high-ceilinged, banking halls that took up prominent sites in the city, for example, the City of London Bank on Ludgate Hill (1890). So also with the insurance companies: Alliance Assurance occupied two large office blocks on St James's Street (1883, 1905), while the Prudential built a sprawling site on High Holborn (1895–1905). The grand bank and insurance headquarters provided not only physical accommodation but also legitimation and authority for their new financial power and possibilities. Such impressive architecture helped ensure a sense of solidity and authority within a complex and seemingly unstable financial sphere. Doyle refers to this instability with financial houses going bankrupt, the consequences of which were felt across the country.

Large buildings included department stores – such as the Civil Service Stores, Harrods and Selfridges – that catered to the developing interest in shopping as a social activity that was aided by the construction of women's lavatories and by changes in social mores that allowed 'respectable' women to travel in public without a male escort.[4] These, however, did not attract the attention of Holmes.

In contrast, hotels, such as the Westminster Palace, Savoy, Carlton, Piccadilly and Ritz, were of interest. Indeed, the Northumberland Avenue hotels are mentioned, as in 'The Greek Interpreter', more than once, and the plot against Sir Henry Baskerville in *The Hound of the Baskervilles* involves the theft of his boots while staying at the Northumberland Hotel, one of the twenty-three near Charing Cross. In the non-Holmes 'The Man with the Watches' (1898), a traveller is defrauded by card sharps 'at one of the Northumberland Avenue hotels'. The Ritz (1906) was the first major steel-framed building in London but could not match the vast Hotel Cecil (1896) on the Strand. With its seven hundred bedrooms, it was said to be the largest in the world, only to be demolished in 1930.

Other large buildings included the gentlemen's clubs, which created a distinctive world of masculinity in and near Pall Mall.[5] Doyle had great fun with them in the case of Mycroft's silent club, the Diogenes Club. Doyle himself had joined the Athenaeum in 1901. Doyle's proposer was George Earle Buckle, editor of *The Times* from 1884 to 1911 and biographer of Benjamin Disraeli. Buckle had also seconded Austen Chamberlain, who was to be a major Conservative politician.[6] Soon after his election, Doyle hosted a members' dinner at the Athenaeum. The strangers present included Edmund Gosse and J. M. Barrie, who was to be elected the following year, while the members present included Anthony Hope, the author of *The Prisoner of Zenda*, the great publishing success of 1894, and Major Arthur Griffiths, Inspector of Prisons and a source for Doyle of information on crime.[7] The club was full of hyper-intelligent people of the same social class, and, if not quite the Diogenes Club, might have suggested it. Probably, Doyle enjoyed teasing his club with the Diogenes, which offered an exaggerated form of the chilly atmosphere noted by members and of the silence rules in the club's South Library. He took one aspect of Clubland *ad absurdum* in a humorous fashion. Separately, in 'The Illustrious Client' (1924), the well-connected Sir James Damery writes to Holmes from the Carlton Club and tells him that he can be found via the club.

Buildings and institutions were not the only distinctive characteristics of London from which writers could draw. Doyle was also one of the very many writers who saw the opportunities of London's fog, and wrote successfully about the problems of visibility in the city. This was a visual equivalent to the deceptions, the throwing 'all pursuit off his track', in 'The Norwood Builder' (1904) that were so significant with the false identities that underlay and explain so many of the mysteries Holmes investigates. Fog was also important for the deceit and disguise so integral to detective and thriller novels.

Fog played a key role in the image of the city – an image that was kept alive until the 1960s and then historicised. In 'The Horror of the Heights' (1913), a gripping non-Holmes story, the aviator Joyce-Armstrong, in his unprecedented high flight into an alien sphere, flies into a cloud which is 'as dark and thick as a London fog'. Foreigners proved especially keen on using fog as a description of London. In 'The Regent's Park Murder' by Baroness Orczy, a short story set in 1907, John Ashley explains his being armed by saying, 'I always carry a revolver about with me in foggy weather'. In *The Fog* (1901), a novel by the American war correspondent Richard Harding Davis, the narrator in London is 'as completely lost as though [he] had been set down by night in the Sahara Desert'.

Doyle frequently depicts London in terms of poor visibility. Thus, 'The Great Brown-Pericord Motor', a non-Holmes story published in *The Cheshire Observer*, 19 December 1891, began: 'It was a cold, foggy, dreary evening in May. Along the Strand blurred patches of light marked the position of the lamps. The flaring shop windows flickered vaguely with steamy brightness through the thick and heavy atmosphere'. More famously, in *The Sign of Four* (1890):

> It was a September evening, and not yet seven o'clock, but the day had been a dreary one, and a dense drizzly fog lay low upon the great city. Mud-coloured clouds drooped sadly over the muddy streets. Down the Strand the lamps were but misty

> splotches of diffused light, which threw a feeble circular glimmer upon the slimy pavement. The yellow glare from the shop-windows streamed out into the steamy, vaporous air, and threw a murky, shifting radiance across the crowded thoroughfare. There was, to my mind, something eerie and ghost-like in the endless procession of faces which flitted across these narrow bars of light – sad faces and glad, haggard and merry. Like all human kind, they flitted from the gloom into the light, and so back into the gloom once more.

Subsequently in the novel, there is a reference to 'the damp fog of the great city'. Air pollution contributed greatly to the fogs; as a result, an increase in respiratory diseases in London in part countered the benefits stemming from action against smallpox and cholera. In 'The Abbey Grange', on a cold morning in the winter of 1897, Holmes and Watson take a cab to Charing Cross Station: 'The first faint winter's dawn was beginning to appear, and we could dimly see the occasional figure of an early workman as he passed us, blurred and indistinct in the opalescent London reek'. The last is very much a hostile response. In 'The Solitary Cyclist', Watson thinks Surrey's heathland 'all the more beautiful to eyes which were weary of the duns and drabs and slate-greys of London'. It is an accurate account not only of building materials but also of the impact of coal smoke. There is a rural counterpart in the dense fog on Dartmoor in *The Hound of the Baskervilles*, but it is described as white, and therefore unpolluted. Surrey, similarly, is found beautiful in Freeman Wills Crofts's *The Hog's Back Mystery* (1933).

A vulnerability to weather, and, indeed, nature, is a theme at the outset of 'The Golden Pince-Nez', which is set in 1894:

> It was a wild, tempestuous night towards the close of November. . . . Outside the wind howled down Baker Street, while the rain beat fiercely against the windows. It was strange there in the very depths of the town, with ten miles of man's handiwork on every side of us, to feel the iron grip of Nature, and to be conscious that to the huge elemental forces all London was no

> more than the molehills that dot the fields. I walked to the window and looked out on the deserted street.

This idea was a commonplace one in the period, one that was a counterpoint to the emphasis on technology. However, the major problem for many was not nature but, rather, the grip of poverty. Paintings such as *The Pinch of Poverty* (1889), by Thomas Kennington, provided a genteel view of poverty, but the reality was generally far harsher. The Reverend Andrew Mearns's tract, *The Bitter Cry of Outcast London* (1883), exposed conditions in the Mint rookery in Southwark, which is around where Marshalsea Road is now located as a result of slum clearance by 1886. In *The People of the Abyss* (1903), the popular American writer Jack London writes:

> For here, in the East End, the obscenities and brute vulgarities of life are rampant. There is no privacy. The bad corrupts the good, and all fester together. Innocent childhood is sweet and beautiful; but in East London innocence is a fleeting thing, and you must catch them before they crawl out of the cradle; or you will find the very babies as unholily wise as you.

Dorset Street in Spitalfields was said to be the worst street in London: "There were pubs every few yards. Bawdy houses [brothels] every few feet. It was peopled by roaring drunken fighting – mad killers'. Many of the poor and casually employed still lived in one-room dwellings, tenements, back-to-backs, rookeries and courts. Many of their walls ran with damp, sanitation was often primitive and poorly swept chimneys contributed to the fug in many homes. In *A Study in Scarlet*, Holmes and Watson travel in South London by means of 'a long succession of dingy streets and dreary byways' to 'a narrow slit in the line of dead-coloured brick. . . . Audley Court was not an attractive locality. The narrow passage led us into a quadrangle paved with flags and lined by sordid dwellings. We picked our way among groups of dirty children, and through lines of discoloured linen'.

In the Holmes stories, there are aspects of a sophisticated metropolitan detective bringing solutions to naïve provincials. However, in practice, London takes on meaning in terms of Holmes's more complex interaction with non-Londoners, as when the arrogance of Londoners is mentioned in 'The Reigate Squires', and also as a sphere in its own right as in 'The Blue Carbuncle', in which Holmes refers to

> 'four million human beings all jostling each other within the space of a few square miles. Amid the action and reaction of so dense a swarm of humanity, every possible combination of events may be expected to take place, and many a little problem will be presented which may be striking and bizarre without being criminal'.

The crowds of London offer opportunities for both criminals and their foes. Holmes, accordingly, advises Sir Henry Baskerville to go to Baskerville Hall:

> 'I have ample evidence that you are being dogged in London, and amid the millions of this great city it is difficult to discover who these people are or what their object can be. If their intentions are evil they might do you a mischief, and we should be powerless to prevent it'.

The Holmes stories repeatedly demonstrated the truth of this warning. In 'The Disappearance of Lady Frances Carfax' (1911):

> neither the official police nor Holmes's own small, but very efficient, organisation sufficed to clear away the mystery. Amid the crowded millions of London the three persons we sought were as completely obliterated as if they had never lived.

Returning from fiction to reality, alongside the continuing structural problems of the city, notably poverty and disease, there were also particular episodes of difficulty. Thus, London was hit hard by the serious economic depression that began in 1877. This depression had led, by the end of the decade, to a marked increase in unemployment and bankruptcy, as well as to much concern about slum conditions and a demand for a new municipal activism.

Meanwhile, London was spreading. Indeed, in the 1890s, the biggest building firm in London was Watts of Catford, a suburban firm. In the hit song 'If it Wasn't for the 'Ouses in between, or, The Cockney Garden' (1894), Gus Elen sings:

> Wiv a ladder and some glasses
> You can see the 'Ackney Marshes
> If it wasn't for the 'ouses in between.

The pace of development was strong. Campaigns to prevent it were few and largely unsuccessful. In 1875, Octavia Hill failed in a campaign to save Swiss Cottage Fields from development. Washington Bacon's *New Large-Scale Ordnance Atlas of London and Suburbs* of 1888 offered twenty-five four-inch maps, but the 1912 edition provided thirty-one, reaching out to Harrow, Chessington, Cheam, Purley, Selsdon, Farnborough and Orpington. Moreover, in areas already covered in the 1888 atlas, there were many new streets and houses, for example in Tottenham, Edmonton, East Greenwich, Hanwell and from West Ham to Barking and Ilford. Highlighting the increasing complexity of navigating the city, a 'shilling map of London' is in a pocket of the murdered man in 'The Six Napoleons' (1904).

New rail lines in the region encouraged commuting. For example, the building of a direct route from London to Southend via Upminster, avoiding the Tilbury detour, opened in 1888, cut the express journey time from ninety-five to fifty minutes and was followed by an alternative route via Shenfield, which opened in 1889. As a result, commuting from Southend into London rose rapidly, as did the population of Southend. So also when rail commuting began from the North Sea coast to Newcastle.

The spread of suburbia and commuting created links but also moved people and groups apart. The poor were now found across London, for example, in the Potteries area of Kensington,[8] not least in order to enable them to serve the needs of the prosperous.

However, there was also a process in which specific areas now accommodated and employed people from distinctly different socioeconomic groups. Doyle's readers would have been well aware of this fact, but it is easily overlooked by modern readers except in the limited sense of the important contrast between the East End and the West End. Instead, London and its hinterland were criss-crossed by isolines of wealth, among other factors, and their resulting gradients. The key perceived difference was one of 'acceptability': a complex matrix of class, cost, status and fashion.

The variety of London very much comes out in the Holmes stories. Thus, in Kensington in 'The Six Napoleons', Holmes goes to 'Pitt Street, a quiet little backwater just beside one of the briskest currents of London life'. In the same story, Watson refers to a journey in which he and Holmes pass 'through the fringe of fashionable London, hotel London, theatrical London, literary London, commercial London, and, finally, maritime London, till we came to a riverside city of a hundred thousand souls, where the tenement houses swelter and reek with the outcasts of Europe', the last a highly pejorative remark for the area that was the setting of works such as Thomas Burke's short story collection set in Chinatown, *Limehouse Nights* (1916). Burke (1886–1945), was born to difficult circumstances in Clapham and did not have an equivalent to Doyle's wealthy relatives and medical education. He became an office boy and began publishing in 1901. *Limehouse Nights*, an account of Chinatown that included interracial relationships, shocked many.[9] Very differently, in terms of power, in 1880 the Royal Albert Dock had been added to London's Docklands, a location which always seems dangerous in Holmes stories due, in part, to its associations with foreignness and lawbreaking.

The Holmes stories give readers an introduction to London's different quarters and tones, and notably so in the quest for the six busts of Napoleon that are being destroyed one by one. Thus, having crossed Hammersmith Bridge, Holmes and Watson walk 'to a secluded road fringed with pleasant houses, each standing in its own grounds', one of which is Laburnum Villa.

Variety was central to London life, as with differing appearances linked to status, occupation and income – notably the City professional, the West End of leisure and the East End of manual labour.[10] London also had a vast array of housing types which was a way in which neighbourhood identity was discerned. By the end of the nineteenth century, the two-up-two-down 'through terrace' was the norm for much of the population. These were solidly constructed and adequately ventilated. From 1875, it was mandatory to provide lavatories in new houses. Moreover, the quality of this housing improved in the 1900s, not least with better insulation. Under the 1894 London Building Act, window area had to be equal to, or greater than, a tenth of the floor area in all new rooms intended for human habitation.

A different type of housing was provided by mansion flats, which became important in parts of London, including Bloomsbury. Doyle has Holmes live at 221B Baker Street, but when the stories began, the Baker Street house numbers only reached the 100s. In *A Study in Scarlet*, the apartment is described in terms of 'a couple of comfortable bed-rooms and a single large airy sitting-room, cheerfully furnished, and illuminated by two broad windows'. While not as fashionable or expensive as more central residential areas, notably Mayfair to the south, Baker Street was a respectable address, not least because it was situated close to both Regent Park and the Baker Street underground station, opened in 1863. The successful novelists Arnold Bennett and H. G. Wells were both to live in a mansion block on the street, Chiltern Court, while William Pitt the Younger had lived at no. 120 in 1803–4, between two periods as Prime Minister.

At every level, new homes were designed to respond to the demand for self-improvement and status. An important aspect of London, which clearly defined manners, customs and social attitudes, was the desire of the lower-middle class to retain what they had: while jealous of their 'superiors' they were horror-struck at the thought of sinking back into the mass of their 'inferiors'. The social politics of this group was depicted by George and Weedon Grossmith in *The Diary of a Nobody* (1892):

> the Pooters rent a house in Holloway rather too close to the railway line (the landlord lets it go cheap because of the noise), and fill their lives with the snobberies they imagine to be typical of a slightly higher class. Delivery men and servants they can ill afford are made to use the rear entrance of what is, in fact, a rather modest town house.

There was far less pretension in the activities recorded in 1895 by the Rector of Bethnal Green, activities that left plenty of time to read about 'true crime':

> a vast majority of the men in your district will have spent their Sundays for the last twenty-five years and their fathers before them, in the following way: they will have lain in bed till about eleven or twelve, having been up early all week; they will then go round when the public houses open, which they do at one; they will have what they call a 'wet' till three . . . they will then have dinner, the great dinner of the week, which the missus has been preparing all morning. Then comes a lie down on the bed in shirt sleeves until five, with a pot of beer and *Lloyd's Weekly*; then follows tea, and after tea a bit of a walk round to see a friend or a relation; then fairly early to bed to make up for a very late Saturday night.

The description is similar to that by George Orwell at the start of his 1946 piece on 'The Decline of the English Murder'. This group of readers was stable as long as employed, but detective writers also explored the plight of the insecure and short-of-money, as in Marie Lowndes's novel *The Lodger* (1913). Although he could receive substantial fees, thanks to his work for royalty and the aristocracy, as in 'The Priory School', Holmes's finances are never explored, which contrasts with Ian Fleming's full disclosure of James Bond's income. Instances reflecting Holmes's interest in money are very rare.

London, meanwhile, was being changed through improvements in transport, although not without competition, as described in Doyle's non-Holmes 'The Story of the Sealed Room,' published in *The Strand Magazine*, September 1898: 'A four-wheeled [horse-drawn] cab, that opprobrium of London, was coming jolting and creaking in one direction, while in the other there was a yellow glare from the lamp of a cyclist'. The volume of traffic reflected the intense web of connections that made up London life. In 'The Third Generation' (1894), a powerful non-Holmes story, Doyle referred to 'The dull roar of the traffic which converged all day upon London Bridge'. In 1899, Sir J. W. Barry estimated that eight horse-drawn buses a minute would pass an observer on Tottenham Court Road,[11] an intensity that posed the problem of disposing of manure.

The application of new power sources was important to transport, first electricity and then the petrol-driven internal combustion engine. Electricity permitted not only Baron Gruner's burglar alarm in 'The Illustrious Client', and the career of the electrical engineer Francis Pericord in 'The Great Brown-Pericord Motor', but also the improvement of the former horse-tram network. London's first electric tramway was established in 1901, running from Shepherd's Bush to Acton, and Newcastle's first electric trams ran that year. Electric trams were quicker and carried more passengers than horse trams and cost less than buses. Steam launches sped travel on the Thames, as dramatically depicted for Holmes and the police in *The Sign of Four*.

As earlier with the trains, however, there was scant cohesion among the tramways that spread rapidly until the beginning of World War One in 1914. The London County Council (LCC) was responsible for central sections, with private operators such as Imperial Tramways in West London, and boroughs such as East Ham active in East London. The trams of Metropolitan Electric Tramways served areas of North London that were to be greatly developed when the underground system spread, such as, for example, Barnet. Towards the close of the period, the spread of suburbia was given greater energy by the development of electric train services, as well as by the establishment of bus networks, with buses using the internal combustion engine. By 1913, London had one thousand motor buses, which had only been introduced there in 1905.

With this pressure of transport, London's streets became essentially means for circulation rather than for sociability, household tasks, leisure, manufacturing, trade and shopping. This change, which was a fundamental aspect of the difference between cities and smaller settlements, helped in the breakdown of communities within London: communities of shared space, as opposed to the shared activities of, for example, religion or sport. People were subordinated to outside purpose, with the utilitarianism of improved traffic taking precedence over other goals; and this emphasis was linked to the regulation of public space and activity by the police. The ability of residents to affect the use of public space was limited, a situation that remains the case today.

Within the more central area, which was too crowded to permit above-ground railways, the underground system provided new transport links. The first underground railway in London, the Metropolitan Railway, opened in 1863, covering a distance of four miles as it linked Bishop's Road, Paddington, via Baker Street to Farringdon in the City. It was a 'cut and cover' tunnel near the surface and, as the trains were steam-hauled, had to tackle the underground production of smoke. The trains were also gas-lit. With its low fares, compared to the horse-drawn bus, the new line was very popular, and the system spread with separate companies constructing individual lines. Relations were not always good, with the Metropolitan Railway having poor ones with the second line, the Metropolitan District Railway. Nevertheless, the Inner Circle (now the Circle Line), which incorporated part of both systems, was completed in 1884. The 'Underground' is referred to in *A Study in Scarlet* and provides a way to try to dispose of a body in 'The Bruce-Partington Plans' (1908), a plot that benefited from the electrification of the line. No other British city had an underground railway until Glasgow opened one in 1896.

The spread of the Underground was helped by the replacement of 'cut and cover' with the use of a tunnelling shield, the basis of the deep-bore 'tube' tunnels, the first of which opened between Tower Hill and Bermondsey in 1870. Eschewing steam-haulage, it was cable-operated. The tube system was also used to construct the City and South London Railway between King William Street in the City and Stockwell, which opened in 1890, now the City branch of the Northern Line. It was the first underground electric railway in the world. This line was followed by the Waterloo and City Line (1898) and the Central Line between Shepherd's Bush and the Bank (1900). The existing District and Metropolitan Railways switched to electricity, with the Circle electrified in 1905. The great success of the Central Line encouraged the building of other lines, notably the Bakerloo, Piccadilly and Hampstead to Charing Cross lines, with the key figure being Charles Tyson Yerkes, an American financier of dubious practices but boundless energy. The Northern line ran from Angel to Clapham in 1901. The Piccadilly, opened in 1906, initially ran from Hammersmith to Finsbury Park, making it the longest line that fed commuters and shoppers from West London into the West End. Sensing the possibilities of expanding London, Yerkes planned an extension for the Hampstead line to Golders Green, which opened in 1907. However, there was no large-scale expansion of the system into Docklands. In 1909, another American, Gordon Selfridge, opened the West End's largest department store, one that occupied an entire block of Oxford Street.

New and existing transport systems created multiple links within London, ensuring new possibilities for individual parts of the city. As a result of such developments and of a rising population, some areas expanded greatly: Acton increased from 3,000 people in 1861 to 3,800 in 1901, while the population of St Pancras, more than 100,000 in 1831, had nearly doubled by 1861 and, by 1901, was 235,000, although, by then, its growth had ceased as areas farther from the centre became the locus of growth. By 1901, the parish of St Mary's, Islington, had a population exceeding 330,000. The fastest growing urban areas in 1891–1901 were inner suburbs: Walthamstow and West Ham, the latter a major centre of manufacturing as well as a county borough, and both linked to central London by the transport system.

London is very much Holmes's domain, in part, as explained in *A Study in Scarlet*, thanks to the 'long walks, which appeared to take him into the lowest portions of the city', a characteristic found within the works of Charles Dickens as well. There can also be an ennui in London, one differently expressed by John Buchan, who, at the beginning of *The Thirty-Nine Steps*, echoes John Watson at the opening of *A Study in Scarlet*. Yet, Watson is released from his boredom by his meeting with Holmes, who is concerned to use science to advance and apply knowledge. London, indeed, was a major centre of science and is presented by Doyle in that light, and not least by the contrast he draws with Oxbridge. Indeed, in 'The Creeping Man' (1923), through the character Professor Presbury of Camford, Oxbridge emerges as unable to understand the limitations of science, which Presbury seeks to use to his own ends.

Doyle uses Holmes to draw attention to the developing nature of detective methods, which indeed were of great interest to him due to his commitment to righting miscarriages of justice, as in his *The Case of Oscar Slater* (1912), which was Doyle's attack on a 1909 conviction in Glasgow that in part rested on a seriously flawed identification parade. In 'The Norwood Builder' (1903), Lestrade is very keen on the evidence from a thumb-mark which he encourages Holmes to examine with a magnifying glass, adding 'will you please compare that print with this wax impression of young McFarlane's right thumb, taken by my orders this morning?'. This was indeed the period when the use of fingerprinting was spreading, but in this case the villain is using a fingerprint to his own end. Holmes trumps Lestrade with additional scientific knowledge, although, characteristically, he does not push it too far:

> 'When those packets were sealed up, Jonas Oldacre got McFarlane to secure one of the seals by putting his thumb upon the soft wax. It would be done so quickly and so naturally that I dare say the young man himself has no recollection of it. Very likely it just so happened, and Oldacre had himself no

> notion of the use he would put it to. Brooding over the case in that den of his, it suddenly struck him what absolutely damning evidence he could make against McFarlane by using that thumb-mark. . . . If you examine among these documents which he took with him into his retreat, I will lay you a wager that you find the seal with the thumb-mark upon it'.

In Doyle's non-Holmes stories, there is also mention of advances in science. Thus, in 'The Horror of the Heights' (1913):

> the fact that something closely resembling the organism of malaria was discovered in this blood, and that Joyce-Armstrong is known to have suffered from intermittent fever, is a remarkable example of the new weapons which modern science has placed in the hands of our detectives.

As another instance of scientific modernity, Holmes also goes in for what would later be termed profiling, and notably so in 'The Golden Pince-Nez' (1904). In 'The Abbey Grange' (1904), he contrasts the burglary with the more normal pattern:

> 'burglars who have done a good stroke of business are, as a rule, only too glad to enjoy the proceeds in peace and quiet without embarking on another perilous undertaking. Again, it is unusual for burglars to operate at so early an hour; it is unusual for burglars to strike a lady to prevent her screaming, since one would imagine that was the sure way to make her scream; it is unusual for them to commit murder when their numbers are sufficient to overpower one man; it is unusual for them to be content with a limited plunder when there is much more within their reach; and, finally, I should say that it was very unusual for such men to leave a bottle half empty'.

The stories provide opportunities to discuss different types of psychological explanation, as when Watson proposes the idea of an *idée fixe* in 'The Six Napoleons' (1904); referring to 'modern French psychologists' without criticizing them. Holmes, however, is sceptical: 'for no amount of *idée fixe* would enable your interesting monomaniac to find out where these busts were situated'.

Profiling rests in part on how Doyle has Holmes explain an aspect of *The Martyrdom of Man* (1872), a secularist Social Darwinian account of human development by William Winwood Reade (1838–1875). He recommends the book to Watson in *The Sign of Four*:

> 'He remarks that, while the individual man is an insoluble puzzle, in the aggregate he becomes a mathematical certainty. You can, for example, never foretell what any one man will do, but you can say with precision what an average number will be up to. Individuals vary, but percentages remain constant. So says the statistician'.

Then the chase begins. Reade, who has already been recommended by Holmes in that story, also wrote on Africa, where he had travelled, and on Druids.

The variety of Holmes's London extends to activities, occupations and areas. Thus, in 'The Red-Headed League' (1891), which he was to describe as his second-favourite Holmes short story, Jabez Wilson describes his pawnbroking business at Coburg Square and, having worked for the League, finds that its head has given a false address, that of a manufactory of artificial knee-caps at King Edward Street near St Paul's. Holmes and Watson visit the fictional square, which is described as

> a pokey, little, shabby-genteel place, where four lines of dingy two-storied brick houses looked out into a small railed-in enclosure, where a lawn of weedy grass and a few clumps of faded laurel bushes made a hard fight against a smoke-laden and uncongenial atmosphere.

The description, however, is not as distinctive as those of London by Dickens and does not grip. Instead, as in this story, the approach is functional. There is a capturing here of the juxtaposition that makes a city so dynamic and also unsettling, one seen in

Booth's maps of social distribution. This was necessary for the plot but also arresting in its presentation, with a prequel to T. S. Eliot's more spectral vision of the London crowd in his poem *The Waste Land* (1922). Watson continues:

> The road in which we found ourselves as we turned round the corner from the retired Saxe-Coburg Square presented as great a contrast to it as the front of a picture does to the back. It was one of the main arteries which convey the traffic of the City to the north and west. The roadway was blocked with the immense stream of commerce flowing in a double tide inwards and outwards, while the footpaths were black with the hurrying swarm of pedestrians. It was difficult to realise as we looked at the line of fine shops and stately business premises that they were really abutted on the other side upon the faded and stagnant square which we had just quitted.

Holmes knows his way through the 'endless labyrinth of gas-lit streets'. That is not an attractive image, as people get trapped in labyrinths. In *A Study in Scarlet*, Jefferson Hope remarks: 'I reckon that of all the mazes that ever were contrived, this city is the most confusing'. Linked to that comes another aspect of London as labyrinth, for Holmes points out how easy it is to vanish amidst its numbers. Yet, as G. K. Chesterton observed in 'A Defence of Detective Stories' (1901), this also gave the detective an epic character:

> Of this realisation of a great city itself as something wild and obvious the detective story is certainly the 'Iliad'. No one can have failed to notice that in these stories the hero or the investigator crosses London with something of the loneliness and liberty of a prince in a tale of elfland.

Returning from India at the start of *A Study in Scarlet*, Watson describes the city as 'that great cesspool into which all the loungers and idlers of the Empire are irresistibly drained . . . the great wilderness of London'. The last is a presentation of urban anonymity but also of a danger. In one of his last Holmes stories, 'The Lion's Mane', published in December 1926, and with Holmes as the narrator, he refers to 'my withdrawal to my little Sussex home, when I had given myself up entirely to that soothing life of Nature for which I had so often yearned during the long years spent amid the gloom of London'.

Many of the stories take place south of the Thames. South London is a particular dislike in the stories, as with Brixton Road, where *A Study in Scarlet* really begins:

> Number 3, Lauriston Gardens, wore an ill-omened and minatory look. It was one of four which stood back some little way from the street, two being occupied and two empty. The latter looked out with three tiers of vacant melancholy windows, which were blank and dreary, save that here and there a 'To Let' card had developed like a cataract upon the bleared panes. A small garden sprinkled over with a scattered eruption of sickly plants separated each of these houses from the street, and was traversed by a narrow pathway, yellowish in colour, and consisting apparently of a mixture of clay and of gravel. The whole place was very sloppy from the rain which had fallen through the night. The garden was bounded by a three-foot brick wall with a fringe of wood rails upon the top.

So also with South London in *The Sign of Four* where the murder takes place in Norwood:

> Long lines of dull brick houses were only relieved by the coarse glare and tawdry brilliancy of public-houses at the corners. Then came rows of two-storied villas, each with a fronting of miniature garden, and then again interminable lines of new, staring brick buildings – the monster tentacles which the giant city was throwing out into the country . . . the howling desert of South London.

In this novel, Watson goes to Pinchin Lane: 'a row of shabby, two-storied brick houses in the lower quarter of Lambeth'. Subsequently, there is a less negative account when Holmes and Watson follow the creosote-sniffing dog Toby into London:

> down the half-rural villa-lined roads which lead to the Metropolis. Now, however, we were beginning to come among continuous streets, where labourers and dockmen were already astir, and slatternly women were taking down shutters and brushing door-steps. At the square-topped corner public-houses business was just beginning, and rough-looking men were emerging, rubbing their sleeves across their beards after their morning wet.

And in 'The Retired Colourman' (1926), in the case of Lewisham, Watson describes:

> the monotonous brick streets, the weary suburban highways. Right in the middle of them, a little island of ancient culture and comfort, lies this old home, surrounded by a high sun-baked wall mottled with lichens and topped with moss.

Holmes tells Watson to cut out the poetry, but Watson is reflecting a sense of individuality and culture lost amidst modernity.

North London also has its problems. In 'The Adventure of the Three Gables', which was published in *The Strand Magazine* in September 1926, Holmes visits Mrs Maberley, who has lived nearly two years in the Three Gables, a house in Harrow Weald:

> A short railway journey, and a shorter drive, brought us to the house, a brick and timber villa, standing in its own acre of undeveloped grassland. Three small projections above the upper windows made a feeble attempt to justify its name. Behind was a grove of melancholy, half-grown pines, and the whole aspect of the place was poor and depressing.

Yet, there is also praise for London and Londoners. In 'The Stockbroker's Clerk' (1893), Watson refers to Hall Pycroft as

> a well-built, fresh-complexioned young fellow with a frank, honest face and a slight, crisp, yellow moustache. He wore a very shiny top-hat and a neat suit of sober black, which made him look what he was – a smart young City man, of the class who have been labelled Cockneys, but who give us our crack Volunteer regiments, and who turn out more fine athletes and sportsmen than any body of men in these islands. His round, ruddy face was naturally full of cheeriness.

This variety of a great city provides the backdrop and personnel for many of Holmes's adventures. So also for those of other writers concerned to emphasise the threats underlying British greatness. Sax Rohmer's Fu-Manchu is a major instance, but there were also threats from fellow nationals. Unsurprisingly, some of those who believed that there were serious threats to the country themselves created secret bodies to counter them, such as the Confederacy, a Conservative secret society founded in 1907 to undermine Free Traders in the constituencies, one followed in 1910 by the Reveille.[12]

In fiction, from the perspective of an author closer to Doyle than Sax Rohmer (the pseudonym for Arthur Sarsfield Ward), comes John Buchan's *The Power-House*. Serialised in *Blackwood's Magazine* in 1913, it appeared as a book in 1916. The threat to Western civilisation comes from Andrew Lumley, a wealthy Englishman, who seeks power and threatens to exploit the vulnerability of an interconnected world. This threat differs significantly from that posed by Professor Moriarty, but there is the same sense of a directing force seeking power and with the ability to strike hard in London. The hero, Sir Edward Leithen, a Tory MP, is conscious of being watched in Piccadilly. That is an aspect of the thin 'sheet of glass' between civilisation and barbarism that was a continual theme for Doyle and for the writers of both detective novels and thrillers.

3

HOLMES'S FORAYS

Rural England

> The crime was committed by a man of medium height with red hair and a cast in the left eye. He limps slightly on the right foot and has a mole just below the shoulder-blade.
> For the moment I was completely taken in.
> You fix upon me a look of dog-like devotion and demand of me a pronouncement à la Sherlock Holmes . . . it is always the clue that attracts you. Alas that he did not smoke the cigarette and leave the ash, and then step in it with a shoe that has nails of a curious pattern.
>
> – Hercule Poirot as reported by Arthur Hastings,
> *The ABC Murders* (1936)

Holmes spent less time in rural England than in its metropolitan counterpart. Moreover, much of his rural investigation was a matter of the South-East, with suburbia and the Home Counties both part of a continuum with the metropolis. This enabled Doyle to offer encomia on rural bliss while also having his detective readily arrive from London. There was in effect an integrated travel system, one in which trains swiftly emanated from London, and travel, by carriage or bicycle or horse or foot, took the detective and others on. Thus, in 'The Golden Pince-Nez' (1904), Holmes and Watson set off from Charing Cross for Chatham at 6:00 a.m., and 'after a long and weary journey' alight 'at a small station some miles from Chatham. While a horse was being put into a trap at the local inn we snatched a hurried breakfast, and so we were all ready for business when we at last arrived at Yoxley Old Place', an arrival predicted for between 8:00 a.m. and 9:00 a.m. It was 'only a reasonable walk to Chatham', they are told.

The train system, which was still expanding up to World War One, is pretty comprehensive, such that in 'Shoscombe Old Place' (1927), Holmes and Watson are able to go for 'the little "halt-on-demand" station of Shoscombe' in Berkshire. However, not all places are easy to reach, not least because of slow or infrequent services or due to inadequately linked transport. In 'The Retired Colourman' (1926), Watson finds Little Purlington in Essex 'not an easy place to reach, for it is on a branch line . . . the train slow. . . . When we at last reached the little station it was a two-mile drive before we came to the Vicarage'. Visiting the Emsworths at Tuxbury Old Hall near Bedford, James Dodd in 'The Blanched Soldier' (1926) finds it 'five miles from anywhere. There was no trap at the station, so I had to walk, carrying my suit-case'. In the non-Holmes 'The Brazilian Cat' (1898), Marshall King goes to Clipton-on-the-March in Suffolk: 'After changing at Ipswich, a little local train deposited me at a small deserted station. . . . I hired a dog-cart [plus driver] at the local inn'.

Resident near Hindhead, Surrey from 1897 to 1907, and Windlesham in Crowborough, Sussex from 1907 until his death in 1930, Doyle was most familiar with this part of rural England and indeed with its excellent rail service to London. Many stories are set there, in part because the individuals involved have long resided in the South-East, but also as a result of people moving there, not least in 'Black Peter' (1904), with Captain Peter Carey, the Dundee seal and whale fisher. Doyle's residence in Surrey and then in Sussex enabled him to understand the perspective of suburbia as an encroachment. Indeed, a significant amount of agricultural land was built over prior to World War One. In *The Valley of*

Fear (1914–15), there is an account of marked rural transformation:

> The village of Birlstone is a small and very ancient cluster of half-timbered cottages on the northern border of the county of Sussex. For centuries it had remained unchanged, but within the last few years its picturesque appearance and situation have attracted a number of well-to-do residents, whose villas peep out from the woods. . . . A number of small shops have come into being to meet the wants of the increased population, so that there seems some prospect that Birlstone may soon grow from an ancient village into a modern town.

Yet, the most memorable rural adventures are further afield, most notably in *The Hound of the Baskervilles*, but also in 'The Adventure of Silver Blaze' (1892). To grasp how readers might have understood these settings, it is necessary to look at the general development of rural England and then at more specific settings, from Devon to Surrey.

Given the master narrative of industrialisation and urbanisation, it is easy today to overlook the continued significance of rural life and agricultural activity in Victorian and Edwardian England. Agriculture was hit hard by the development of transoceanic food imports – notably of meat from Australasia, Argentina and North America and of grain from the last – imports that Doyle was to present in 1914 as vulnerable to submarine attack. Refrigerated holds in large steamships aided meat imports, as did developing techniques in meatpacking. The extension of railway systems overseas, the geopolitical implications of which for British maritime power troubled Halford Mackinder (see chapter 5), also brought food for export to ports such as Buenos Aires. Once transported to Britain, shipments were then unloaded in the expanding harbour facilities, notably in Liverpool – Britain's main North Atlantic port – London and Southampton.

All this competition helped produce a sustained agricultural depression in Britain. This was not true of all products, however;

milk, fruit and vegetables required a freshness that aided domestic production such as, for example, milk in the West Country and market gardening near cities. Yet, except for these products, competition was very hard. It was accentuated by the development of European options, most obviously with Danish bacon but also with German sugar beets and Eastern European grain.

The resulting squeeze on food prices benefited urban workers but hit their agricultural counterparts hard. Employment, rents and profits all declined. So also did the local towns that had existed primarily to process products and service communities. Additional disruption to earlier agricultural methods came with the spread of technology in which machinery replaced workers and, notably, manual farm work, as in the threshing scene in Thomas Hardy's *Tess of the d'Urbervilles* (1891). So also was agriculture disrupted by the railway changing the methods and geography of distribution and processing.

The pressure on the rural economy lessened the value of land, and certainly so relative to capital. The economics of rural estates were far worse than is suggested by visiting many of the stately homes of the period. In 1897, Herbrand Russell, 11th Duke of Bedford, wrote about his 'ruined' estate.[1] Rent rebates were common: 10 per cent on the Blanchland estate of Lord Crewe's Charity in County Durham from 1887 until 1893, and on most of the estate's holdings the 1895 rent was equal to or less than it was in 1870. Rents there did not improve until the 1900s. H. Rider Haggard's *Rural England* (1902) is a detailed non-fiction work, especially on East Anglia, and indeed an example of the novelist as social observer, which Doyle also was in some respects. The agricultural depression hit arable farming particularly hard on the heavier soils such as Essex, where 30 per cent of the arable area was officially 'derelict'. More generally, routine tasks such as hedge-laying were badly delayed, and many fields were chronically neglected and overtaken by thistles and dandelions. In the non-Holmes 'The Jew's Breastplate' (1899), Doyle refers to

Rural Britain saw social tension, notably in Highland Scotland, but also in England. In 1888, Henry, 3rd Earl of Sheffield (1832–1909) – a Sussex landowner who lived close to where Doyle was to settle and also Holmes to retire (as noted in 'The Second Stain') – received a letter. Signed 'Jack the Ripper', it included the following passage:

> 'my duty to let you know, as I think you do, or you would not have the heart to turn out an old tenant like poor Mrs Grover out of her home after such a hard struggle to maintain and bring up her family . . . you and your faithful steward want it all. . . . My knife is nice and sharp'.[3]

This was not a mystery requiring Holmes. Nothing happened to the earl, Mrs Grover was staying with her children after a fall, and Edward Grover, a failed butcher, admitted to writing the letter. Failed butchers were not the type of character that featured in stories by Doyle, or indeed others. This was not, however, an isolated episode. In another example of rural tension, the earl, a former Conservative MP, wrote an open letter in 1889 to the secretary of Sussex County Cricket Club, explaining his resignation as president, in which he referred to two and a half years of pestering by anonymous threats. The unmarried earl, who was rumoured to be homosexual, died abroad. In *The Valley of Fear*, Doyle counterpoints rural Sussex and Pennsylvania mining towns. In northern Sussex, John Douglas, the American who rents Birlstone, and his English wife, find a very different response from particular social groups, as Watson describes:

> He was cheery and genial to all, but somewhat offhand in his manners, giving the impression that he had seen life in social strata on some far lower horizon than the county society of Sussex. Yet, though looked at with some curiosity and reserve by his more cultivated neighbours he soon acquired a great popularity among the villagers, subscribing handsomely to all local objects, and attending their smoking concerts and other functions. . . . The good impression which had been produced

> by his generosity and by his democratic manners. . . . His wife, too, was popular with those who had made her acquaintance, though, after the English fashion, the callers upon a stranger who settled in the county without introductions were few and far between.

Rural tension was seen far more clearly in the novels of Thomas Hardy (1840–1928). In *The Mayor of Casterbridge* (1886), for example, the countryside is presented as prey to both North American grain imports and the corrosive pressures of often new urban norms on traditional rural life. Doyle's reflection of rural tension is somewhat more conventional. In 'The *Gloria Scott*' (1893), for example, a poaching gang is the menacing background in the Norfolk setting. Poaching remained commonplace and was a challenge both to landowners and to police forces. Rural tension was, in large part, a product of long-lasting issues, of which hunting rights were one. These brought tension and conflict between landlords and the rural population, notably in the shape of poaching, but landlords could also compete over hunting and shooting. In Matthias McDonnell Bodkin's 'Murder by Proxy' (1897), Colonel Peyton and Mr Neville have neighbouring estates and dispute shooting rights, Neville calling the Colonel 'a common poacher'.

At the same time, an extension of state power altered the equations of local influence through the development of policing. It involved not simply establishing police forces, which had occurred earlier in the nineteenth century, but also negotiating their relationships with other officials and local society. The key issue here, one that bridged the two relationships, was that between police officers and the landed élite, for it was the latter that provided the officials in rural society.

The position of this élite itself was changing greatly, due to the problems of the rural economy and the formation of the County Councils, both of which accentuated questions of power and authority. Under the Local Government Acts of 1888 and 1894, elected county and town councils took over functions formerly performed by magistrates and the Poor Law Unions. The first act alienated Conservative landowners but was pushed through by a Conservative government in an attempt to pre-empt a more radical measure from a future Liberal government.

The role of the police in detection was particularly problematic because it entailed questioning across social ranks and exposing the difficult dynamics of landed dynasticism and personal relationships. This is a subtext to the Holmes stories, both insofar as the police were concerned and with reference to Holmes. In *The Valley of Fear*, Inspector MacDonald says that he has worked with Holmes before and that 'He plays the game', to which the detective replies:

> 'My own idea of the game, at any rate. I go into a case to help the ends of justice and the work of the police. If ever I have separated myself from the official force, it is because they have first separated themselves from me. I have no wish ever to score at their expense'.

In practice, however, this account leaves out the independent roles of those they have dealt with which could elucidate differences between Holmes and his contemporaries.

Doyle is very different from Hardy in his response to the crises of rural England, but it is an issue in the background of the Holmes stories. The foundation of the National Trust in 1895 gave institutional form to a widespread concern about the disappearance of rural England and Wales but also to a belief that something could be done that did not necessarily involve action through the traditional rural order. Although it came to be, in large part, about tourism and consuming 'heritage', the National Trust was initially about preservation. As such, it reflected a ruralism that became more pronounced as England urbanised. Thus, Hardwicke Rawnsley, one of the founders of the National Trust, launched a public campaign that blocked plans for railway lines into the Lake District and for further quarrying in Borrowdale and into Ennerdale and Ullswater. Rawnsley had complained: 'You will soon have a Cook's tourist railway up Scawfell – and another up Helvellyn – and another up Skiddaw. And then a connecting line, all round'.

As the countryside came to encapsulate national values, so emerged a desire to preserve it, either free of obvious human impact or of the conditions of a worked environment on what was seen as a human scale. The nature of both were presented by Doyle. He also captured a sense of landscape as a repository of and inspiration for identity and history, and as a key medium between past and present.

This is an aspect of the environmental determinism, or at least influence, that became more significant in academic thought and public discussion during this period. The rise of environmentalism looked back to eighteenth-century notions of the role of geography in culture and society,[4] and to the nineteenth-century interest in nationalism and evolution. These concepts combined to suggest an agenda of political history, domestic and international, in which environmentally moulded nation-states played a crucial role, displacing the dynastic interests of ruling houses in favour of what were styled as national interests. In the eighteenth century, the thesis that objective national interests existed had developed rapidly. In large part, this thesis was a product of the Enlightenment proposition that humans live in a universe governed by natural laws which proclaim, among other things, the existence of 'nations'. These were defined through a mixture of geography, language, culture, physical features and even traits of personality. The 'interests of nations', essentially, were to be understood in terms of protecting their geographical, cultural and physical (i.e. security) integrity.

Such ideas became more prominent in the nineteenth century as states were increasingly defined in nationalist terms. This was a process that led to greater interest in ethnic and environmental factors. It was environmental influence that apparently could best explain the differing political trajectories of various ethnic groups, the processes by which they had become nations and states with particular characteristics and interests. Far from being an alternative to nationalism, environmentalism could make these processes appear natural, necessary and inevitable. Doyle's interest in continuity (see chapter 9) was important to his strong sense of national identity.

Trained mostly in the natural sciences, nineteenth-century geographers also assumed a close relationship between humanity and the biophysical environment. They sought to probe this relationship in terms of the environmental control that they took for granted. Halford Mackinder, later a leading geopolitical thinker who took a degree in history, after one in animal morphology, wrote in his 1887 paper 'The Scope and Methods of Geography', of 'an interaction between man and environment'. Environmentalism was an attractive method for the geographers and historians of successful and expanding states.[5]

The inevitable triumph of the 'civilised' was a frequent theme of this period, as with the Oxford geographer Hereford George (1838–1910), author of *Relations of Geography and History* (1901).[6] This was an influential book which appeared in new editions in 1903, 1907, 1910 and 1924, the last of which was reprinted in 1930 – an instance of prewar ideas extending into the interwar period. George stressed the role of geographical influences, not least on strategy such as the 1898 British campaign in Sudan and in the Second Boer War (1899–1902), both of which greatly influenced Doyle. George also argued that human action could, in turn, affect the environment. The significance of geography in the shape of landscape was central to the plot in *The Hound of the Baskervilles* (1901). Two years after its publication, Emil Reich claimed, in his *New Student's Atlas of English History*, 'The paramount importance of geography as the basis of a study of history has been brought home to Englishmen by the late war in South Africa'.

Although Doyle's literary action ranges much further, to India and notably to the United States, with the physical geography captured in the account of Utah, he does not have Holmes leave Britain other than for his Swiss adventure with Moriarty and the briefly mentioned long aftermath, which is not used, as it readily could have been, as the setting for adventures described later.

These international adventures, however, would have taken Holmes from the familiar settings that readers expected – settings that were social as well as geographical. Instead of ranging wider, the ideas of a close relationship between landscape and people are primarily captured in his treatment of England in the Holmes stories. This relationship might be shrunk by railways and the post, standardized by the press, regulated by the police and united by a common nationality and humanity, but still there are significant differences. In 'The Copper Beeches', Doyle has Watson applaud the beauty of the Hampshire farmland from the train, whereas Holmes argues that 'the smiling and beautiful countryside' offers the seclusion that makes 'hidden wickedness' easier:

> 'You look at these scattered houses, and you are impressed by their beauty. . . . I look at them, and the only thought that comes to me is a feeling of their isolation, and of the impunity with which crime may be committed there . . . they always fill me with a certain horror. It is my belief, Watson, founded upon my experience, that the lowest and vilest alleys in London do not present a more dreadful record of sin than does the smiling and beautiful countryside. . . . Think of the deeds of hellish cruelty, the hidden wickedness which may go on, year in, year out, in such places, and none the wiser'.

That hidden menace, however, does not prevent others hoping and dreaming. In 'The Crooked Man', Henry Wood dreams 'of the bright green fields and the hedges of England', while, in 'The Resident Patient', Watson, in the heat of a close, rainy London August, yearns 'for the glades of the New Forest or the shingle of Southsea', both of which could be readily reached from London by rail. In 'The Dancing Men', the 'clear eyes and florid cheeks' of Hilton Cubitt from rural Norfolk 'told of a life led far from the fogs of Baker Street. He seemed to bring a whiff of his strong, fresh, bracing, east-coast air with him as he entered . . . this man of the old English soil'. This adventure takes Holmes and Watson on a train to North Walsham followed by a seven-mile carriage ride to Ridling Thorpe Manor.

> There was much around us to interest us, for we were passing through as singular a country-side as any in England, where a few scattered cottages represented the population of to-day, while on every hand enormous square-towered churches bristled up from the flat green landscape and told of the glory and prosperity of old East Anglia. At last the violent rim of the German Ocean appeared over the green edge of the Norfolk coast.

It is a passage that certainly did not capture the often leaden character of the North Sea, while, in my experience, the church towers do not bristle. In 'The Solitary Cyclist', it is the turn of the country near Farnham in Surrey: 'The heath was covered with golden patches of flowering gorse, gleaming magnificently in the light of the bright spring sunshine'.

Holmes, however, has a very different perspective; in 'The Resident Patient':

> neither the country nor the sea presented the slightest attraction to him. He loved to lie in the very centre of five millions of people, with his filaments stretching out and running through them, responsive to every little rumour or suspicion of unsolved crime. Appreciation of Nature found no place among his many gifts, and his only change was when he turned his mind from the evil-doer of the town to track down his brother of the country.

Similarly, 'the glories of the landscape' at Capleton in 'Silver Blaze' are 'all wasted' on Holmes. 'The Lion's Mane', however, finds Holmes, later in life, in a very different mood: 'my little Sussex home, when I had given myself up entirely to that soothing life of Nature for which I had so often yearned during the long years spent amid the gloom of London'.

Capleton, like Dartmoor as a whole, is an England close by rail, but very different from the feel of the Home Counties. In 'Silver Blaze', there are references to the sparsely inhabited nature north of Dartmoor and subsequently, of the stables at King's Pyland:

> The country round is very lonely, but about half a mile to the north there is a small cluster of villas which have been built by a Tavistock contractor for the use of invalids and others who may wish to enjoy the pure Dartmoor air. Tavistock itself lies two miles to the west, while across the moor, also about two miles distant, is the larger training establishment of Capleton. . . . In every other direction the moor is a complete wilderness, inhabited only by a few roaming gipsies.

Tavistock, which was on the train route, is referred to as a 'quaint old Devonshire town', while nearby Dartmoor in this story lacks the brooding neo-Gothic character of *The Hound of the Baskervilles*. In 'Silver Blaze', Holmes and Watson arrive at the stable at King's Pyland:

> our driver pulled up at a neat little red-brick villa with overhanging eaves, which stood by the road. Some distance off, across a paddock, lay a long grey-tiled outbuilding. In every other direction the low curves of the moor, bronze-coloured from the fading ferns, stretched away to the sky-line, broken only by the steeples of Tavistock, and by a cluster of houses away to the westward, which marked the Capleton stables.

Later, in 'Silver Blaze' there is again a favourable reference to the moor:

> The sun was beginning to sink behind the stables of Capleton, and the long sloping plain in front of us was tinged with gold, deepening into rich, ruddy brown where the faded ferns and brambles caught the evening light.

If 'the glories of the landscape' appeared 'all wasted upon [Watson's] companion', it was because Holmes was 'sunk in the deepest thought'. There is no reference in this story to a monstrous hound. Indeed, the dog of note is that which does not bark in the night-time because he knew the midnight visitor. In addition, Holmes is threatened with a dog by Silas Brown when he visits the Mapleton stables.

A physical and a psychological contrast is initially drawn a decade later in *The Hound of the Baskervilles*, in which Doyle has more room to write than in 'Silver Blaze' and more of a need to create atmosphere, which indeed is central to both puzzle and plot. Watson notes in *The Hound* that Devon viewed from the railway is a lusher aspect of well-settled cultivation:

> the brown earth had become ruddy, the brick had changed to granite, and red cows grazed in well-hedged fields where the lush grasses and more luxuriant vegetation spoke of a richer, if a damper, climate.

And then there is Dartmoor, initially seen 'like some fantastic landscape in a dream'.

Subsequently, there is in this novel a sense of the menace underneath civilisation: 'behind the peaceful and sunlit country-side there rose, ever dark against the evening sky, the long, gloomy curve of the moor, broken by the jagged and sinister hills'. Holmes, nevertheless, is sceptical about the idea of a problem specific to Dartmoor: 'A devil with merely local powers like a parish vestry would be too inconceivable a thing'. This is an instance of the dry wit that is present in many of the stories. As with Agatha Christie, a speedy approach to the text can lead to a tendency to overlook the humour, but it rises readily to the cautious bait.

Holmes, meanwhile, is successfully able to visit Dartmoor in his mind thanks to a major development of the previous century, one repeatedly referenced in the stories: more comprehensive mapping. Indeed, that is an aspect of the novelist's method and skill – providing accounts of fictional places, but doing so in a fashion that suggests that they have a precise location that can be readily mastered. The Ordnance Survey had mapped the entire country and at a scale that permitted the differentiation of individual fields. Alongside the standard coverage at one inch to the mile, there was mapping at six and twenty-five inches to the mile.

Holmes goes to Devon at first 'in spirit': 'I sent down to Stanford's for the ordnance map of this portion of the moor, and my spirit has hovered over it all day. I flatter myself that I could find my way about'. Based in Covent Garden – and with Edward Stanford II, Cartographer to the Queen and then to Edward VII – Stanford's were the sole agents for Ordnance Survey Maps in England and Wales. Holmes thereby is able to outline the geography of the environs of Baskerville Hall. So also with the 'large ordnance map of the neighbourhood' Holmes obtains to understand and highlight the geographical features of the Priory School in the short story of that title. In the cold, bracing atmosphere of the Peak Country of Derbyshire, the school faces to the north:

> a great rolling moor . . . a peculiarly desolate plain. A few moor farmers have small holdings, where they rear sheep and cattle. Except these, the plover and the curlew are the inhabitants until you come to the Chesterfield high road. There is a church there, you see, a few cottages, and an inn. Beyond that the hills become precipitous.

Doyle's interest in the South-West of England allowed him to explore Celticist themes. 'The Devil's Foot', published in *The Strand Magazine* in December 1910, took the geography further, beyond Devon, with Holmes and Watson on holiday at Poldhu on the Lizard Peninsula in Cornwall, in a story set in 1897, in order to help the former recuperate from the strain of his constant hard work in and near London. There is an attempt to capture the ambivalent nature of the coast:

> From the windows of our little whitewashed house, which stood high upon a grassy headland, we looked down upon the whole sinister semicircle of Mounts Bay, that old death trap of sailing vessels, with its fringe of black cliffs and surge-swept reefs on which innumerable seamen have met their end. With a northerly breeze it lies placid and sheltered, inviting the storm-tossed craft to tack into it for rest and protection. Then

> comes the sudden swirl round of the wind . . . and the last battle in the creaming breakers.

The last is a wonderful phrase. Doyle continues with a different sense of history:

> On the land side our surroundings were as sombre as on the sea. It was a country of rolling moors, lonely and dun-coloured, with an occasional church tower to mark the site of some old-world village. In every direction upon these moors there were traces of some vanished race which had passed utterly away, and left as its sole record strange monuments of stone, irregular mounds which contained the burned ashes of the dead, and curious earthworks which hinted at prehistoric strife. The glamour and mystery of the place, with its sinister atmosphere of forgotten nations, appealed to the imagination of my friend, and he spent much of his time in long walks and solitary meditations upon the moor.

Holmes also displays his scholarship on Celticist themes, and, through him, Doyle's: 'The ancient Cornish language had also arrested his attention, and he had, I remember, conceived the idea that it was akin to the Chaldean, and had been largely derived from the Phoenician traders in tin. He had received a consignment of books upon philology'.

At the close of this story, Holmes goes back 'to the study of those Chaldean roots which are surely to be traced in the Cornish branch of the great Celtic speech'. This is an aspect of the fascination of the period with civilisational roots and routes, not least the diffusion of languages and the spread of ancient peoples. In contrast to these Devon and Cornwall adventures, for which there is rational explanation which Holmes is there to unravel, 'The Terror of Blue John Gap', a Doyle story published in *The Strand Magazine* (August 1910), has no Holmes. It begins with Dr James Hardcastle going, in April 1907, to Derbyshire in order to help his recovery from tuberculosis, 'the usual morning cough'. He finds the Peak District 'picturesque in the extreme' and explores the limestone caves, notably Blue John. There is a local legend of 'the Terror' that lives in the cave and seizes sheep. Hardcastle, at first, dismisses the tale of the roaring made by the monster, assuming the noise's source to be an underground water system, as Holmes might have done. Yet, when he goes into the cave, he senses the monster. The police reject the account, while the doctor encounters a 'monstrous inchoate creature', firing at it, but not killing it. The local poor then seal the cave. Prefiguring *Dr Challenger and the Lost World* (1912), Hardcastle suggests that the monster was the product of the subterranean evolution of a species of cave bear that had been able by a rift in the mountain to wander into the outer world.

This is an atypical literary depiction of Doyle's rural England. Instead, as with others,[7] he generally offers a romantic quality to the idea of rural life, but also provides a reaction to disquiet about aspects of urban life. In 'Black Peter', Doyle certainly presents the iron workings of the Weald as having fallen victim to 'the North'. However, as so often with his stories, the process itself is historicised and not therefore discussed as a present plight. In 'The Man from Archangel', a non-Holmes short story by Doyle published in *London Society* in January 1885, the narrator, John McVittie, who had been a lawyer in a Midlands town, leaves the 'vile, smoke-polluted town' for a remote inheritance in rural Caithness. There he seeks refuge from, as he describes it, 'the swarming, restless race of which I am a member', including the officials in the county town of Wick.

Within the British Empire, to describe yourself as 'English' was the norm, including for people who by geography rather than ethnicity were Irish or Scots. As an added aspect of the primacy of Englishness, there were many cases of upper-class or professional people who were born and lived most of their lives outside the British Isles – with, usually, the critical exception of having been educated at an English public school – who still called themselves English. They could be simultaneously English and Scottish, Welsh or Irish, with English being their wider identity. Thus, in 1915, the kilt-wearing Scottish general Sir Ian Hamilton

(1853–1947) described Horatio Kitchener (1850–1916), whose family home was in Ireland, as the 'idol of England' with no sense of incongruity.[8] While the English tended not to differentiate themselves from Britishness, there was also a crucial multinational character to Britishness. Most particularly, Scots benefited greatly from Britain and its empire. The English essentially called the shots, certainly in financial terms, but the Scots (and Welsh and many of the Irish) largely acquiesced, partly because of the argument of Britishness. Moreover, they could be the first to correct any foreigners who called them 'English'.

That Scotland retained considerable independence within the United Kingdom also militated against political nationalism. It had its own established church and educational system, as well as a distinctive legal system. Furthermore, in 1885, the Scottish Office and Secretary were created, the first secretary of state for Scotland since 1746.

Yet, alongside an awareness of distinctive features and a different heritage, nationalism was weak in Scotland, in large part due to its identification with the idea of Britain and the benefits of the British Empire. There was a re-emergent cultural identity, with kilts and literary consciousness, but no real drive for independence. The religious dimension, so obvious in Ireland, was lacking. Launched in 1853, the National Association for the Vindication of Scottish Rights pressed for administrative devolution and cabinet-level representation but was not explicitly nationalist. The notion of 'North Britain' was rejected by the late nineteenth century in favour of that of Scotland, but it was an increasingly anglicised Scotland.

Five of the ten prime ministers between 1880 and 1935 were Scottish. As in the eighteenth century, the Scots were heavily represented in the army. Furthermore, Scotland was not only an aspect of imperial Britishness, as with the military, politics and trade of Scotland, but also a local imperial identity, the same fundamentally as being British and Canadian. Individual careers reflected the significance of British links. Liberal Prime Minister William Gladstone, born in England to two Scottish parents, retained a

Scottish connection, but Liverpool, Oxford, London and Hawarden in Wales were also crucial places in his life and experience.

However, with important variations of their own, the Scots subscribed to the prevalent Whig interpretation of history. This was a British public myth that offered a comforting and glorious account that appeared appropriate for a state that ruled much of the globe and was exporting its constitutional arrangements to other parts of the world.

At the same time, thanks to improved transport and more leisure, Britain was becoming better known. Consisting of thirty-one sheets, *Philips' Clear Print Half-Inch Cycling Map of England and Wales* first appeared in 1903, taking forward a genre of maps first produced in 1876. Demand rose greatly, with the press runs of Bartholomew's cycling maps rising from two thousand in the early 1890s to sixty thousand in 1908, and the mechanisation of folding ensured that the maps could be made more user friendly. The first national road atlas for cars was *Pratt's Road Atlas of England and Wales for Motorists* (1905), which was published by the Anglo-American Oil Company. Charles Pratt was an oil company director, and Pratt's a name of 'Perfection Motor Spirit'. A Scotland and Ireland atlas followed in 1907. Britain was becoming more accessible.

4

SOCIETY

> 'It's no wonder my uncle felt as if trouble were coming on him in such a place as this. It's enough to scare any man. I'll have a row of electric lamps up here inside of six months, and you won't know it again, with a thousand-candle power Swan and Edison right here in front of the hall door'.

Arriving with Watson at Baskerville Hall, Sir Henry Baskerville, a new baronet from the New World in a new century,[1] proposes at once to banish the sombreness of the past that has made him shudder.

As with the differences within the Baskerville family, society for Holmes is principally a matter of the individuals he comes across. There is an emphasis on individuals and their propensity to good or evil – a propensity influenced by heredity, which in part reflects the widespread interest of the period in eugenics. This propensity is reflected in the continued interest in guides to character, not least in terms of physiognomy, or the craniology that interests Dr Mortimer in *The Hound of the Baskervilles*. Thus, in 'The Empty House', Watson has a 'good look' at the captured Colonel Sebastian Moran:

> It was a tremendously virile and yet sinister face which was turned towards us. With the brow of a philosopher above and

> the jaw of a sensualist below, the man must have started with great capacities for good or for evil. But one could not look upon his cruel blue eyes, with their drooping, cynical lids, or upon the fierce, aggressive nose and the threatening, deep-lined brow, without reading Nature's plainest danger-signals.

Another instance of an individual who demeans his group is provided through Watson's description of the wealthy Lord Mount-James in 'The Missing Three-Quarter'. With an emphasis on clothes and conversation, and not physiognomy, he is introduced as peculiar and quickly becomes mean:

> a queer little old man jerking and twitching in the doorway. He was dressed in rusty black, with a very broad-brimmed top-hat and a loose white necktie – the whole effect being that of a very rustic parson or an undertaker's mute. Yet, in spite of his shabby and even absurd appearance, his voice had a sharp crackle, and his manner a quick intensity which commanded attention.

Lord Mount-James screams at Holmes that he will not spend a penny to find his missing nephew, and even when frightened 'the noble miser only offers £10'. Holmes subsequently reveals that his 'sympathies in this matter are entirely against that nobleman'.

Heredity as opposed to environment is a frequent issue, as exemplified in an exchange about Sir Henry shared between Watson and Dr Mortimer in the train as it entered Devon:

> 'I never saw a Devonshire man who did not swear by his county', I remarked.
>
> 'It depends upon the breed of man quite as much as on the country', said Dr Mortimer. 'A glance at our friend here reveals the rounded head of the Celt, which carries inside it the Celtic enthusiasm and power of attachment. Poor Sir Charles's head was of a very rare type, half Gaelic, half Ivernian in its characteristics'.

Holmes argues strongly for heredity in 'The Empty House' (1903):

> 'I have a theory that the individual represents in his development the whole procession of his ancestors, and that such a sudden turn to good or evil stands for some strong influence which came from the line of his pedigree. The person becomes, as it were, the epitome of the history of his own family'.

Indeed, ancestral (or family) history was a key theme for Doyle, one that was not only demonstrated in his historical novels. Heredity, not ability, is also the crucial issue with Sherlock Holmes's brilliant adversary, Moriarty:

> 'the man had hereditary tendencies of the most diabolical kind. A criminal strain ran in his blood, which instead of being modified, was increased and rendered infinitely more dangerous by his extraordinary mental powers'.

So also with non-Holmes stories. Lord Linchmere explains Sir Thomas Rossiter to Dr Hamilton in 'The Beetle-Hunter':

> 'he comes from a stock which is deeply tainted with insanity. He has more than once had homicidal outbreaks, which are the more painful because his inclination is always to attack the very person to whom he is most attached'.

Stereotypes play a role. Sir Thomas is introduced as 'a tall, thin figure, curiously angular and bony', but, before he later launches his mad attempt at murder, he has 'the silhouette of a bulky and misshapen dwarf'.

The Holmes stories don't emphasize the often stark reflections Doyle offered elsewhere, for example in 'The Curse of Eve' (1894):

> birth, and lust, and illness, and death are changeless things, and when one of these harsh facts springs out upon a man at some sudden turn of the path of life, it dashes off for the moment his mask of civilisation and gives a glimpse of the stranger and stronger face below.

This story, of the biting anxieties of childbirth, which include medical cupidity and the cruelty of Nature, ends with a successful birth, and a concluding paragraph whose dark philosophy would be far better remembered were it in a Holmes story, which circulated much more widely:

> So he sat in silence with his hand in hers. The lamp was burning dim and the first cold light of dawn was breaking through the window. The night had been long and dark, but the day was the sweeter and the purer in consequence. London was waking up. The roar began to rise from the street. Lives had come and lives had gone, but the great machine was still working out its dim and tragic destiny.

As we can see from 'Eve's' story, Doyle is sensitive to the position of women, as with Irene Adler and also Violet Hunter in 'The Copper Beeches'. He possibly shows this best in 'The Doctors of Hoyland' (1894), a non-Holmes short story in which James Ripley is concerned about competition for his medical services from a new doctor, the highly talented Verrinder Smith, on whom he calls only to discover to his surprise that the woman he meets is not a wife but, instead, the doctor:

> He had never seen a woman doctor before, and his whole conservative soul rose up in revolt at the idea. He could not recall any Biblical injunction that the man should remain ever the doctor and woman the nurse, and yet he felt as if a blasphemy had been committed.

In a dialogue that captures the attitudes of the period, Ripley tells Smith that 'Ladies are in danger of losing their privileges when they usurp the place of the other sex', and that he does 'not think medicine a suitable profession for women and that [he has] a personal objection to masculine ladies'. Smith brilliantly replies, 'if it makes women masculine that *would* be a considerable deterioration'. And she points out that a paper of his in the *Lancet* is flawed because it fails to draw on the latest research. Moreover,

Smith proves a good doctor who wins over Ripley's former patients and also banishes superstition. There is wit in the writing:

> Mrs Crowder, who had always regarded the birthmark upon her second daughter Eliza as a sign of the indignation of the Creator at a third helping of raspberry tart which she had partaken of during a critical period, learned that, with the help of two galvanic needles, the mischief was not irreparable.

In the event, Ripley has a compound fracture. Smith successfully tends him, leading Ripley to reject his brother's pejorative views about women doctors, apologise to Smith, and propose to her, only for Smith to tell him she is off to a Parisian vacancy and does not intend to marry.

The Holmes stories very much address the position of women and accomplish this through characterisation and plot. Women are presented as able and willing to seek the services of the great detective. Many, however, are oppressed by men who seek to control them – whether fathers, brothers, husbands or would-be spouses. The pressure is psychological, but also physical. In a long-standing pattern in fiction, incarceration is a common theme, as is physical violence. Surveillance is a regular element of this pressure. Thus, Holmes emerges as a rescuer, a chivalric character made more so by his lack of lust as a drive. There is a quasi-Wagnerian aspect indeed to some of the presentation of the truly noble hero.

Holmes also applauds women who have what he sees as quality, while himself fending off the idea of marriage. Furthermore, at the close of *The Sign of Four*, instead of congratulating Watson on his engagement to Mary Morstan, Holmes ruminates about the risk that love poses to the faculties of reason:

> 'I think she is one of the most charming young ladies I ever met, and might have been most useful in such work as we have been doing. She had a decided genius that way; witness the way in which she preserved that Agra plan from all the other papers of her father. But love is an emotional thing, and what-

> ever is emotional is opposed to that true, cold reason which I place above all things. I should never marry myself, lest I bias my judgment'.

Watson, in contrast, is presented as both normal and a role model, in part through his successful domesticity, having shared very cramped quarters with Holmes. Watson's wife, in turn, is ready to allow him to accompany Holmes on missions. Yet, just as Holmes eventually returns from the Reichenbach Falls, so Watson is released by widowerhood to renew a closer relationship with Holmes. Rational male friendship is a key element. Subsequent suggestions of a sexual element are unconvincing and not supported by the stories.

Industrial urban society served women little better than rural society had. In both cases, women were affected by social and ecological challenges similar to those of men, but they also faced additional problems. Like most men, most women had to cope with gruelling labour and debilitating diseases; but aside from the perils of giving birth, their legal position was worse. This was a reflection of a culture that awarded control and respect to men, and left little role for female merit or achievement. The restrictive nature of the work available to women, and the confining implications of family and social life, together defined the existence of the vast majority of women. For the celebration of Victoria's Golden Jubilee in 1887, the women and children of the town of Ashby-de-la-Zouche sat down to a tea of sandwiches, bread and butter, and cake in the marketplace, while the men had earlier had a hearty meal of roast beef, mutton, potatoes, plum pudding and beer, which had been prepared by women.

Industrialisation ensured that more, predominantly single, women worked in factories, while it reduced rural opportunities such as spinning. Women generally moved into the low-skill, low-pay, 'sweated' sector as they were denied access to the new technologies. Female factory workers were generally worse treated than men, a practice in which the trade unions (which were male organisations) cooperated with the management. Both condemned the women woollen workers of Batley and Dewsbury for organising themselves in an 1875 dispute. Definitions of skills, which affected pay, were controlled by men and favoured them; skilled women, such as the weavers of Preston or Bolton, were poorly recognised. In contrast, women in the pottery industry were able to maintain status and pay despite male opposition.

Divorce was costly and therefore not a possibility for the poor. As a result, former practices of 'self-divorce' continued, while cohabitation was another option, though offering most women no economic security. Women suffered because marital desertions were generally a matter of men leaving, with the women bearing the burden of supporting the children: poverty made some men heedless of the Victorian cult of the family and patriarchy. This cult was strengthened by the normal belief that the home was the key way to maintain morality, which was the basis for the drama in some of the Holmes stories, for example 'The Second Stain', which, in turn, drew on the use of this idea by other writers. This drama is sometimes presented in terms of a destabilising character in gender relations linked to the suffragette movement. While attractive to some literary critics, this is not a convincing interpretation.

Doyle made reference to the problems of divorce for those who were not poor. In 'The Devil's Foot', Sterndale complains that he could not marry Brenda Tregennis: 'for I have a wife who has left me for years and yet whom, by the deplorable laws of England, I could not divorce'. In 'The Abbey Grange', the wealthy Kent landowner Sir Eustace Brackenstall is a drunkard who beats his wife, Mary, who declares to Holmes and Watson:

> 'To be with such a man for an hour is unpleasant. Can you imagine what it means for a sensitive and high-spirited woman to be tied to him for day and night? It is a sacrilege, a crime, a villainy to hold such a marriage is binding. I say that these monstrous laws of yours will bring a curse upon the land – Heaven will not let such wickedness endure'.

Doyle was a supporter of divorce reform, and this is an instructive deployment of Heaven against the idea of the sanctity of the marriage vows.

The horror of control by a husband is most strongly presented by Doyle in a powerful non-Holmes story, 'The Case of Lady Sannox', published in *The Tatler* in November 1893, a newly launched monthly with the writer Jerome K. Jerome as one of the two co-editors. (Other notable contributors included Kipling, Twain, Wells and Zangwill.) The 'notorious' Lady Sannox is clearly depicted as an adulteress. A former actress, she 'had a liking for new experiences, and was gracious to most men who wooed her'. Lady Sannox is married to a man who appears much older than she and focusses on gardening. She has a scandalously open affair with the highly talented surgeon Douglas Stone, a sensualist who has a 'mad passion' for her. Stone is tricked by Lord Sannox into operating on the face of his wife, his lordship then grimly remarking, 'I had long intended to make a little example'. Stone goes mad and Lady Sannox, her face mutilated, becomes a nun. In 2008, in an instance of bridging to the non-Holmes stories, an American radio series called 'The Further Adventures of Sherlock Holmes' had Holmes investigate the reason for Stone's breakdown.

A large proportion of working-class couples lived together out of wedlock, often in what were called 'folk marriages'. At any rate, social and economic pressures helped to drive women towards co-habitation or marriage and also, whether they were unmarried or married, towards employment. While useful, and indeed a should-be factor in the plot of 'The Solitary Cyclist', the Married Women's Property Acts of 1870 and 1882, which established these property rights, could only mean so much to the poor. Nevertheless, co-habitation and, even more, marriage offered most women a form of stability, albeit precarious. That helps illuminate the nobility of Godfrey Staunton in 'The Missing Three-Quarter'. In love with his landlady's daughter, he married her. Dr Armstrong explains:

> 'She was as good as she was beautiful, and as intelligent as she was good. No man need be ashamed of such a wife. But Godfrey was the heir to this crabbed old nobleman, and it was quite certain that the news of his marriage would have been the end of his inheritance'.

This was not always the course of such relationships. Many, indeed, were more exploitative. However, for Staunton to be a hero, that was not the acceptable outcome. Instead, there was the very different one of a good death (albeit without a cleric) and a classic Victorian deathbed scene, of pictorial, notably pre-Raphaelite, clarity, when consumption of the most virulent kind struck in the 'house of grief':

> A woman, young and beautiful, was lying dead upon the bed. Her calm, pale face, with dim, wide-opened blue eyes, looked upwards from amid a great tangle of golden hair. At the foot of the bed, half sitting, half kneeling, his face buried in the clothes, was a young man, whose frame was racked by his sobs.

The marital prospects of unmarried mothers were low, with the significant exception of widows with children of a first marriage, particularly if the widows possessed some property. As a result, single women often resorted to abortion, which was treated as a crime and was hazardous to health, while unmarried mothers often became prostitutes or were treated as such. The Holmes stories do not address the issue of unmarried mothers.

The absence of an effective social welfare system and the low wages paid to most women ensured that prostitution, either full- or part-time, was the fate of many. Part-time prostitution was related to economic conditions. Again, prostitutes are not part of the Holmes stories, though the implications are that the vicious Baron Gruner is prostituting women.

While sexual pleasure was generally given discreet approval within marriage, it was harshly treated, in the case of women, outside it, as well as being against the dominant norms of male behaviour.[2] The Foundling Hospital in London, established in

1741 to deal with abandoned babies, in the nineteenth century only accepted infants from mothers who could prove that they had had sex against their will or on promise of marriage and were otherwise of irreproachable conduct, a policy designed to exclude prostitutes, who were a large group.

Doyle deals with venereal disease in 'The Third Generation' (1894), a well-crafted and strong story that does not involve Holmes. The thoughtful and experienced Dr Horace Selby tells the young visiting Sir Francis Norton, 'There are many thousands who bear the same cross as you do'. The deeds of the baronet's debauched grandfather 'were living and rotting the blood in the veins of an innocent man' – and that enabled Doyle to discuss one of his favourite subjects, heredity, which he considers in terms of what was taught when he was a medical student.[3] Like his father, Sir Francis is no reprobate, and he denounces his fates: '"Talk about the sins of the father! How about the sins of the Creator!" He shook his two clenched hands in the air, the poor, impotent atom with his pin-point of brain caught in the whirl of the infinite'.

Selby replies by saying that humans so far are but 'half-evolved creatures in a transition stage', an argument that captures the interest of Doyle, and others, in science fiction as a means to consider the future. Because of the issue of passing on the disease, Selby tells him that he will have to cancel his planned marriage. The baronet leaves with the burden of the past upon him: 'it looked to the doctor's eye as though some huge and sombre figure walked by a manikin's side and led him silently up the lonely street'. Sir Francis dies that night under the wheels of a horse-drawn wagon, and Selby realises that this is no accident. The tone is far more sombre than those of the Holmes stories. Suicide is not a theme Doyle generally discussed.

Women, single, co-habiting and married, suffered from the generally limited and primitive nature of contraceptive practices. Frequent childbirth was exhausting, and many women died giving birth, ensuring that a large number of children were brought up by stepmothers. Near the apex of industrial society and wealth, Joseph Chamberlain's first two wives (cousins) died in childbirth, in 1863 and 1875 respectively, leaving him with responsibility for six children. His younger American third wife, by whom he had no children, survived him. Female pelvises were often distorted by rickets during malnourished childhoods, while there was no adequate training in midwifery. As a result, obstetric haemorrhages were poorly managed and often fatal. It was not until the introduction of sulphonamides after 1936 that mortality figures fell substantially. Birth control was, however, developing. For example, in Scotland, marital fertility declined appreciably between 1881 and 1901.

Women often did very arduous jobs, such as coal-carrying in the mines, or work in the fields. In 1851, 229,000 women were employed in agriculture, but this number fell to 67,000 in 1901 in large part due to the agricultural depression. A common form of work was domestic service. Household tasks, such as cleaning and drying clothes, also involved much effort. It was possible in the hierarchy of service to gain promotion, but, in general, domestic service was unskilled and not a career. Wages were poor and pay was largely in kind, which made life very hard for those who wished to marry and leave service. The working conditions, however, were generally better and less hazardous than those of the factories, where repetitive work for many hours was expected.

Service was a category that involved both men and women. Doyle took it for granted that his readers would be fully informed of the gradations, which were subtle and varied. Thus, Milverton has an 'under-gardener'. In 'The Musgrave Ritual', Reginald Musgrave, although a bachelor, describes how he has, at his country seat of Hurlstone, 'a considerable staff of servants . . . in the pheasant months I usually have a house party, so that it would not do to be short-handed. Altogether there are eight maids, the cook, the butler, two footmen and a boy. The garden and the stables, of course, have a separate staff'. At Birlstone, in *The Valley of Fear*, John Douglas and his wife have eight servants in the house. More modestly in 'The Crooked Man', Colonel and Mrs Barclay have 'a coachman and two maids' for their villa. They lack inherited wealth. Mrs Hudson, Holmes's landlady, employs a page and a live-in maid.

For both men and women, service also offers an opportunity to shine or be base. Selling secrets about employers to Milverton is an aspect of the latter. In contrast, Bannister in 'The Three Students' is an instance of the good servant:

> 'I was butler to old Sir Jabez Gilchrist, this young gentleman's father. When he was ruined I come to the college as servant, but I never forgot my old employer because he was down in the world. I watched his son all I could for the sake of the old days. . . . Wasn't it natural, sir, that I should save him, and wasn't it natural also that I should try to speak to him as his dead father would have done, and make him understand that he could not profit by such a deed?'

This is a case of speaking directly to the reader, as well as to Holmes, and the former is thereby invited to share the latter's forgiveness. There are also bad or apparently bad masters. In 'The Priory School', Reuben Hayes, the publican of the Fighting Cock inn, complains of the Duke of Holdernesse, his former master: 'I was his head coachman once, and cruel bad he treated me. It was him that sacked me without a character on the word of a lying corn-chandler'. In reality, although Holdernesse is certainly arrogant, however, Hayes is a 'rascal', a brutal husband and responsible for the death of Heidegger, the German master.

Women from the social élite came to have more opportunities in this period. Indeed, the fictional Lady Molly Robertson-Kirk is propelled to head Scotland Yard by Baroness Orczy, the very popular *Lady Molly of Scotland Yard* being published in 1910. There was higher education for women in both Cambridge and Oxford, though they were not permitted to take degrees for many years to come. At Aberdeen University, it was formally agreed in 1892 that women be admitted to all faculties, but none studied law or divinity, they were not offered equivalent teaching in medicine and there was unequal access to the Bursary Competition. Women students took no positions of influence at Aberdeen, and the student newspaper, *Alma Mater*, was hostile, presenting them as unfeminine or flighty and foolish: the men clearly found it difficult to adjust to female students, although their numbers and influence increased in the 1900s and especially during World War One. Indeed, by 1939, nearly a quarter of British university students were women.

The general notion of equality was one of respect for separate functions and development, and the definition of the distinctive nature of the ideal female condition was one that, by modern standards, certainly did not entail equality. Women's special role was defined as that of home and family and was used to justify their exclusion from other spheres while also explaining why they deserved protection.[4] To a certain extent, such issues were meaningless for most women, because their economic conditions and the nature of medical knowledge and attention ensured that their circumstances were bleak. Thus, Mrs Lyons points out to Watson in *The Hound of the Baskervilles* that a woman could not go alone in the evening 'to a bachelor's house'. The bachelor in question is the highly respectable and far-from-young Sir Charles Baskerville.

The articulate and public challenge to gender roles focussed on the idea of the 'new woman'. On the one hand, the degree to which the journalist and novelist Eliza Linton (1822–98) could write, in works for women, so extensively against the 'new woman', as in *The Girl of the Period and Other Essays* (1883), is an indication of the fears that were aroused. On the other hand, the practical impact of the idea of the 'new woman' is easily overstated, even for middle-class (let alone working-class) women. In both practice and discussion, the 'separate spheres' ideology displayed resilience and also adaptability. Moreover, in the treatment of women, it is important to notice nuances and shifts: it is only from the misleading perspective of hindsight that Victorian society and culture appears as a monolith. Recent work, for example, has re-evaluated notions of Victorian sexuality in order to suggest that the image of universal repression was misleading, not least in Queen Victoria's own enjoyment of sex.

Certainly, Doyle allows for variety, both by individual characters and by type. Indeed, he explicitly refers to types as with Edith Presbury in 'The Creeping Man': 'a bright, handsome girl of a conventional English type'. As was conventional at the time, Doyle presents his sexually exciting women as foreigners, while the British women of note are very different. Lady Hilda Trelawney Hope, the daughter of the Duke of Belminster, is 'the most lovely woman in London. . . . The subtle, delicate charm and the beautiful colouring of that exquisite head . . . a queenly figure'. Prior to her marriage she had written 'an indiscreet letter . . . a foolish letter, a letter of an impulsive loving girl. I meant no harm, and yet he [her husband] would have thought it criminal'. Violet de Merville in 'The Illustrious Client' is 'demure, pale, self-contained, as inflexible and remote as a snow image on a mountain' with 'a voice like the wind from an iceberg'.

In contrast, comes Isadora Klein – Spanish by descent, Brazilian by birth. Having become a very rich and lovely widow, 'there was an interval of adventure when she pleased her own tastes. She had several lovers. . . . She is the "*belle dame sans merci*" of fiction. When her caprice is satisfied, the matter is ended'. She is 'roguish and exquisite' and has 'a challenging smile'.

Outside Doyle's Holmes stories there are bad women, notably Lady Sannox but, more clearly, in 'The Nightmare Room', Lucille Mason, the French wife of a wealthy American banker, who, formerly a famous dancer and 'the heroine of a dozen extraordinary romances', is having an affair and seeking to poison her husband. She is described as 'a devil' lurking within.

> Nature had placed there some subtle mark, some indefinable expression, which told that a devil lurked within. It had been noticed that dogs shrank from her, and that children screamed and ran from her caresses. There are instincts which are deeper than reason.

The last is a suitable phrase for much of Doyle's writing, although this story ended with rare humour and deserves reading.

Meanwhile, although the élite were socially less dependent than is generally assumed, and than their legal situation might suggest, successive extensions of the franchise did not bring the vote to women. The suffragette movement pressing for the vote for women in national elections was a prominent aspect of a more widespread articulate and public challenge to gender roles. The militant tactics of the Women's Social and Political Union founded by Christabel and Emmeline Pankhurst in 1903 were designed to force public attention but had only limited political impact. Parliamentary support for the cause, including among Conservatives, increased considerably in the 1890s, but a limited vote for women was not introduced until 1918, and then as part of a general revision of the franchise arising from World War One.[5] Less dramatically, but also indicative of pressure from women for a different society, the Co-operative Women's Guild, founded in 1884, had one hundred branches and six thousand members by 1889. Campaigning for working women's rights, the guild also pressed for a different society, arguing in the 1900s for divorce reform, pensions and better schools.

Alongside counter-currents, there was definitely an incremental process of change. Women were admitted to London degrees in 1878, and married women gained the full right to own property in 1882. Whereas, after debate in both Houses of Parliament, the London Government Act of 1899 excluded women from serving as councillors or aldermen for the new metropolitan boroughs, another Act in 1907 gave women the right to sit as borough councillors: the first was passed by a Conservative government, the second by a Liberal one.[6]

Women were police officers from 1915 and could be magistrates from 1919. Doyle did not deploy female detectives, but others did. James Redding Ware (1832–c.1909), writing under the pseudonym of Andrew Forrester, introduced Miss Gladden in *The Female Detective* (1864), a professional who is not keen on the regular police. So also with Edward Ellis's *Ruth the Betrayers; or, The Female Spy* (1862–63), and W. S. Hayward's *The Revelations of a Female Detective* (1863–64). R. D. Blackmore's *Clara Vau-*

ghan (1864) centres on the quest to discover a murderer by the victim's daughter. Mathias McDonnell Bodkin provided Dora Myrl, *Lady Detective* (1900), a professor's daughter who had studied medicine at Cambridge only to fail to get patients. Having been a journalist, she becomes a detective who benefits from the opportunities presented by the bicycle. The development of the safety bicycle in 1885 had greatly encouraged bicycling, and notably by women, but Holmes never utilized the contraption. In *The Capture of Paul Beck* (1909), Bodkin has his two detectives marry.

If gender is a key element in the Holmes stories, so also are the assumptions and expectations surrounding class. Indeed, in 'The Lion's Mane', Maud's father, Mr Bellamy, objects to '[his] girl picking up with men outside her station', a remark that helps to present him in the unattractive light that his attitude has already indicated he deserves in full. Doyle's representation of the poor is generally positive, with an emphasis on Holmes's ability to engage with them, not least when in disguise. There is a paternalism at play, particularly with his young Baker Street Irregulars, and this offers a parallel to the crusading philanthropists of the period such as William Booth, Thomas Stephenson, Thomas Barnardo and Wilson Carlile.

Doyle also presented another instance of the commitment of the expanding Victorian middle class to reform and appropriate behaviour, a course much encouraged in, and by, novels. Deference was eroded as middle-class commentators pressed for improvement. This pressure was directed as much against the habits of the Establishment and inherited privilege as it was against those of the poor. In 'The Naval Treaty', with the candour that both Doyle and Holmes share, Doyle refers to 'that not too common type, a nobleman who is in truth noble'. Rational organisation, meritocratic conduct and moral purpose, not least in the pursuit of justice and the protection of the weak, were the goals. Holmes befits this model, as do those in the élite Doyle praises. Many are not aristocrats, and thus not members of the Conservative-dominated House of Lords, a case in point being Sir Henry Baskerville, although he is a landowner. He is romanticised in a passage that captures a strong sense of an identity of man, place and role, one that is to be differently expressed in the defence of the Empire. Watson describes Baskerville's first sight of Dartmoor:

> I read upon his eager face how much it meant to him, this first sight of that strange spot where the men of his blood had held sway so long and left their mark so deep. There he sat, with his tweed suit and his American accent, in the corner of a prosaic railway-carriage, and yet as I looked at his dark and expressive face I felt more than ever how true a descendant he was of that long line of high-blooded, fiery, and masterful men. There were pride, valour and strength in his thick brows, his sensitive nostrils, and his large hazel eyes. If on that forbidding moor a difficult and dangerous quest should lie before us, this was at least a comrade for whom one might venture to take a risk with the certainty that he would bravely share it.

At the same time, Holmes does not capture all elements of the ideal understanding of true nobility and proper masculinity.[7] In 'The Missing Three-Quarter', published in *The Strand Magazine* in August 1904, Holmes is thought ignorant by Cyril Overton, a Cambridge undergraduate, because he has never heard of Godfrey Staunton:

> 'I didn't think there was a soul in England who didn't know Godfrey Staunton, the crack three-quarter, Cambridge, Blackheath, and five Internationals. Good Lord! Mr Holmes, where *have* you lived?'

which would have been an appropriate response given the nature of the press in this period. Holmes replies:

> 'You live in a different world to me, Mr. Overton, a sweeter and healthier one. My ramifications stretch out into many sections of society, but never, I am happy to say, into amateur sport, which is the best and soundest thing in England'.

This is an implicit criticism of professional sport, and Holmes subsequently comments on how 'the ruffians of the Turf get at a race horse'.[8] However, in *The Sign of Four*, Holmes recalls that he had been an amateur boxer who had fought three rounds with the prize-fighter McMurdo 'at Alison's rooms on the night of your benefit'. McMurdo refers to 'that cross-hit of yours under the jaw. . . . You might have aimed high, if you had joined the fancy', which leads Holmes to respond, 'if all else fails me, I have still one of the scientific professions open to me'. Doyle himself was a good cricketer, adept at both bowling and batting, and wrote several cricketing works including *The Story of Spedegue's Dropper* (1928).[9]

A very different form of unity was provided by the more national world of retailing. Control by national chains became more pronounced, and public limited companies developed accordingly. This was part of the process by which the local and regional levels of activity and organisation were increasingly subordinated to the national. John Sainsbury opened his first dairy in London in 1869, Thomas Lipton his first grocery in Glasgow in 1871. By 1900, Sainsbury had forty-seven provisions stores, and by 1914, Lipton had five hundred. In 1894, Marks & Spencer was founded. In 1883, Julius Drewe and his partner opened a shop on London's Edgware Road called the Home and Colonial Stories. By 1890, there were 107 shops in Drewe's company, and by 1906 more than 500. Drewe did the buying, and encouraged the drinking of Indian, not Chinese, tea to gain commercial advantage. He also entered the Establishment, becoming a Justice of the Peace in 1900, deciding that he had Norman antecedents, accumulating a Devon estate and commissioning a country house, Castle Drogo, on the edge of Dartmoor in Devon.

Attitudes about race, ethnicity and nationality were also part of the social equation. We will address these in the upcoming chapters on Holmes and the outside world (6–8), but they should be remembered as part of social dynamics and of the snobbery and deference that played a role in social attitudes. Holmes navigated these with skill. Doyle had his own views and expressed them, not least through his strong criticism of the law on divorce. At the same time, Doyle skilfully crafted Holmes, a character who, while capable of change, was sufficiently distinctive to be able to move at all levels of society without being owned by any.

Doyle also presents social indicators as political, and notably so in the case of Scott Eccles in 'Wisteria Lodge' (1908). Watson comments on how a

> solemnly respectable person was ushered into the room. His life history was written in his heavy features and pompous manner. From his spats to his gold-rimmed spectacles he was a Conservative, a Churchman, a good citizen, orthodox and conventional to the last degree.

Meanwhile, alongside improvements,[10] the context for life for much of the population was grim. For both men and women, there was persistent and justified concern about the 'state of the nation'. Infant mortality rates were high: in the mining communities of North-East England, half the total deaths occurred in the range 0–5 years and a high proportion in 5–15. In 1885, 30.6 per cent of Newcastle's population was still living in dwellings of only one or two rooms. Furthermore, industrial pollution was a serious problem there and elsewhere. Gastro-intestinal disorders linked to inadequate water and sewerage systems were responsible for Bradford's very high infant mortality rate. More generally, the supply of fresh cow's milk became badly infected in the 1880s and 1890s, leading to a serious increase in diarrhoea in inner cities in hot weather and a rise in infant mortality, especially as the practice of breast feeding decreased. In reality, the situation in Doyle's Britain, while not as bad, was not terribly encouraging. Watson was discharged from the army due to 'enteric fever, that curse of our Indian possessions', typhoid.

Poor urban sanitation, housing and nutrition were blamed for the physical weakness of much of the population. The army found this a serious problem at the time of the Boer War and World War One, the Metropolitan Police thought their London recruits physically weak, and defeats at the hands of the visiting New Zealand All Blacks rugby team in 1905 led to discussion about a supposed physical and moral decline arising from the country's urban and industrial nature. This discussion took up long-established themes.[11]

In his *Poverty, a Study of Town Life* (1901), Seebohm Rowntree determined that 27.8 per cent of York's population were living below the poverty line. He mapped the position of the pubs and their relationship to poverty, shading the map in four colours from lilac, 'The poorest districts', to green, 'Districts inhabited by the servant-keeping class'. York's central streets, where the wealthy lived, had very few pubs. Rowntree was critical of expenditure on drink, but noted of the pubs:

> 'Many of the songs are characterised by maudlin sentimentality; others again are unreservedly vulgar. Throughout the whole assembly there is an air of jollity and an absence of irksome restraint which must prove very attractive after a day's confinement in factory or shop'.

There was also concern at the apparent extent of atheism among the urban working classes, while some politicians, such as Winston Churchill, emphasised the threat to Imperial stability allegedly posed by social distress within Britain, and advocated reform as the best means of defence. William Booth had already founded the East London Revival Society in 1865 and, in 1878, it was reorganised as the Salvation Army. The Boy Scout movement was launched in 1908 by Robert Baden-Powell, a hero of the Boer War, in order to revive and to occupy the martial vigour of the nation's youth. The movement rapidly became a national and international institution.

Government action was another response. 'We are all Socialists nowadays', declared Sir William Harcourt, the Liberal chancellor of the exchequer, in a speech at the Mansion House in 1895. He was referring to the creation of public utilities – 'gas and water Socialism' – and to the concern for social welfare that was such an obvious feature of late Victorian values and that played a role in the amelioration of living conditions, especially the decline of deadly epidemic disease, such as the diphtheria that kills Victor Trevor's sister while on a visit to Birmingham, as mentioned in 'The *Gloria Scott*' (1893). The bacterium responsible for diphtheria was first recognised in 1883. It had caused the death in Germany of Queen Victoria's second daughter, Alice, in 1878.

Urban and rural sanitary authorities and their districts, responsible for the maintenance of sewers and highways, were inaugurated in England and Wales by the 1872 Public Health Act following the recommendations of a report by the Sanitary Commission (1871). These districts were based on town councils, existing local boards of health in urban areas and boards of guardians in rural areas. The Rating and Local Government Act of 1871 set up the central machinery in the shape of the Local Government Board. In respect of the local machinery of rural and urban sanitary authorities, the Public Health Act of 1875 was a consolidating measure. The Public Health (Scotland) Act of 1867 established the appointment of sanitary inspectors there.

Meanwhile, the supply of clean water was improved or initiated, and London at last acquired a sewerage system appropriate for the capital of a modern empire. From 1859, under the direction of the determined Joseph Bazalgette, chief engineer to the Metropolitan Commissioner of Sewers (a body established in 1847), an effective drainage system was finally constructed. Fully completed in 1875, this pioneering system contained eighty-two miles of intercepting sewers. These took sewage from earlier pipes that had drained into the Thames and transported it instead to new downstream works and storage tanks from which the effluent could be pumped into the river when the tide was flowing into the North Sea. A large number of steam pumping stations provided the power. Storm-relief sewers followed in the 1880s. In part, the storm-relief system used London's rivers other than the Thames, completing the process by which these had been directed underground. This concealment of the rivers made their use for this sewage system acceptable. Whereas Doyle sets 'The New Catacomb' (1898),[12] a spooky non-Holmes story, in the ancient catacombs near Rome, Holmes is sent in London to Limehouse, but not on any mystery into the sewers.

In Glasgow, the civic government was associated with the provision of pure water and with the individual purity of teetotalism. The provision of plentiful supplies of clean water was not only an engineering and organisational triumph, but also part of the process by which rural Britain was increasingly subordinated to the cities, one, moreover, seen in the expansion of the rail system. Manchester, for example, looked to the distant Lake District to supplement supplies from the nearby Pennines: the corporation purchased the Wythburn estate, stopped the local lead industry in order to prevent water pollution and, despite overwhelming local opposition, gained parliamentary approval in 1877 for the drowning of the Thirlmere Valley.

Across the country, typhus virtually disappeared by the 1890s, typhoid was brought under partial control, and death rates from tuberculosis and scarlet fever declined. Yet, in *A Study in Scarlet*, Holmes and Watson are told about the problems posed by negligent landowners. Constable Rance informs them: 'I knew that them two houses in Lauriston Gardens was empty on account of him that owns them who won't have the drains seed too, though the very last tenant what lived in one of them died o' typhoid fever'. There were indeed such issues.

The sole infection seriously to affect adults in 1900 was tuberculosis, but the childhood killers were still rampant. The burial records of the Bonner Hill cemetery in Kingston, Surrey, indicate that from 1855 to 1911 one-third of all burials was of children aged four or under. Surrey was very much an area of activity by Holmes. Diphtheria and measles were particularly serious killers. Neither was tackled adequately by medical provision, and the situation was exacerbated by the number of damp houses and by crowded conditions, including sharing beds.

Improved diet, thanks, in part, to a significant fall in food prices due to free trade and improvement in transoceanic transport, played an important role in the decline in mortality rates, which in

Newcastle fell from 30.1 to 19.1 per thousand between 1872 and 1900. Medical advances, not least the replacement of the 'miasma' theory of disease by that of 'germs', were important. However, mortality contrasts between registration districts persisted. There was a noticeable, though not invariable, relationship between life expectancy and population density, and thus poverty: crowded cities, such as Liverpool, having very much higher mortality rates. Using the 1901 census, *The Survey Gazetteer of the British Isles* (1904) produced instructive maps showing per capita death rates, maps for children under the age of one, and maps for deaths from tuberculosis. These variations underlay the comments, made by Doyle and others, on the differing parts of cities – most notably, London.

Public health problems, however, also existed in small towns and rural areas, including Sussex, an area of activity by Holmes. Reports on the situation in the small Somerset town of Bruton in the 1870s and 1880s graphically described insufficient and defective toilet arrangements, inadequate sewerage disposal and a lack of clean water. A reluctance to spend money ensured, however, that, as in mid-century London, plans to improve the situation were delayed, and, though the sewerage system was finally upgraded, Bruton did not construct a water-supply system in the Victorian period.

Social welfare was linked to the growing institutionalisation of society that led to the construction of schools, workhouses and asylums. In *The Sign of Four*, Holmes is able, in disguising himself successfully, to impersonate 'the proper workhouse cough' – a cough that reflected the poor health of many who went to the workhouses and their role in spreading infectious disease. Far more than just clothes are involved in his disguises. In 1851, the Wiltshire asylum was opened in Devizes, replacing private institutions for the insane run for profit. By 1914 a basic national network of infant and child welfare centres had been created. Health-visiting was expanding. Educational authorities had been made responsible for the medical inspection of schoolchildren. Isolation, tuberculosis, smallpox and maternity hospitals and sanatoria were established by local authorities. Far from unconstrained capitalism, this was an increasingly regulated society. For example, in 1888, the county councils assumed responsibility for most of the turnpike roads, and the turnpike trusts were wound up. Yet, to a considerable degree, these councils reflected the existing social hierarchy that was very much present in the Holmes stories. Thus, the heads were members of the local élite.

Period costume dramas on television and film, notably *The Shooting Party*, *Upstairs Downstairs* and *Downton Abbey*, suggest that it was a highly attractive world that was to be swept away by war. These works offer an image of class, gender and political stereotypes that dramatically underplays the dynamism and energy of the period. In particular, there was a widespread conviction among politicians, writers and key sections in society that change was inevitable. Many saw it as necessary and beneficial. The aristocracy indeed opposed the Liberal Party because it sought not only to preserve its political position, but also to resist what appeared to be an entire ethos of change centring on policies regarding the extension of state power, collectivism and the destruction of the Union with Ireland. The aristocracy saw a danger that democracy might entail the poor plundering the rich,[13] or, in the eyes of its supporters, the social justice of redistribution. There was a realisation that the change also seen in other aspects of life, notably technology and the economy, might affect social power and politics.

Technology was certainly potent, and, as such, played a significant role, if not the driving force, in Doyle's plot narrative. In *The Sign of Four*, the steam launch that takes Holmes and Watson on their chase on the Thames is a repeated hymn to the surging power of machinery:

> The furnaces roared, and the powerful engines whizzed and clanked, like a great metallic heart. Her sharp, steep prow cut through the still river-water and sent two rolling waves to right and to left of us. With every throb of the engines we sprang and quivered like a living thing. One great yellow lantern in our

> bows threw a long flickering funnel of light ahead of us. . . . We flashed past barges, steamers, merchant-vessels . . . the frail shell vibrated and creaked with the fierce energy which was driving us along.

Captain Peter Carey in 'Black Peter' commanded the Dundee steam sealer *Sea Unicorn* in 1883–84.

Meanwhile, also regarded as a means through which to improve the social environment, the use of electricity was rapidly spreading. A primary reason for its swift adoption was that it was cleaner than coal. John Tenniel's *Punch* cartoon of 6 December 1882, 'The Coming Force – Mr Punch's Dream', satirises the enthusiasts, capturing their sense of excitement and anticipation of new frontiers as an earlier coal-based world of fog, chimney sweeps and coalmen succumbs. And entrepreneurs sought to make this imagined new world a reality. Thus, Birmingham, for example, that year saw the first demonstration of electric lighting and, in 1889, the foundation of the Birmingham Electric Supply Ltd. This was a new England of great potential, one represented in 'The Solitary Cyclist' – a story set in 1895 but published in 1903 – by the young woman seeking Holmes's services, Violet Smith, and Cyril Morton, the electrical engineer to whom she is engaged and who becomes 'the senior partner of Morton and Kennedy, the famous Westminster electricians'.

Also mixed into the late-century technological surge was the introduction of the petrol engine. The first original full-size British petrol motor was produced in 1895, and in 1896 the first commercial motor company was established. That same year, Parliament repealed legislation that required automobiles to follow a man carrying a red flag, instead allowing them to drive, independently, at a speed up to fourteen miles per hour.

Thanks to the impact of technology, science fiction seemed increasingly relevant as well as potent in the imaginative landscape. *The Time Machine* (1895) was the first major novel by H. G. Wells, prophet of New Liberalism, whose scientific futurism seemed increasingly appropriate in the rapidly changing world.

The novel's protagonist, the 'Time Traveller', goes to the year 802,701, where he finds a dystopia with two human species – the aesthetic Eloi and the crude Morlocks – the latter being the descendants of subterranean labourers. This vision, a warning about the social and cultural divisiveness of modern Britain, reflects Wells's interest in evolution. This theme is strongly echoed in Doyle's novel *The Maracot Deep* (1929), by the divisions depicted in Atlantis between the underwater Atlanteans and their slaves.

Like science fiction, Doyle's Spiritualism was a popular means of understanding reality in a world in which formal religion seemed to be losing relevance or, at least, losing potency as an intellectual framework. In 'Silver Blaze', Holmes refers to the deceit and greed of Silas Brown, the dishonest manager of Lord Blackwater's horse-training establishment at Mapleton through a religious trope: 'the devil had shown him how he could hide the horse until the race was over'. This was not the approach most obvious to those interested in psychology. In 'The Yellow Face', the reference is less directly religious. Holmes tells Grant Munro, 'we have had the good fortune to bring peace to many troubled souls'. 'God Almighty' is cited by James Armitage in 'The *Gloria Scott*'. In a more significant passage, Holmes puts his faith in reason to establish purpose in faith, notably so in 'The Naval Treaty', in which he explains:

> 'There is nothing in which deduction is so necessary as in religion. . . . It can be built up as an exact science by the reasoner. Our highest assurance of the goodness of Providence seems to me to rest in the flowers. All other things, our powers, our desires, our food, are really necessary for existence in the first instance. But this rose is an extra. Its smell and its colour are an embellishment of life, not a condition of it. It is only goodness which gives extra, and so I say again that we have much to hope from the flowers'.

5

POLITICS

I have established a right of way through the centre of old Middleton's park. . . . We'll teach these magnates that they cannot ride roughshod over the rights of the commoners, confound them! And I've closed the wood where the Fernworthy folk used to picnic. These infernal people seem to think that there are no rights of property, and that they can swarm where they like with their papers and their bottles.

– Mr Frankland in *The Hound of the Baskervilles* (1901)

The papers were full of the disappearance of Mingey's daughter. Disappearances, apparently, were the order of the day; tunnel murders were no longer in fashion . . . there were leaders on the subject. . . . It appeared that no one was safe. . . . The *Morning Star* maintained that Parliament ought to interfere. The *Morning Star* always believed in the omnipotence of Parliament, mainly because it was against the Government. . . . One enterprising journal offered a prize of a life's subscription . . . for the most probable solution sent in by one of its readers on a detachable coupon.

– Frank Richardson, *2835 Mayfair* (1907)[1]

When evaluated by Watson in *A Study in Scarlet*, Holmes's knowledge of politics is presented as 'feeble'. This is better than the nil returned for literature, philosophy and astronomy, but not by much. Earlier in the story, Watson notes:

> Of contemporary literature, philosophy and politics he appeared to know next to nothing. Upon my quoting Thomas Carlyle, he inquired in the naivest way who he might be and what he had done.

This presentation of Holmes is reprised in 'The Five Orange Pips'. The stories, indeed, largely support Watson's evaluation. When Watson, Holmes and Athelney Jones dine in *The Sign of Four*, Holmes speaks on five topics, none of which is political. Social convention plays a role in the topics selected, but so does authorial convenience, the consistency of character and considerations about readership.

The distinctive and permitted role of Holmes in his chosen career is affected more by the nature of government than by politics. He has to be accepted by the police. Indeed, like the discussion of the omniscient and politically well-connected Mycroft Holmes in 'The Bruce-Partington Plans', Sherlock Holmes reflects the idea of the individual polymath as the solution to problems. Indeed, in his character as polymath, he is the natural counterpart to the master-criminal. Despite the limitations outlined by Watson, Holmes is revealed as an anti-criminal polymath.

In contrast to the individual working alone, the volume of material, complexity of issues, and need for a structure of routine had led, and was continuing to lead, to new or newly formal governing processes, systems and institutions. As administration became more bureaucratic, administrators were increasingly trained and made to specialise, resulting in the bureaucratic information state, one with bureaucratic processes and an ethos that relied on using information. Mycroft Holmes represents both in microcosm. Doyle's description of him reflects the idea of government as a machine, one that encourages support for the mechanisation of process,[2] and that is reflected in the presentation of Moriarty in 'The Final Problem' as a 'deep organising power . . . a brain of the first order' who plans with great care. In this context, it is scarcely surprising that Moriarty is a mathematician, reflecting, in part, the prestige of the discipline. In *The Valley of Fear*, Holmes provides a view of Moriarty's system:

> 'a chain with this Napoleon-gone-wrong at one end and a hundred broken fighting men, pickpockets, blackmailers, and cardsharpers at the other, with every sort of crime in between. His chief of the staff [*sic*] is Colonel Sebastian Moran . . . he pays him . . . six thousand a year. That's paying for brains, you see – the American business principle. . . . It's more than the Prime Minister gets.[3] That gives you an idea of Moriarty's gains and of the scale on which he works'.

Official recorded information, meanwhile, was becoming more pervasive and insistent. Indeed, *The Importance of Being Earnest* (1895) reveals that Cecily Cardew's eighteen years are recorded with an impressive number of certificates. To cope with the new scale of activity, the Civil Service had moved over to the use of press copies and stencil duplicating for documents in the late 1870s and 1880s.

Holmes, however, like his successor James Bond, is an individualist who essentially works on his own, and not the conventional product of an institution operating by way of protocol. As part of a tradition of gentleman detectives, Doyle has Holmes as the recourse of all ranks when government fails. This is the heroic approach to policing and justice, one that emphasises the individual, and not the team or the institution. It is an approach that is necessary for the fiction. Holmes meets prime ministers and cabinet ministers, but without having anything political to discuss other than the specific tasks of the moment. These tasks focus on international developments and not on their domestic counterparts. However, no such luxury was left to readers. While we will address imperial and foreign issues in subsequent chapters, here we provide an account of the domestic political background to understand the context for Doyle's fiction.

We will look at national politics and then at their London counterpart, but let us refer beforehand to Holmes's clear commitment to reform in 'The Naval Treaty' (1893), a short story published at a time of Liberal government, that of William Gladstone's last ministry. Taking the train through South London, Holmes presents the 'Board schools' as 'brick islands in a lead-coloured sea', a reference to John of Gaunt's speech in Shakespeare's *Richard II* (2.1): 'precious stone set in the silver sea', before continuing: 'Lighthouses, my boy! Beacons of the future! Capsules, with hundreds of bright little seeds in each, out of which will spring the wiser, better England of the future'. It is difficult to see how Doyle could have been clearer. Passed by a Liberal government under Gladstone, the 1870 Elementary Education Act for English and Welsh children between five and twelve divided the country into school districts under education boards, and stipulated a minimum level of educational provision in each district. 'Board schools' were introduced where existing parish provision was inadequate, for Gladstone did not want to see existing Church of England schools lose their independence.

Supervision by central government was a major part of the new system. Founded that year, the Endowed Schools Commission redistributed endowments and reformed governing bodies. In what was at once, allowing for crosscurrents, a struggle between central and local government, Liberals and Conservatives, Nonconformists and the Church of England, and tax-and-spenders and their opponents, the provisions of the Act were vigorously resisted. Thus, in Ealing, tenacious efforts by the Church of England sought to protect denominational education and block the introduction of state schools.

Doyle's support for the Act might appear to mark him out simply as a liberal, but its key protagonist, William Forster (1818–86) was an opponent of Irish nationalism and Home Rule (Irish self-government within the Empire), and a keen supporter of Imperial federation and disagreed with Gladstone over policies in Sudan and South Africa. As such, Forster, had he lived longer, would have been a Liberal Unionist like Doyle.

Passed by Gladstone's Liberal government in 1884, the Third Reform Act extended the franchise so that about 63 per cent of the entire adult male population received the vote. However, the percentage who could vote was closer to 40 per cent than 63 because so many people changed address, and because a voter needed eighteen months' continuous residence before he could vote. In 1885, the Conservatives (colloquially known as the Tories) were defeated in the first election held with the new franchise, with many rural electors voting against their landlords.

Nevertheless, many tenants continued to support the landowners, and county families often continued to provide the local MPs as well as the members of the new County councils. This was certainly the case with Sussex, where Doyle was to settle. The Conservatives had a solid control of parliamentary seats such as Horsham, where their candidate won 65 per cent of the vote in 1892, and 61 per cent in an 1893 by-election, and was returned unopposed in 1895 and 1900. Sir Walter Barttelot, the MP for West Sussex from 1860 until 1885, and then for Horsham until his death in 1893, came from a long-established Sussex family. His first wife, Harriet, was the daughter of Sir Christopher Musgrave, 9th Baronet, which provides a link to the Holmes story. In Lewes, the Conservative candidate was unopposed in 1886, 1895 and 1900, and won 71 per cent of the vote in 1892. Sir Henry Fletcher, the 4th Baronet, was MP for Horsham from 1880 to 1885, and for Lewes from 1885 until his death in 1910. He changed his name to Henry Aubrey-Fletcher in 1903 to reflect his inheritance from the Aubrey estate. The 6th Baron, another Henry (1887–1969), wrote under the pen-name Henry Wade, with an impressive series of novels published from 1926 to 1957.

It was therefore perfectly plausible in 'The Musgrave Ritual' (1893) for Reginald Musgrave, the heir to the estate, to be 'member for the district'. The Musgraves had established themselves in western Sussex in the sixteenth century. His being a MP is not germane to the plot, but was simply a product of status and thus part of a rapid sketching of context. Edward Krehbiel's 1916 analytical map of the eight general elections of 1885–1910 showing political consistency demonstrated clearly the significance of Scotland and Wales to the Liberals, and of Southern and South-East England to the Conservatives.

Proposals for Home Rule for Ireland, introduced by Gladstone, were defeated in 1886 and 1893 at Westminster, where they divided politicians. Conservatives led the resistance, and the Conservative Party changed its name to the Unionist Party in 1886; but the defeat of the First Home Rule Bill in that year was due to the defection of ninety-three Liberal Unionists from Gladstone's third government, a group among whom Joseph Chamberlain was prominent. Doyle had already criticised Gladstone in 'Crabbe's Practice', a non-Holmes short story published in the Christmas edition of *The Boy's Own Paper* in December 1884. The hero, Thomas Waterhouse Crabbe, who, like Doyle, finds it difficult to establish himself as a doctor on the South Coast of England, was a medical student in Edinburgh who is described as a genius – and not the usual weak physical type, but rather a 'powerfully built, square-shouldered fellow, full of vitality. . . . A muscular Christian too, and one of the best Rugby forwards in Edinburgh'. The narrator, Jack Barton, encounters Crabbe at 'one of the Bulgarian Atrocity meetings held in Edinburgh in '78', meetings that were part of Gladstone's energetic campaign against Disraeli and his foreign policy, notably his failure to act against the brutal Turkish rule of Bulgaria:

> the invectives which speaker after speaker was hurling at the Conservative ministry. The audience seemed enthusiastically unanimous. A burst of cheering hailed every argument and sarcasm. There was not one dissentient voice. The speaker paused to moisten his lips, and there was a silence over the hall. Then a clear voice rose from the middle of it: 'All very fine, but what did Gladstone –'. There was a howl of execration and yells of 'Turn him out!' But the voice was still audible. 'What did Gladstone do in '63?' it demanded.

Crabbe is thrown out, subsequently joking to Barton that that was his way of escaping a crowded hall; but the story also strongly captured the idea of Gladstone as a hypocrite given to opportunistic moralising. The British had done nothing about the Russian suppression of a Polish rebellion in 1863. The Conservatives under Benjamin Disraeli adopted the notion of a patriotic foreign policy with bellicose tones in the late 1870s, although the Liberals were also offering patriotic rhetoric a decade later.[4]

Home Rule split the Liberals, not the first or the last occasion when Ireland was of great significance for British politics. At Easter 1887, Gladstone wrote in his diary, 'now one prayer absorbs all others: Ireland, Ireland, Ireland'. Doyle was to stand (unsuccessfully) for Parliament in 1900 and 1906 as a Liberal Unionist, and therefore against Home Rule.

The political hegemony of the Liberals, who had returned to office in January 1886 after a brief Conservative minority ministry, was destroyed that July, as the Conservatives, under Robert Cecil, 3rd Marquess of Salisbury, won the general election. Nevertheless, the Liberals, still under Gladstone, now elderly, half-blind and half-deaf, won the 1892 election, in part because the Liberal Unionists did badly.[5] Set in 1889, *The Hound of the Baskervilles* notes that Sir Charles Baskerville had been mentioned as the probable Liberal candidate for Mid-Devon at the next election, which would have been 1892. In practice, Devon was not always good territory for the Liberals; separately, other than for Irish reasons, politicians were not murdered in this period.

Notwithstanding the 1892 result, the Conservatives dominated the period 1886–1905 with the support of the Liberal Unionists, with whom they eventually merged. Salisbury (Prime Minister 1885–86, 1886–92, 1895–1902) and his nephew and successor, Arthur Balfour (1902–5), opposed Home Rule and followed a cautious policy on domestic reform. The cultural basis of Liberalism was under challenge and the mix of Conservative policies, attitudes and resonances was more attractive to the electorate.[6] Salisbury, a Marquess and owner of the palatial Hatfield House, one of the palaces the British domesticate as 'stately homes', derived most of his disposable income from urban property, including London slums, which made George Bernard Shaw's focus on slum landlordism in his play *Widowers' Houses* (1892) particularly notable. Salisbury is presented by Doyle as Lord Bellinger, the prime minister, in 'The Adventure of the Second Stain', a secret-papers mystery, which was published in *The Strand Magazine* in December 1904, but set in 1888. He is 'austere, high-nosed, eagle-eyed, and dominant', and is described as 'twice Premier of Britain' as Salisbury was at that time. The subsequent descriptions are supportive: 'the quick, decisive manner for which he was famous . . . the quick, fierce gleam of his deep-set eyes . . . the keen scrutiny of those wonderful eyes'.

Much of Salisbury's cabinet were peers, while the government was nicknamed 'Hotel Cecil' as it contained so many Cecil family members. Doyle refers to that in 'The Naval Treaty' (1893), when Percy Phelps informs Watson that 'through my uncle's influence, I obtained a good appointment at the Foreign Office'. In case that was not clear enough, Watson notes that 'his mother's brother was Lord Holdhurst, the great Conservative politician', and Phelps tells Holmes: 'When my uncle became Foreign Minister in this Administration he gave me several missions of trust'. Salisbury was foreign secretary as well as prime minister. Balfour's mother's brother was Salisbury. Like Phelps, Balfour had been to Cambridge, and, like Phelps, he was unmarried. Balfour was also indolent, indeed lazy.

Similarly, alongside professionalisation, there was a continued dominance of diplomacy by the social élite, as Doyle noted in the non-Holmes 'The Brazilian Cat' (1898): 'at least there would be found some post in that diplomatic service which still remains the special preserve of our privileged classes', an expectation that in at least this case proves mistaken for the narrator, the nephew of a peer. The 1914 report of the Royal Commission on the Civil Service noted that twenty-five out of the thirty-seven attachés recruited to the diplomatic service in 1908–13 were from Eton, and, in his *Democracy and Diplomacy: A Plea for Popular Control of*

Foreign Policy (1915), Arthur Ponsonby, a radical, anti-war MP, complained:

> A small number of men, associating only with others of their own class, and carrying on their intercourse in whispers, cannot fail to have a distorted perspective, a narrow vision, and a false sense of proportion. A tradition of intrigue has been carried down from the Middle Ages, but it is not only out of place, but positively dangerous, in the twentieth century.

Ponsonby's remedy, diplomats with 'a constant sense that they are the servants of a people, not the puppets of a court, or even the tools of a government',[7] was not the world of Phelps.

Although married, Trelawney Hope in 'The Second Stain' also has echoes of Balfour in his relationship with Salisbury, for whom he is 'Secretary for European Affairs, and the most rising statesman in the country'. He is described as 'dark, clear-cut, and elegant, hardly yet of middle age, and endowed with every beauty of body and of mind', which possibly captures some of the ambiguities of Balfour's high reputation, notably frequent questions about his sexuality. Balfour was also very bright, although he proved himself incapable of rising to the challenge of providing a perceptive lead to advance the causes he supported, notably a strong Empire.[8]

The Conservatives were in power from 1874 to 1880, 1885 to 1886, 1886 to 1892 and 1895 to 1905.They benefited not only from hostility to the Liberals and Irish Home Rule, but also from more positive support, notably the ability to tap populist themes and to couch their policies in nationalist terms. The Conservatives put considerable emphasis on imperialism abroad (both spreading empire and imperial sentiment) and at home (in Ireland), hitting the Liberals on both issues. Indeed, proposals for Home Rule for Ireland were defeated in part because they divided the Liberals as well as energised the Conservatives. The Liberal Unionists were in coalition with the Conservatives from 1895. Far from being politically and socially rigid, the Conservatives also displayed an openness to social trends, as with a willingness to recruit Catholics and to mobilise female support. The latter proved particularly useful after women gained the vote in national elections in 1918, but they had earlier won many female votes in municipal elections.

In 1894, Gladstone was succeeded, as Liberal leader and prime minister, by Archibald, 5th Earl of Rosebery (1847–1929), whose landed wealth had been enhanced by marriage to Hannah de Rothschild, the wealthiest British heiress of her day. A bibliophile and sportsman as well, he was a character who could have come straight from a novel. Hannah was to die from typhoid and Bright's disease in 1890, and Rosebery never remarried. Called a 'Snob Queer' by John, 9th Marquess of Queensberry, the obsessive foe of Oscar Wilde, Rosebery may have had bisexual tendencies. As an instance of the prominence of racing and its links with the social élite, both of which emerge in the Holmes stories, Rosebery's horses won the Derby in 1894, 1895 and 1905.

There was also, however, growing pressure for more radical political and social policies. Political opinion began increasingly to coalesce and polarise along social and class lines, and the landed interest largely broke from the Liberals after 1886. Joseph Chamberlain's 'unauthorised' Liberal programme of 1885 called for land reform and was followed in 1891 by the Liberals' Newcastle programme, which also called for Home Rule, Welsh and Scottish disestablishment, free education, a reduction in factory work-hours, electoral reform, and the reform or abolition of the House of Lords. That year, the Scottish Liberals pressed for land reform in the Highlands, an eight-hour day for miners and an extension of the franchise. In 'The Naval Treaty' (1893), Watson tries with no success to interest Percy Phelps in 'societal questions'.

The social order could be harsh as well as inegalitarian. In 1891, Tom Masters, a thirteen-year-old Northamptonshire farm labourer, was whipped by his employer for insolence. However, calls for a more radical Liberalism led to accusations that Liberalism was increasingly a threat to stability and a product of sectional interests. This pressure encouraged an opposing coalescence of opinion in defence of property and order, and helped lead right-wing Liberals to join the Conservatives. Taxes were a key issue. The spread in the power and activity of government had led to new commitments, for example by school boards, and these commitments pushed up the rates (local property taxes). Rising tax demands pressed on a society that was less buoyant and, crucially, less confident economically, than that of the middle decades of the nineteenth century, and this hit support for the Liberals.

The relatively benign 1890s gave rise to a more troubling situation in the following decade, and there was no Edwardian calm to British politics, despite subsequent suggestions to that effect from the vantage point of the even more troubled postwar world. Instead, Edward VII's reign (1901–10) was a period of uncertainty and tension. Indeed, these years, running on to the outbreak of World War One in 1914, while often seen as a continuation of the late nineteenth century, can be regarded, conversely, as its dissolution, a dissolution that had already gathered pace before the war.

The twentieth century opened with Britain already at war. The Boer War (1899–1902), which arose from the British attempt to dominate Southern Africa, was very different in scale to World War One but proved far more difficult than military and political leaders had anticipated. Moreover, in the early 1900s, the national debt was rising substantially, and politicians were unsure about how best to respond to growing industrial militancy, as well as to widespread concerns about national efficiency and separate pressures for social reform. War and domestic issues were linked in anxiety about Britain's strength relative to other powers, particularly Germany. Rudyard Kipling's poem *The Islanders* (1902) saw the British as weak and self-regarding, concerned with trinkets and 'the flannelled fools at the wicket or the muddied oafs at the goals', references to cricket and football. Far from there being any general complacency, there was a widespread feeling that something had to be done, a feeling exacerbated by very serious defeats in the early stages of the Boer War. Furthermore, to pay for the war, the government raised taxes, including income tax from 8d to 1s 3d (3 to 6 new pence) per £ of income and borrowed £135 million.

What was to be done was less clear. Salisbury and the Conservatives, then called Unionists because of their support for the existing constitutional arrangements in Ireland, won in October 1900 what was termed a 'Khaki Election' because it was held when the Boer War was arousing patriotic sentiments and going well, while the Liberals were publicly divided over the merits of the war. There was an overtly pro-Boer group, denouncing an 'immoral' war allegedly waged in the interests of greedy plutocrats, Rosebery's liberal imperialist wing, and the more cautious tactical approach of the leader of the party from 1899 to 1908, Henry Campbell-Bannerman, who focused on the iniquities of government policy leading up to the war while patriotically supporting the war effort itself. In contrast, most of the electorate had no such doubt about the expansion of empire. Only 184 Liberals were elected and no fewer than 163 government supporters were elected unopposed.[9]

Doyle tried first for Parliament in this election. He stood in Central Edinburgh as the Liberal Unionist candidate, but his rival, the Liberal Party candidate, won with 3,028 votes to Doyle's 2459. This was a safe Liberal seat, and Doyle had been selected for what was a no-hoper. Nationally, however, Doyle was in more tune with the mood in the 'Khaki Election'. The Liberals had little response to a government enjoying patriotic popularity on the basis of relief at victory and (crucially) the return of economic prosperity and lost their overall majority of Scottish seats for the first time since 1832. Although 1900 is an instance of the general proposition that governments (not oppositions) win or lose elections, that was also one in which the opposition actively acted to make itself unelectable. In his autobiography, Doyle revealed that he did not enjoy electioneering. However, as a supporter of the Boer War, he was keen to do his bit, and he did so. This would not have hurt his subsequently receiving a knighthood.

Financially successful, Doyle could have afforded to be an MP, whereas in 1895, Matthias McDonnell Bodkin stood down as MP for North Roscommon on the grounds that he could not afford to lose the earnings he would otherwise gain as a lawyer. MPs were not paid until the 1911 Parliament Act. Instead, in short stories from 1897, Bodkin launched a Holmes substitute, Paul Beck, 'the rule of thumb' detective, a far from arrogant, but also multi-talented, alternative to Holmes.

The 1900 electoral victory could not, for long, conceal important weaknesses in the Conservative position, including the inability to respond successfully to the growing demands of organised labour. The elderly Salisbury also failed to take advantage of the general election in order to reorganise and strengthen the government, and very few middle-class politicians were brought into office. The Liberals, moreover, were helped by the still-considerable strength of their Nonconformist constituency.

A political freneticism on the part of some reflected the sense that real issues were at stake. The first lightning bolt was hurled by Joseph Chamberlain, colonial secretary from June 1895 to September 1903, who, concerned about the pressure of international competition, sought to replace free trade by tariffs (import duties), with, in addition, a system of imperial preference to encourage trade within the empire. The revenue produced by tariffs was to be spent on social welfare, thus easing social tension without increasing taxes. To Chamberlain, this policy offered imperial revival, populism and an opportunity to strengthen the Conservative government, but, in fact, his policy divided and weakened the party. Imperial revival was an aspect of the interest in 'national efficiency', one that Holmes can be seen as providing through his deductive powers and rigorous compilation of information.

Much needed to be done. Poor urban housing, sanitation, and nutrition were widely blamed for what was seen as the physical weakness of much of the population, and this perception encouraged the Liberals, Labour, and, also, Conservative paternalists to support measures for social welfare, notably the New Liberalism of the 1900s and 1910s. Concern about England/Britain as a physical space affected by the pressures of urbanisation was related to anxieties about the country as a moral sphere and political system. This was fired up further by the crises of the early stages of the Boer War.

A new order, political and governmental, that was meritocratic and professional was exemplified by Chamberlain. A self-made businessman,[10] he despised the amateurism and inherited privilege of aristocratic politicians such as Spencer, Marquess of Hartington (1833–1908). Liberal leader in 1875–80, and subsequently the leader of the Liberal Unionists until 1903, Hartington became the 8th Duke of Devonshire in 1891 and was lord president of the Council from 1893 to 1903. He was possibly the unsympathetic 6th Duke of Holdernesse in 'The Priory School', which appeared in *The Strand Magazine* in February 1904. Much interested in horseracing, Devonshire's long-term mistress was the courtesan Catherine Walters, who was followed by the German-born Louisa, Duchess of Manchester, whom, in turn, he married in 1892 after she was widowed in 1890. In the story, with reference to Holdernesse,

> It is an open secret that the duke's married life had not been a peaceful one, and the matter had ended in a separation by mutual consent, the duchess taking up her residence in the South of France.

Holmes reproaches the arrogant Duke. The precariousness of some of the aristocracy was clear in the case of the Manchesters. George, the 8th Duke (1853–92), went bankrupt in 1890 and was a drunk who married Consuelo Yznaga, a New York–born Cuban, for money. William, the 9th Duke (1877–1947) further exhausted the family finances, despite marrying a wealthy American in 1900.

Earlier, in 'The Reigate Squire', published in *The Strand Magazine* in June 1893, Holmes had emphasised the need not to share social suppositions in favour of those he terms county magnates, a singularly pejorative remark that challenges the idea of the unity of rural society advanced by many Conservatives:

> The Inspector had overlooked it because he had started with the supposition that these county magnates had had nothing to do with the matter. Now, I make a point of never having any prejudices.

That remark serves both to describe Holmes's practice of following wherever facts may lead him, but also a social position, that of a meritocrat wary of inherited privilege. Thus, the politics of the Holmes stories are social as well as party. This provides the great detective with more space in which to manoeuvre and from which to find fault.

The popularity of Chamberlain's tariff policy was compromised, because it was presented as a taxation on food imports that would hit the urban working class by increasing the price of food. In an instructive instance of the importance of the public dimension, Chamberlain's campaigning gesture of 1903, when he held up two loaves of similar size to demonstrate that the tariffs he proposed would not have a great effect on consumers, was hijacked by opponents who contrasted the protectionist 'little loaf' with the current 'big loaf'. The cheap big loaf was the key representation in posters, postcards and parades; a readily grasped image suited to an age of democratic politics. The Free Trade campaigners and the Tariff Reformers both actively sought popular support in the localities.

Furthermore, the tariff issue united the Liberals and increased their popularity, thus demonstrating the political limitations of tariff reform for the Conservatives. Never under-estimating the credulity of their audience, Liberal speakers focused on the price of food and ignored the wider questions posed by the challenges to the British economy represented by free trade, especially the serious competition for British industry. As a result both of their stance on cheap food and of their willingness to seek the support of organised labour, the Liberals were far better placed than the Conservatives to give voice to popular pressure for social reform and, more generally, for change, although such pressure was far from universal.

A case for Free Trade and against Protectionism was offered in *The Hound of the Baskervilles*, which was serialised in *The Strand Magazine* from August 1901 to April 1902. Holmes praises a newspaper defence of Free Trade:

> 'You may be cajoled into imagining that your own special trade or your own industry will be encouraged by a protective tariff, but it stands to reason that such legislation must in the long run keep away wealth from the country, diminish the value of our imports, and lower the general conditions of life in this island. . . . Don't you think that is an admirable sentiment?'

However, this may be considered a joke by Doyle, and one that would have been understood as such by his contemporary readers.

Unable to unite the party over tariff reform, or to offer solutions on questions such as social reform, Salisbury's successor, Arthur Balfour, resigned as prime minister on 4 December 1905. He hoped that, once in government, the Liberals would divide, providing the Conservatives with an opportunity to win the imminent general election. This proved a major miscalculation. The election, held in January 1906, led to a Liberal landslide, with the Liberals gaining 401 seats to the Conservatives' 157. The Liberals had recovered well from earlier divisions over Ireland and the Boer War. Doyle stood as a Liberal Unionist for Hawick Burghs in southern Scotland but was beaten anew. Doyle received 2,444 votes, but the Liberal incumbent, Thomas Shaw, who had held the seat since 1892, won 3,125. The swing to the Liberals was 3.8 per cent, which was not a bad result for Doyle in a year of Liberal triumph, but that was scant consolation. In the following election, a by-election in 1909, the Liberals held the seat, defeating another prominent Unionist, the geopolitician Halford Mackinder, whose views offer an instructive perspective for considering those of Doyle; the two men were both keen supporters of the Empire.

Growing pressure for more radical policies had led political opinion to coalesce and polarise to a considerable extent along social and class lines, with the working class increasingly Liberal and the less-numerous middle and upper classes Conservative. In 1891, Gladstone had called for a reduction in factory work hours, electoral reform, and the reform or abolition of the House of Lords. In 1903, the Liberals secretly allied with Labour, in part because they saw a shared class interest, the two parties agreeing not to fight each other in certain seats lest they help the Conservatives. This cooperation was helped by common hostility to tariffs and by Labour anger with the Conservative government's attitude towards trade unions. In the 1906 election, the majority of Liberal candidates included pledges for social reform in their election addresses to their would-be constituents.

The Conservatives were regarded as overly linked to sectional interests – the employers, the agricultural interest, the Church of England, and the brewers (who were unpopular with the Nonconformist temperance lobby) – and had not acquired any reputation for competence. They were blamed for the mismanagement of the Boer War and suffered from the sour taste the conflict had left. Furthermore, Balfour was unable to unite his party. He was also no populist and a poor campaigner. In the 1906 election, the Conservatives lost some of their urban working-class support, while the Liberals took the former Conservative strongholds of London and Lancashire, and also made important gains in rural and suburban parts of southern England, the Conservative heartland. Many of the latter gains were lost in the two general elections of 1910, but the Liberals then retained Lancashire and London, ensuring that they were the major party in all the leading industrial areas. This was not the party that Doyle backed.

Politics was developing towards what was to be its class-orientated character for much of the twentieth century. The foundation of trade unions reflected the growing industrialisation of the economy, the rise of larger concerns employing more people, and, by the end of the nineteenth century, a new, more adversarial and combative working-class consciousness. Moreover, the trade union lodge complemented or displaced the chapel as the main meeting place for men in many working-class communities. The Trades Union Congress (TUC), a federation of trade unions organized in 1868, was responsible for spreading unionism from the skilled craft sector to the more numerous semi-skilled and unskilled workers whose interests had not initially been represented, and TUC support led, in 1900, to the formation of the Labour Representation Committee, the basis of the Labour Party. Some working-class militants looked to a Marxist tradition: the Social-Democratic Federation pioneered the development of socialism in the 1880s and was Britain's first avowedly Marxist party. Most, however, looked to Labour. For example, the decision of the South Wales miners in 1906 to affiliate with the Labour Party marked the beginning of the end of Liberalism's hold over the Welsh urban working class.

British society did not seem beneficent to the growing numbers who were gaining the vote and becoming more politically aware, while many commentators were concerned about the relative weakness of Britain, economically and politically, compared to the leading Continental states. British industries no longer benefited from cheaper raw materials, energy and labour. Foreign competition was responsible for closures, as in 1901 of the Tudhoe Ironworks in County Durham, which employed 1,500 men. Similarly, in Gateshead, the major ironworks ceased trading in 1889 and 1909, the chemical industry declined from the 1880s and the railways works was much cut in 1910.

There was less confidence that British institutions and practices were best. In the 1890s and early 1900s, there was much interest in the German educational system, and much envy of its 'practical' orientation. Salisbury was not alone in being pessimistic about the future of the Empire. These varied strands of disquiet were to lead to fresh pressure for reform and new political divisions in the period up to World War One. The British could take pride in the spread of Empire and the triumphalism of Queen Victoria's Golden and Diamond Jubilees in 1887 and 1897, but the domestic divisions of the first half of the nineteenth century, which had diminished or disappeared in its prosperous third quarter, were re-emerging, taking on new forms, and being accentuated by fresh sources of tension. Economic change brought significant levels of social disruption, and social and political developments, both international and domestic, encouraged unease.[11]

In 1909, Louis Blériot flew across the channel. 'Britain is no longer an island' reflected the press baron Lord Northcliffe.[12] In 1904, Leo Amery, a journalist who was to become a Conservative politician, emphasised the onward rush of technology when he told the Royal Geographical Society in a discussion after a paper presented by Mackinder, that sea and rail links and power would be supplemented by air, and then

> a great deal of this geographical distribution must lose its importance, and the successful powers will be those who have the greatest industrial basis. It will not matter whether they are in the centre of a continent or on an island; those people who have the industrial power and the power of invention and of science will be able to defeat all others.[13]

This matched Doyle's view on submarines, on which see chapter 9.

Greater radicalism contributed to, and in part reflected and sustained, a sense of doubt, if not a crisis of confidence in society. The demand for reform was matched by a pressure for security in a competitive international environment, the two combining to produce an uneasiness about present and future that fed into debates about the condition of the people and calls for National Efficiency: competence in government and a more vigorous and better-educated populace.

Some prominent Liberals, especially the dynamic David Lloyd George (1863–1945), a Welsh solicitor who became chancellor of the exchequer from 1908 to 1915 (and prime minister from 1916 to 1922), sought to change the state of the people by undermining the power and possessions of the old landed élite and by providing assured social welfare. As with much else in politics, problems provided a key context. Indeed, the New Liberalism of the Liberal Reforms was as much to do with propping up the tottering Poor Law than bringing about social reform and social harmony.

In 1909, Lloyd George announced a 'People's Budget'. Proposing redistributive measures in order to give force to his views about the necessary nature of society for Britain to improve, this budget raised direct taxation on higher incomes, and prepared the way for taxes on land. The Liberals lessened the concern about redistribution by planning no tax increases on annual earned income below £2,000, a figure that then excluded the middle class; but the notion of redistributive taxation was indeed a threat to this group. Just as it had earlier rejected measures against pubs, the House of Lords rejected the budget, only for two general elections in 1910 to return a Liberal government that was dependent on support from Labour and the Irish Nationalists. That of January 1910 saw the Liberals with 274 seats and 43.5 per cent of the popular vote, and the Conservatives with 272 and 46.8 per cent. In that of December, the Liberals gained 272 seats and 44.2 per cent and the Conservatives 271 and 46.6 per cent. Aside from the passage of the budget, the Parliament Act of 1911 replaced the Lords' ability to veto Commons' legislation with the right only to delay it, an Act only passed as a result of the threat of creating many more peers to pack the Lords with Liberal supporters, the policy already followed in order to push through the 'Great' or First Reform Act, that of 1832.

Shot through with uncertainty, the entire dispute was accompanied by strident social criticism of the aristocracy. In 1911, H. G. Wells, in his novel *The New Machiavelli*, presented Richard Remington as narrator, a fictional politician who advocated a 'trained aristocracy', universal education, feminism, and a more perfect, and thus stronger, Britain. Somewhat differently, Doyle's stress on ancestral houses is a call for continuity and incremental development, but, in contrast to the idea of inherited talent, he also very much emphasised professionalism in his presentation of Holmes first introduced in *A Study in Scarlet*:

> 'I'm a consulting detective. . . . Here in London we have lots of Government detectives and lots of private ones. When these fellows are at fault, they come to me, and I manage to put them on the right scent. They lay all the evidence before me, and I am generally able, by the help of my knowledge of the history of crime, to set them straight. There is a strong family resemblance about misdeeds, and if you have all the details of a

> thousand at your finger ends, it is odd if you can't unravel the thousand and first'.

To a degree, this is the individual case reduced to the system. As with Hercule Poirot, Holmes can solve a problem from his room even though others can see 'every detail for themselves'.

> 'I have a kind of intuition that way. Now and again a case turns up which is a little more complex. Then I have to bustle about and see things with my own eyes. You see I have a lot of special knowledge which I apply to the problem, and which facilitates matters wonderfully'.

This is not the aristocratic amateur, however talented, as later with Dorothy L. Sayers's creation Lord Peter Wimsey.

In 1911, Lloyd George's National Insurance Act provided for unemployment assistance and for all males eligible for insurance to be registered with a doctor who was to receive a fee per patient, irrespective of the amount of medical attention required. Thus, with the key exclusions of children and most women from the health proposals, and of unskilled workers from the unemployment provisions, exclusions that reflected costs as well as notions of entitlement, there was already considerable provision of public welfare support prior to the establishment of the National Health Service in 1948. At the same time, the 1911 legislation reflected the determination to align private commitment to one's own future alongside state security.

The legislation of the Liberal government was designed to provide an environment for further regulation, as with the first Town Planning Act, passed in 1909, but the context was one of social and political division. In 1906, the Liberals passed a Trade Disputes Act that gave the trade unions immunity from actions for damages as a result of strike action, and thus rejected the attempts of the courts, through the Taff Vale case of 1901, to bring the unions within the law. The latter verdict had threatened to make strike action prohibitively expensive. The Liberals thus appealed to the working class, although, despite the populist and collectivist strain in 'New Liberalism', the Liberals were unhappy with using the language of class, unenthusiastic about powerful trade unions, and did not adopt working-class candidates.

Welsh church disestablishment was pushed through in 1914, although, with the intervention of war, it was not implemented until 1920. Irish Home Rule was far more of a key issue, but the Liberal government initially side-lined it. In 1900, while standing for Parliament, Doyle pressed for an Ireland united 'upon a base of national unity and Imperial loyalty' and deplored sectarianism there. He praised Sir Horace Plunkett, a talented Anglo-Irish Unionist MP, and called for 'a body of reasonable and temperate men who will intervene between the bigots and fanatics of either party'.[14]

In a fashion that was diametrically opposite to what Doyle had urged, the determination of the Ulster Protestants, who were in a minority in Ireland, to resist Home Rule took the country to the brink of civil war in 1914. The formation of the Ulster Unionist Council (1905) and the Ulster Volunteer Force (1913) revealed the unwillingness of the Ulster Protestants to subordinate their sense of identity to Irish nationalism. They were assisted by the Conservatives (after their merger with the Liberal Unionists in 1912, the Conservative and Unionist Party), who did their best to resist the Home Rule Bill introduced by the Liberal government in 1912. The Bill, twice rejected by the House of Lords, was passed in an amended form in 1914, with the proviso that it was not to be implemented until after the war. The crisis defined the political forces in Ireland and gave a powerful impetus to the consciousness of the Ulster Protestants. The authority and power of the British state was challenged in a fashion that was far more potent and threatening than the Boer War.

Prior to World War One, the Liberal Party, with its desire for the cooperation of capital and labour, and its stress on class harmony for all except the aristocracy, still displayed few signs of decline at the hands of Labour, and also showed much confidence in its future. Another general election was due by 1915, and, although the Conservatives were in better shape than they had been after the 1906 election, there seemed many reasons to assume that they would face, after their two in 1910, a fourth election defeat, not least because they had fewer allies than the Liberals.

At the same time as the economic challenges highlighted by Chamberlain, there were also the fresh possibilities generated by new inventions. By 1907, the Britannia Foundry at Derby included a motor cylinder line making four hundred to five hundred parts a week for car manufacturers, such as Jowett Motors of Bradford. There were 132,000 private car registrations by 1914, as well as 51,167 buses and taxis on the road and 124,000 motorcycle registrations. There was also change in the sheer scale of activity. The cotton industry was well established, but in 1900–9, fifteen million spindles added 35 per cent to the industry's capacity.

So also with London, an area of dynamic change which had a political trajectory that is in the background to the Doyle stories, although more for the readers than for driving the plots. As a result of electoral reform and the newly expanded public politics, political power, there and elsewhere, was becoming more populist. Institutional reform accompanied the transition, as earlier governmental practices and political compromises seemed unacceptable and as both political parties sought to benefit from the change. In 1884, the Liberal government supported the London Government Bill, which proposed to establish a single authority for London, incorporating the city, the vestries and the Metropolitan Board of Works. Strong opposition from within London led, however, to the abandonment of the legislation.

In turn, the Local Government Act of 1888, a measure passed by a Conservative government, created county councils and county boroughs, with London being organised in terms of the new directly elected London County Council (LCC), which covered 117 square miles. Nevertheless, the Conservative-dominated City of London retained the powers of a municipal borough and was excluded from the LCC area, while Greater London, the built-up area beyond the LCC, a largely Conservative area to which Holmes frequently went, was also excluded.

The first elections to the new body were held in 1889 and led to victory by the Progressives (or Liberals). The first Chairman of the LCC was Rosebery, who was to become Liberal prime minister in 1894. As chairman from 1889 to 1890, Rosebery, a Scottish magnate, proved a critic of slum-landlordism, and, thereby, of Salisbury. More generally, the LCC, the world's largest municipal authority, took an activist role in trying to expand its powers and improve London life, a role based on a strong sense of mission and a capacity to produce information on which policy could be based.

The politics of London were also transformed as the Conservatives benefited from the long-term expansion of the middle classes, and, instead of being rural, became an increasingly urban- and suburban-based party. In this, the Conservatives profited from hostility to the perceived radicalism of Gladstonian Liberalism, which drove the newly anxious middle classes, ironically the beneficiaries of the meritocratic reforms of the first Gladstone ministry, into the Conservative camp. The Conservatives, in turn, had become a party defending the property of the many, rather than social privilege.

In 1882, Salisbury wrote of the rise of 'a great Villa Toryism which requires organization'. Many of those Holmes goes to help live in such villas. This middle-class move away from the Liberals in part reflected a reaction based on self-interest, namely opposition to the spread in the power and activity of local government, which led to new commitments, not least by school boards, pushing up municipal rates. As also with subsequent rallies to the Conservatives in London, rising tax demands pressed on a society that, in the 1880s, a period of recession, was less buoyant and, crucially, less confident economically, than it had been. London's electoral weight itself had increased due to the Redistribution of Seats Act (1885), which was designed to make the number of MPs proportional to the voting population, although some seats, such as rapidly growing Croydon, had a disproportionately large electorate. Whereas twenty-five Liberal MPs had been elected from the London area in 1892, in 1895 the Unionists (Conservatives allied with

Liberal Unionists) won fifty-three seats compared to only eight for the Liberals.

These results reflected the strength of a metropolitan Conservatism that was separate from the more suburban villa-dom. The former was the product of the appeal of Conservatism to significant working-class and lower-middle-class interests.[15] Indeed, London was on average markedly Conservative in the period 1885–1910, a fact that was significant in the composition of Holmes's readership. Working-class support for the Conservatives in London owed something to opposition to immigration, to support for drinking (threatened by Liberal advocacy for temperance), and to the backing of workers who had a degree of rights in their work, for example costermongers who saw their pitches as freeholds.[16] Drunkenness is often linked in the Holmes stories to brutality, as with James Browner, the murderer in 'The Cardboard Box' (1893), and Captain Peter Carey in 'Black Peter' (1904). However, Holmes is no temperance advocate.

Prefiguring the situation for the Greater London Council faced by the Conservative government of Margaret Thatcher in the 1980s, the Conservatives were worried by the radicalism of the LCC, a concern freely expressed in the newspapers read by Holmes, such as the *Daily Telegraph*. The Progressives became more radical in their language, composition and policy, and also pressed for greater attention to the East End. Conservative concerns led, in 1899, under the Government of London Act passed by the Conservative government, to the transfer of several of its roles to twenty-seven new metropolitan boroughs, alongside the City of London. In the event, the Conservatives, then called Municipal Reformers, gained control of the LCC in 1907, retaining it until 1934. As a major mark of civic pride as well as a functioning headquarters, County Hall was designed for the LCC by Ralph Knott in 1909, and begun in 1911 on an area of former factories, wharves and houses, although it was not to be opened until 1922.

While politics was developing towards a class-orientated character, the social order could be harsh as well as inegalitarian. A London campaign against street prostitution, launched in 1883, came to an end, in 1887, amid public complaints and parliamentary questions about the blackmailing of poor prostitutes, bribery of the police, and police harassment through arrests. Such criticism helps explain the varied view of police officers in the Holmes stories. By then, the Metropolitan Police were commanded from Scotland Yard, which had been bought by the Home Office in 1886 for £186,000. Doyle's mention of it is of a new facility. He can be critical of the police in the Holmes stories, but generally takes a positive view of them, as in 'The Three Garridebs' (1924): 'There may be an occasional want of imaginative intuition down there, but they lead the world for thoroughness and method'. Charles Dickens espoused the same opinions in his novels.

A radical political current was also coming to the fore, one that had survived from Chartism. Radical clubs were most active in London and provided the background for the First International Workingmen's Association in 1864, the Reform League demonstrations of 1866–67, the Manhood Suffrage League in the mid-1870s, the agitation in the early 1880s around the refusal to allow an avowed atheist, Charles Bradlaugh, to take his seat in the House of Commons, the Socialist revival in the 1880s, the breaking of clubland windows by demonstrators in 1886, and the major London demonstrations in 1887.

In light of the presentation in *The Valley of Fear* of class war as really anti-societal criminality, it is instructive to consider the response to 'Bloody Sunday', November 13, 1887, at Trafalgar Square, the totemic centre of Empire. A meeting called by the Metropolitan Radical Association in protest against the government's failure to tackle unemployment was banned. Large numbers of police sought to block the entry march into the square, which led to a violent clash involving more than four hundred arrests and about two hundred casualties, notably two deaths. The previous year, riots by the unemployed in central London included attacks on expensive Piccadilly stores. There were rumours of widespread unrest among the South London poor.[17] These reports and the surrounding concerns would have affected the perception of London by the readers of fiction.

In turn, radical pressures from within the Liberal Party were supplemented, in London and elsewhere, by the creation of more explicitly working-class movements, both political and industrial. The development of trade unions reflected a new, more adversarial and combative working-class consciousness. There were major strikes in the London gasworks and docks in 1888–89, which helped radicalise the local Progressives, and, in 1900, the Labour Representation Committee, the basis of the Labour Party, was created. In *The Sign of Four*, Holmes sardonically comments on the workers leaving the Jacobson's Yard on the Thames: 'Dirty-looking rascals, but I suppose everyone has some little immortal spark concealed about him. You would not think it, to look at them'.

In 'The Six Napoleons' (1904), Morse Hudson, a picture-dealer on the Kennington Road, is ready to find a political current in lawlessness:

> 'What we pay rates and taxes for I don't know, when any ruffian can come in and break one's goods. . . . A Nihilist plot, that's what I make it. No one but an Anarchist would go about breaking statues. Red republicans, that's what I call them'.

This is mockery, for the attack on the busts is simply criminal in intent, but the story reflected the febrile character of the belief in conspiracies at a time of undoubted anarchism. This theme was developed by Joseph Conrad in *The Secret Agent* (1907), which was set in London in 1886, but possibly based on the Greenwich Bombing of 1894, an anarchist failure. Robert Louis Stevenson and his wife Fanny in *The Dynamiter* (1885) were also more politically engaged than Doyle in the Holmes stories. Separately, the Hudson character in 'The Six Napoleons' captures the sense that government, both local and national, was accountable.

The Labour Party increasingly defined radical politics and Labour developed strong local roots, notably in the East End. Electoral victories, such as those of Keir Hardie in West Ham, South, in 1892, and of Will Crooks at the Woolwich by-election in 1903, became more frequent. This allowed radical issues to be presented in Parliament, with Crooks advancing the cases for unemployed workers and a minimum wage. Labour's support and activities were strongest in the East End, and far weaker in West London, which, instead, was much more integrated into a service economy. The Labour Party and the trade unions thus added another level to the spatial differentiation within London. The strength Labour was to show in London after World War One and the introduction of universal adult suffrage in 1918 was not yet apparent. However, the rise in trade-union and Labour activity led to new public occasions and displays, as with the May Day Procession in Central London in 1912. Photographs of the scene make clear the nature of such occasions with large numbers of mostly male walkers, smartly dressed with jackets, ties and collars, marching escorted by the police. Brass bands were in attendance.

At the same time, troops were deployed to contain violent strikes in South Wales in 1910 and Liverpool in 1911, while London Docklands, in 1911–12, faced serious labour problems as a result of Syndicalist agitation. On a long-standing pattern, such problems stoked fears about radicalism. In 'The Lost Special', a story without Holmes published in *The Strand Magazine* in August 1898, the loss of a specially hired train between Liverpool and Manchester in 1890 leads to the question in *The Times*: 'Is there a secret society of colliers, an English *Camorra*, which is capable of destroying both train and passengers? It is improbable but it is not impossible'. In practice, this is a misdirection designed to cast critical light on the press; and, acting on behalf of corrupt members of the French élite, it is a French fraudster who is responsible.

More radical views were also disseminated. In 1885, the group variously termed the 'Hampstead Marx Circle' or 'Hampstead Historic Society', which included George Bernard Shaw and Sidney Webb, began meeting to discuss the work of Karl Marx. Two years later, an English translation of *Das Kapital* appeared in London. Webb's *London Programme* (1891) pressed the Progressives to expand LCC powers to include control over gas, water, transport and the building of public-sector housing. Greater radicalism contributed to, and, in part, reflected, a situation of sustained doubt, if not a crisis of confidence, in late Victorian society. The demand for reform was matched by a pressure for security, the two combining to produce an uneasiness about present and future that fed into debate about the condition of the people. Concern about the extent of London's poverty, and the associated social problems, encouraged enumeration and analysis, led to calls for public action, promoted charitable missions and resulted in unease, variously sympathetic and critical, about an apparently volatile situation. Clement Attlee, Labour prime minister from 1945 to 1951, was converted to socialism by visiting, in 1905, Haileybury House, a boys' club in Stepney run by members of his old school, and he took over as manager of the club two years later.

The wider social politics of the period served as the backdrop to the Holmes stories. In the case of London, they helped explain the appeal of a detective who could act successfully in such a foreboding human-scape. Holmes both understands this world and can confront and overcome its villains, while also remaining untarnished. Danger and bravery are at stake, as well as understanding, for the police and for Holmes. In 'The Red Circle' (1911), in an implicit counterpoint to the bravery of Imperial conflict and an appropriately proud rejection of American pushiness, Doyle notes:

> Our official detectives may blunder in the matter of intelligence, but never in that of courage. Gregson climbed the stair to arrest this desperate murderer with the same absolutely quiet and business-like bearing with which he would have ascended the official staircase of Scotland Yard. The Pinkerton man had tried to push past him, but Gregson had firmly elbowed him back. London dangers were the privilege of the London force.[18]

6

HOLMES AND EMPIRE

> The whole course of future history depends on whether the Old Britain beside the Narrow Seas have enough of virility and imagination to withstand the challenge of her naval supremacy, until such time as the daughter nations shall have grown to maturity, and the British Navy shall have expanded into the Navy of the Britains.
>
> – Not Doyle but his fellow Liberal Unionist, Halford Mackinder in his *Britain and the British Seas* (1902)

The imperial agenda of the Liberal Unionists among whom Doyle was politically active was that of Mackinder who, like Doyle in 1906, stood unsuccessfully for Parliament for Hawick. Like Doyle, Mackinder wanted to see strengthening at home and imperial development – the latter indeed a federalist empire. Like Doyle, Mackinder was also interested in medicine. The son of a provincial doctor, Mackinder had studied medical geography and sought to relate diseases to environmental conditions.[1] Both men were part of the energy of ideas in Britain at the turn of the century.

Empire is always present in the Holmes world. London is the centre of imperial networks and Empire a source of renewal and material wealth for Britain. This is seen in *The Hound of the Bas-*

kervilles. Sir Charles's wealth comes from the South African goldfields. Before he returns to Britain, his successor, the young baronet, Sir Henry, has spent his entire adult life in Canada on the prairies, and he represents youth, virility and a confidence in the future also seen in the Australian-born characters in the stories.

Empire indeed helped bring Britain wealth. It dominated the production of many important goods. Gold and diamonds came from South Africa; wheat, copper, timber and fish from Canada; tin from Malaya; cocoa from Ghana; palm oil from Nigeria; cotton from Egypt; tea from India; and sugar from the West Indies. Britain was also the largest overseas investor and the greatest merchant shipper in the world, as well as the centre of the world's financial system: commodity prices, shipping routes and insurance premiums were all set in London, as was the meridian on which time zones were based from 1884. The expansion of the service sector, focused on the City of London, was fundamental to Britain's economic strength and influence. Thanks to its prominence in submarine telegraphy, Britain was also at the centre of the world's communications. The landing point for suboceanic cables was Porthcurno Beach in Cornwall.

Empire was very important to Britain, both in Doyle's life, and for the Holmes stories. In Britain, Empire was staged in music-hall, melodrama and blackface minstrelsy, and across all of society. Exhibitions, such as *The Empire of India* seen in London in 1895, or the *Stanley and Africa* held five years earlier, were much visited. Furthermore, more than 2.5 million visitors thronged the naval exhibition on the Thames embankment from May to October 1891.[2]

So also with new technology. Jack Hunt, a private in the Scots Guards, described, in a letter to his brother, the British entry into Pretoria, the capital of Transvaal, in 1900 during the Boer War: 'When we marched into the market square headed by Lord Roberts to raise the flag, they took our photo by the cinematograph so I expect you will see it on some of the music-halls in London'.[3]

Earlier that year, large London crowds, many of them clerks and medical students, applauded the relief of Mafeking from a long Boer siege. Its commander, Robert Baden-Powell (1857–1941), became an iconic figure. Joining the army in 1876, he had already served extensively before the siege of Mafeking: in southern Africa, West Africa and India. Baden-Powell presented the Fourth Anglo-Ashanti war of 1895–96 in West Africa, in which he served, as a moral cause intended to pacify and develop the area, and to stop slave-trading and raiding. He was promoted to major-general after holding Mafeking, where his second-in-command was Lord Edward Cecil, the fourth son of Salisbury, who had earlier served in Sudan, including at the crucial battle of Omdurman in 1898. Like Doyle, Baden-Powell was a keen advocate of Empire and believed that it was a means to build character. He wrote much and was seen as a good storyteller. Both men also regarded Germany as a threat.[4]

Empire was not simply a matter of power politics, military interests, élite careers and an ideology of mission and purpose that appealed to the propertied and the proselytising. It also had relevance and meaning throughout a society affected by the growth of popular imperialist sentiment. On the one hand, this influence was reflected in the jingoistic strains of popular culture such as music-hall ballads and the images depicted on advertisements for mass-produced goods. In *The Sign of Four*, Jonathan Small 'earned a living at this time by my exhibiting poor Tonga at fairs and other such places as the black cannibal. He would eat raw meat and dance his war-dance: so we always had a hatful of pennies after a day's work', the pennies referring to coins thrown in by ordinary citizens. On the other hand, many of the workers watching Tonga appear to have been pretty apathetic about imperialism.

Empire reflected and sustained widespread racist assertions and assumptions, both of which were amply demonstrated in the literature and press of the period. Empire also provided the occasion and stimulus for a new concept of exemplary masculinity focusing on soldier heroes such as Wolseley, Gordon, Roberts, Kitchener and Baden-Powell, who, in a fusion of martial prowess, Protestant zeal and moral manhood, were all seen as national icons. Their victories were gained at the expense of numerous non-Europeans, often slaughtered by the technology of modern weaponry, as in Kitchener's victory at Omdurman (Sudan) in 1898. The zealous Charles Gordon, who died unsuccessfully defending Khartoum against the Mahdists in 1885, was presented as a quasi-saint resisting a vast force of Muslims and sacrificing himself to that end. The impact of such controversial imperial events was enough to threaten prominent politicians such as Gladstone, who was held responsible for the failure to send a relief force until too late. In 'The Resident Patient', Watson looks at his newly framed picture of Gordon. Kitchener's success was regarded in Britain as the appropriate response and as a purging of guilt.

Military figures frequently appear in the Holmes stories, although, in *The Hound of the Baskervilles*, Holmes, unusually, breaks rank by allowing himself to be seen as a military commander:

> 'Good morning, Holmes', said the baronet. 'You look like a general who is planning a battle with his Chief of the Staff'.
>
> 'That is the exact situation. Watson was asking for orders'.

In general, Holmes is more careful in explaining his position. He is no soldier other than on the front line against crime and conspiracy. Doyle deploys Holmes at the highest rank of the political system, so that he is able to make a prime minister hold him in respect. However, there is not the comparable setting with the most senior army ranks. Nor is there any echo of the political rifts over the army in the 1890s. Sir Garnet Wolseley, the commander-in-chief from 1895 until 1900, loathed politicians and wanted a larger army, only to have to accept greater government control. Moreover, Wolseley's network competed with the protégés of Lord Roberts, the head of the Indian army, and Wolseley's successor.[5]

Instead, the senior ranks of the army come into play in the Holmes stories as retired figures concerned about their interests, including their children. Many are part of county society. In 'The

Blanched Soldier', there is not only Godfrey Emsworth, who had played a brave role in the Boer War, but also his father Colonel Emsworth – 'Emsworth, the Crimean V. C.'. There was no shortage of VCs in the pages of detective novelists. In 'Murder by Proxy' (1897) by Matthias McDonnell Bodkin, Colonel Peyton 'had distinguished himself in a dozen engagements, and has the Victoria Cross locked up in a drawer of his desk'. Needless to say, the Colonel is a positive character.

In discussing the Emsworths, James Dodd presents 'the fighting blood' as hereditary. The Crimean War of 1854–56, in which Russia lost to an alliance made up of Britain, France, the Ottoman Empire and Sardinia, is also referred to in 'The Golden Pince-Nez': 'Mortimer, the gardener, who wheels the bath-chair, is an Army Pensioner – an old Crimean man of excellent character'. Philip Green, the hero in 'Lady Frances Carfax', is 'the son of the famous admiral of that name who commanded the sea of Azof [*sic*] fleet in the Crimean War'. There were individuals who matched these characters. Thus, Colonel Alexander Sebastian Leith-Hay of Leith Hall (1818–1900) served in the Crimean War and in the relief of the besieged British garrison at Lucknow in 1857 during the Indian Mutiny, bringing home the jewellery of the Nawab of Oudh and a white cockatoo.

In the Holmes stories, Colonel Emsworth is not the only military figure to pose problems, although he is not a criminal. Similarly, the obdurate Colonel Ross owns the horse Silver Blaze but is no criminal. At the humble level, in 'The Naval Treaty', the commissionaire at the Foreign Office is a Coldstream Guards veteran, which seems to excuse his falling asleep in his box. There can also be villains, as in the fraudster uncovered in *The Sign of Four*. Thaddeus Sholto notes of his father:

> 'Major John Sholto, once of the Indian Army. He retired some eleven years ago, and came to live at Pondicherry Lodge, in Upper Norwood. He had prospered in India, and brought back with him a considerable sum of money, a large collection of valuable curiosities, and a staff of native servants. With these

> advantages he bought himself a house, and lived in great luxury'.

However, all was not well, as the story reveals.

In 'The Crooked Man', the death of Colonel Barclay of the Royal Mallows is the puzzle. Holmes notes:

> 'The Royal Mallows is one of the most famous Irish regiments in the British Army. It did wonders both in the Crimea and the Mutiny, and has since that time distinguished itself upon every possible occasion. It was commanded by James Barclay, a gallant veteran, who started as a full private, was raised to commissioned rank for his bravery at the time of the Mutiny, and so lived to command the regiment in which he had once carried a musket'.

In practice, Barclay's compromised reputation provides the essence of the story of this apparent Victorian hero.

Alongside the occasional flaw, the idea of imperial masculinity as noble was frequently presented in Holmes stories, as with the Australian sea captain in 'The Abbey Grange' (1904):

> Our door was opened to admit as fine a specimen of manhood as ever passed through it. He was a very tall young man, golden-moustached, blue-eyed, with a skin which had been burned by tropical suns, and a springy step which showed that the huge frame was as active as it was strong.

Captain Croker himself uses the commonplace language of Empire, addressing Holmes's requirement that he comes clean about events: 'I believe you are a man of your word, and a white man', the latter a racist commonplace for being honest.[6] To complete the account, Watson becomes 'a British jury . . . and I never met a man who was more eminently fitted to represent one', and Holmes the judge, and Croker is swiftly cleared. In *The Hound of the Baskervilles*, Sir Henry Baskerville is a positive force. His vigour is indicated by his lack of smartly dressing 'the part'. Indeed, returning from Canada, Sir Henry has to remedy this by purchasing new clothes and boots. Manliness was a matter not only of supporting the cause of imperial federalism but also of meeting the pressure for conscription, or, at least, volunteers.

The adventures of Holmes's longer foreign stories were located in India and the United States. Imperial struggle, notably the sieges of the Indian Mutiny and the Boer War, offered drama for the entire country. Imperial clashes were re-enacted in open-air spectacles in Britain: the tableau and pageant became art forms. Newspapers spent substantial sums on the telegraphy that brought news of imperial conflict. Moreover, army service was a glorious route out of the slums for many working-class men. The Protestant and Catholic churches of Britain devoted their resources to missionary activity outside Europe, particularly, though not only, within the Empire, which they endorsed as a means of facilitating Christian missions.

Empire was a crucial component of British nationalism, especially towards the end of the century. The imagery of government fuelled this: Victoria was made Empress of India in 1876; the journal *Punch*, an influential creator of images, popularised Empire in its cartoons; and public buildings were decorated with symbols of Empire. The expansion of Empire was seen as furthering moral, as well as national, goals, by spreading what was seen as liberal government and the rule of law, and by providing opportunities for Christian proselytism.

Whereas Agatha Christie had her protagonists follow Empire (formal or informal) abroad, as in *The Man in the Brown Suit*, *Death on the Nile* and *They Came to Baghdad*, that was not the practice for Holmes. He could readily have taken a steamer to Cape Town, Kingston or Halifax, but did not do so, and indeed, was less travelled than Doyle.

Yet, Empire was very much present in the Holmes stories because of its presence in Britain. This was a highly varied phenomenon. It included Britons who had lived abroad before coming home, as with the Honourable Philip Green in 'Lady Frances Carfax', who, having been 'a wild youngster', makes his money in

South Africa. In 'The Solitary Cyclist', Violet Smith's uncle: 'Ralph Smith . . . went to Africa twenty-five years ago, and we have never had a word from him since'. In response to an advertisement in *The Times*, she '"met two gentlemen, Mr Carruthers and Mr Woodley, who were home on a visit from South Africa. They said that my uncle was a friend of theirs, that he died some months before in poverty in Johannesburg, and that he had asked them with his last breath to hunt up his relations"'.

There were many born in Empire who came to Britain, as with Jinny O'James, 'the mature woman of the world' with a past, and Professor James McMurdo O'Brien, the two Australians in the non-Holmes 'A Physiologist's Wife' (1890). Australia is again at the fore in 'Lady Frances Carfax', with Holmes telling Watson

> 'that we are dealing with an exceptionally astute and dangerous man. The Rev. Dr Schlessinger, missionary from South America, is none other than Holy Peters, one of the most unscrupulous rascals that Australia has ever evolved – and for a young country it has turned out some very finished types. His particular speciality is the beguiling of lonely ladies by playing upon their religious feelings, and his so-called wife, an Englishwoman named Fraser, is a worthy helpmate . . . he was badly bitten in a saloon-fight at Adelaide in '89'.

There was also Empire as a source of wealth and a focus for investment. Thus, in 'The Dancing Men', set in 1898, Holmes reveals to Watson his knowledge that the latter had chosen not to invest in South African securities, which are subsequently clarified to mean the goldfields. In 'The Stockbroker's Clerk', Hall Pycraft is quizzed on the stock price of New Zealand Consolidated and British Broken Hills, the latter a reference to the Broken Hill Proprietary Company, which was founded in 1885 to work the silver-rich Broken Hill ore body found in Australia in 1883. Readers would have been expected to understand the reference. Canadian Pacific Railway shares are part of the loot in 'The Adventure of Black Peter'. There were also in this story South American securities, from Argentina, Costa Rica and Brazil. The varied products from Empire mentioned in the stories include the 'Penang lawyer' type of walking stick referred to in 'Silver Blaze'.

The Britons going abroad can be sometimes unworthy, such as James Armitage, who is transported in 1855 for fraud in the 'The *Gloria Scott*', which falls victim to a very violent convicts' rising that also dooms the ship. Like his compatriot Evans, Armitage then makes his money in the Australasian diggings, where he is able to lose his former identity, and the two men return to England as 'rich colonials' and buy into rural status, only to be exploited as a result of the *Gloria Scott*. At the close, Armitage's heartbroken son, Trevor, like Gilchrist in 'The Three Students', leaves England in an act of imperial cleansing. Trevor goes 'out to the Terai tea planting, where I hear that he is doing well'. The Terai is an area of northern India and southern Nepal, some of which Britain had annexed from Nepal in 1816. Tea cultivation was successfully introduced in the Darjeeling Terai in 1862 and helped supply Britain's apparently insatiable demand for this product of Empire.

The villain in 'The Priory School', James Wilder, the Duke of Holderness's secretary and his unacknowledged illegitimate son, who has 'always a taste for low company', is sent 'to seek his fortune in Australia'. The assumption is that he would fit in there, and, at least, find opportunities. In Wilde's *The Importance of Being Earnest* (1895), Jack Worthing proposes to send the spendthrift Algernon to Australia, although the latter responds that he would 'sooner die', and, told the choice is 'this world, the next world, and Australia', replies 'The accounts I have received of Australia and the next world, are not particularly encouraging'.

In 'The Veiled Lodger', to India, but for different reasons, goes 'a young Edmunds, of the Berkshire Constabulary. A smart lad that! He was sent later to Allahabad'. Set in 1890, though published in 1927, the story that details his career reflects the extent to which the British presence in India increasingly moved from the military to the police. Later in the story, Edmunds is revealed to have been a detective.

The most contentious presentation of the Empire to modern eyes would be in *The Sign of Four* with Jonathan Small's description of the Mutiny and the subsequent account of Tonga, the Andaman Islander. Small's account of his earlier life is the deep history of the story but does not come until the close of it, thus providing both a lengthy denouement and a second narrative for the novel, one shot through with a degree of drama and violence even greater than the river chase involving Holmes and Watson.

Going out to India as a soldier, Small loses a leg to a Ganges crocodile, thus providing an additional exoticism and a reminder of the hazards of India, military service and life. Small then becomes an estate overseer, finding both a role and stability, only to encounter the horror of the Mutiny:

> 'One month India lay as still and peaceful, to all appearance, as Surrey or Kent; the next there were two hundred thousand black devils let loose, and the country was a perfect hell . . . the whole sky was alight with the burning bungalows. . . . Dawson's wife, all cut into ribbons . . . hundreds of the black fiends . . . a fight of the millions against the hundreds . . . nothing but torture and murder and outrage . . . fanatics and fierce devil-worshippers'.

Small was then recruited under threat of death by three Sikhs into a conspiracy to kill a Hindu pretend-merchant transporting a duplicitous rajah's jewels. In an instructive note about tensions between the non-British inhabitants of India, Abdullah Khan, one of the Sikhs, tells Small that he, Khan, cannot trust Hindus, 'But the Sikh knows the Englishman, and the Englishman knows the Sikh'.

The murder is discovered. Sent to the prison settlement at Blair Island on the Andamans, when he was 'bullied by every cursed black-faced policeman who loved to take it out of a white man', including a 'vile Pathan', Small cures and befriends a young Islander, and the two men escape to hunt down the officer who had tricked Small on the prison colony. Tonga, the Islander, is earlier identified by Holmes, and a gazetteer that describes them as fierce, intractable, hideous and cannibals offers a disturbing background. To a degree, it captured the willingness of the indigenous inhabitants to reject the constraints of British India.

In the subsequent chase on the River Thames, the language becomes far more derogatory, and unnecessarily so. Tonga becomes 'this savage, distorted creature . . . never have I seen features so deeply marked with all bestiality and cruelty . . . half-animal fury . . . unhallowed dwarf . . . venomous, menacing eyes'. Subsequently, Tonga is described by Small as 'that hell-hound . . . the little devil'. Fired at by Tonga with a poisoned dart, Holmes and Watson shoot together and hit Tonga, who falls into the river.

This novel has an ironic counterpart in modern cultural politics. Visiting Port Blair on South Andaman Island, I noted the memorialisation at the Cellular Jail of the 'firebrand revolutionaries against the brutalities of the British barbarisms', in the words of the plaque erected in 1979 by the then Indian prime minister, Morarji Desai. There is no mention, there or elsewhere, of the islands only being Indian because India succeeded to the British imperial position: benefiting from their firepower and amphibious capability, the British had overcome opposition by the local indigenous population in the late 1850s.

When Doyle wrote his account, the prisoners there were kept in miserable circumstances. Small himself gets a little hut and takes part in ditch digging, yam planting, and, far more easily, drug dispensing. The Cellular Jail for political detainees, a different form of regimentation, was not built until 1896–1906, and its single cells were designed to help limit the spread of disease.

Changing memorialisation was, and is, also the case with the Mutiny. The emphasis in Doyle's day was on the brutal treatment of British women and children, especially the massacre at Kanpur (Small's Cawnpore) of over two hundred people in 1857, the details of which still have the capacity to shock.[7] The fate of the women and children were also at issue in the Holmes short story 'The Crooked Man'. Now the emphasis has moved, instead, to British atrocities. These were indeed harsh, plentiful and not restricted to the rebel soldiers. Indeed, alongside hostility to the massacres by the rebels, there was criticism in Britain about the harsh and often arbitrary nature of the reprisals.

Doyle's treatment of the Andaman Islanders reflects the sense of civilisational conflict and progress, and the defence of British imperialism, seen also in his non-Holmes *The Tragedy of the Korosko*. This appeared as a serial in *The Strand Magazine* in 1897, as a book in 1898 and, in an adaptation by Doyle, as the play *Fires of Fate* (1909), which, in 1923, became a film. The story is very much set in the here-and-now of the British conflict with the Mahdists of Sudan. In the novel, Cecil Brown presents the Dervishes (Mahdists) as uncompromising believers in destiny, the proof of how bigotry leads towards barbarism, and a dire threat to the civilisation of Egypt which is protected by Britain. Brown feels that Britain has taken on the excessive burdens of being the global policeman, only for Colonel Cochrane to argue that he has

> 'a very limited view of our national duties . . . behind national interests and diplomacy and all that there lies a great guiding force – a Providence in fact – which is for ever getting the best out of each nation and using it for the good of the whole. When a nation ceases to respond, it is time that she went into hospital for a few centuries, like Spain or Greece – the virtue has gone out of her. A man or a nation is not placed upon the earth to do merely what is pleasant and what is profitable. . . . That is how we rule India. We came there by a kind of natural law, like air rushing into a vacuum'.

There is also an opportunity for Doyle to advance his view of Anglo-American Manifest Destiny:

> the English-speakers are all in the same boat . . . we and you have among our best men a higher conception of moral sense and public duty than is to be found in any other people . . . these are the two qualities which are needed for directing a weaker race. . . . The pressure of destiny will force you to administer the Whole of America from Mexico to the Horn.

The *Korosko*, a boat on the Nile, has a fate very different to that in Agatha Christie's *Death on the Nile* (1937), but, by then, Egypt, and indeed the entire course of the White Nile, are under apparently stable British control.

A hero of Empire featured in 'The Devil's Foot', an effective Holmes story which was published in 1910, but set in 1897. The tall, craggy, fierce-eyed Leon Sterndale, 'the great lion-hunter and explorer' with a 'tremendous personality', kills the villainous Mortimer Tregennis with a rare West African ordeal poison he 'obtained under very extraordinary circumstances in the Ubanghi country'. Having in effect been his judge, Holmes, impressed by the 'lawless lion-hunter', lets him go to Central Africa to complete his work.

Explorers were famous in Britain and the West. Henry Morton Stanley (1841–1904), who had made his fame as an explorer of Central Africa, was the Liberal Unionist MP for Lambeth North in 1895–1900, having been defeated for the seat by a Liberal by a narrow margin in 1892. Stanley did not stand in 1900. Ernest Shackleton, the polar explorer, and an Anglo-Irishman opposed to Irish Home Rule, was a Liberal Unionist candidate for Dundee in 1906, but did badly in that Liberal stronghold where Churchill was to be easily elected as a Liberal in a 1908 by-election.

Reference to lions in 'The Devil's Foot' underlined the extent to which the tropics were associated with danger, not least dangerous animals. This was seen, for example, 'with the giant rat of Sumatra, a story for which the world is not yet prepared', as mentioned by Holmes in 'The Sussex Vampire'. So also in the index of his notes and items he retains, with 'Venomous lizard or gila. Remarkable case, that!'

A somewhat different hero of Empire is Holmes himself in his years of post–Reichenbach Falls deception, as described in 'The Empty House'. He travelled for two years in Lhasa, passed through Persia and Mecca, and visited the Sudanese capital Khartoum, which would have been a very brave mission, before giving the Foreign Office a report. There is not, however, in this travel novel, the suppressed violence of Colonel Sebastian Moran, a hunter 'in the dark jungle of criminal London'. The jungle is an image that Doyle frequently uses, including for the upper atmosphere in the non-Holmes 'The Horror of the Heights' (1913). Once Moran, an excellent 'heavy game shot', in many respects like a tiger himself, is captured, Holmes scorns him by describing his capture in terms of the standard tiger-hunting technique in India. Hunting is frequently used also as a descriptor for Holmes, but his ethos and methods are different from Moran's. The use of such language identifies Holmes in terms of manliness and both rural and imperial values and practices. Thus, in 'The Abbey Grange', while tracking down a visitor from Australia, he remarks of the steamer lines that 'we will draw the larger cover first'. In contrast to Holmes, Moran is very much a child of Empire. While born in London, in 1840, and educated at Eton and Oxford, he was the son of the onetime British envoy to Persia, and had served with the Bangalore Pioneers in India, including in the Second Afghan War in which Watson had been wounded. The author of two books on his hunting exploits in India, he was obliged to leave it and the army due to his unacceptable behaviour there.

In 'The Speckled Band', set in 1883, and Doyle's favourite Holmes short story, Dr Grimesby Roylott has to go to Calcutta to try to rescue himself from being an 'aristocrat pauper'. A successful doctor, but lacking in self-control, he is convicted and imprisoned there for beating his native butler to death: Roylott was angered by robberies in the house. Released from prison, he brings back to Surrey his love of strong Indian cigars and his passion for Indian animals. One plays a crucial role in the plot, although the account of the snake is not fully accurate.

Africa, as a land of extremes, emerged in another context in 'The Blanched Soldier', a story set in 1903 in which James Dodd, a veteran of the Middlesex Corps of the Imperial Yeomanry as Holmes ascertains, seeks the detective's help to find his wartime friend, Godfrey Emsworth, only to discover that the latter, when wounded in the Boer War, had staggered into a leper colony and become ill. In Doyle and most popular fiction, Africa is very much the testing ground of imperial manliness, unlike the Asian adventures of the day, whether relieving the Legations of Beijing from Boxer besiegers in 1900 or accompanying Younghusband and his expedition to Lhasa in 1904.

Manliness is shown in both exploration and hunting, and there are elements of each in Holmes's adventures in Britain. Thus, in 'Black Peter', Holmes, Watson and Inspector Hopkins wait among the bushes at night in order to find Peter Carey's killer. Watson treats humans and animals as interchangeable in character:

> It brought with it something of the thrill which the hunter feels when he lies beside the water-pool and waits for the coming of the thirsty beast of prey. What savage creature was it which might steal upon us out of the darkness? Was it a fierce tiger of crime, which could only be taken fighting hard with flashing fang and claw, or would it prove to be some skulking jackal, dangerous only to the weak and unguarded? In absolute silence we crouched amongst the bushes, waiting for whatever might come . . . an absolute stillness . . . it was the darkest hour which precedes the dawn.

A different form of identification of humans and animals was provided by Holmes's description of Charles Augustus Milverton, in the impressive story of that name published in 1904:

> 'Do you feel a creeping, shrinking sensation, Watson, when you stand before the serpents in the Zoo and see the slithery, gliding, venomous creatures, with their deadly eyes and wicked, flattened faces? Well, that's how Milverton impresses me'.

London Zoo had been opened initially to a membership society in 1828, and then to the public in 1847, with the reptile house following two years later, being followed by a replacement in 1882, and another in 1926. Milverton was based on the half-Portuguese blackmailer Charles Augustus Howell (1840–90), who was found in Chelsea with his throat slit and a coin in his mouth. Milverton is far from manly.

There is also an element of necessary hunting in the 'campaign' against Milverton, whom Holmes has compared to 'the Evil One', the Devil. This campaign is described by Watson with a Gothic flourish: 'As a flash of lightning in the night shows up in an instant every detail of a wide landscape'. Holmes himself uses the image of 'a sporting duel between this fellow Milverton and me'. In breaking into Milverton's house, there is an air of the tropics: having used his burgling kit which, Holmes remarks, contains 'every modern improvement which the march of civilisation demands', he and Watson confront 'the thick warm air of the conservatory and the rich, choking fragrance of exotic plants [which] took us by the throat'.

The impact of Empire on Britain is found throughout the stories, including those set far from the ports. Thus, in 'Silver Blaze', the trainer on guard, Ned Hunter, has 'curried mutton' for dinner, the strong, spicy taste of which provides an opportunity to drug him. In addition, Mrs Hudson offers curried chicken for breakfast in 'The Naval Treaty'. In *A Study in Scarlet*, the suspect smokes a Trichinopoly cigar, one made of Indian tobacco that was popular in Britain during this period.

The heyday of the Holmes stories marked a high point in London's grand imperial history. London provided the setting for Victoria's Golden and Diamond Jubilees in 1887 and 1897. Prominent visitors, such as the Khedive of Egypt in 1900, were entertained by the mayor and corporation of the city. Whitehall had new government offices, notably the New War Office (1899–1906) and the New Government Offices (1899–1915). The Mall was conceived as a great ceremonial route with, at one end, Buckingham Palace's new façade as well as the enormous Victoria memorial in the *rond-point* in front of the palace, and, at the other, Admiralty Arch (1912), which provided an opening onto Trafalgar Square and the north end of Whitehall.

The Empire was expanded greatly in the late nineteenth century. There were setbacks along the way to imperial expansion, especially at Isandlwana (1879) and Maiwand (1880) at the hands of the Zulus and Afghans respectively. The latter saw Watson, an army doctor, wounded, while 962 of the outnumbered 2,500-strong British force were killed and the colours of a regiment were lost. The flavour of this very difficult imperial conflict can be readily captured, as the Reverend Alfred Cane writes of a sortie against the village of Deh Khoja:

> We began by shelling the place. There was no reply so 800 of our infantry advanced to the attack when at once a galling fire was opened on them from loop holes round the village. Our men rushed on and entered the village on the south side but only to find it filled with armed men firing from the windows, doors and roofs. It was a hopeless task . . . had to return in hot haste under the same heavy fire.[8]

Nevertheless, the British were usually successful in battle, notably over the Zulus in 1879, in particular at Ulundi, and the Second Anglo-Afghan War ultimately led to British victory: Ayub Khan, who had been victorious over the British at Maiwand on 27 July, was decisively defeated at Kandahar on 1 September after an epic relief march by General Roberts from Kabul to Kandahar in August. Victory at Tel el Kebir (1882) left Britain dominant in Egypt, while the fate of Sudan was settled at Omdurman in 1898, when artillery, machine guns and rifle fire devastated the attacking Mahdists, with 31,000 casualties for the latter and only 430 for the Anglo-Egyptian force. The writer Hilaire Belloc observed in *The Modern Traveller* (1898):

> Whatever happens we have got
> the Maxim Gun; and they have not.

Technology and resources were not at stake only on the battlefield. In 1896, the British invading force built a railway straight across the desert, from Wadi Halfa to Abu Hamed. Extended to Atbara in 1898, it played a major role in the supply of the British forces. A succinct Doyle Sudan contribution was 'The Début of Bimbashi Joyce', which, while involving a mystery, was not a Holmes story. It was published in *Punch* on 3 January 1900, and then in *The Green Flag and Other Stories of War and Sport*, a Doyle short-story collection, published on 27 March, and in *McClure's Magazine* in the United States that May. This was very much an account of the Mahdists, and barbaric Sudan is described in the opening paragraph as 'That country of darkness. Sometimes the sunset would turn those distant mists into a bank of crimson, and the dark mountains would rise from that sinister reek like islands in a sea of blood'. British force was presented as benign: 'it was time for civilisation to take a trip south once more, travelling, as her wont is, in an armoured train'. British command emerges in a positive light.

The same collection was led off by 'The Green Flag', a story first published in the *Pall Mall Magazine* in June 1893 that depicted how imperial service redeemed Irishness and in particular those involved in the Land League. Set also in Sudan, this story told of an attack by a far larger number of Mahdists or 'fanatics'. Each side benefits from artillery, which obliges the British to rely on bravery. The 'fighting blood' of the Irish was crucial, but there was a clash of identities: 'You are not fighting for England. You are fighting for Ireland, and for the Empire of which it is part,' remarks Captain Foley.

The Mahdists are described as looking 'like a blast of fiends from the pit.[9] And were these the Allies of Ireland? . . . the murder of the wounded, the hacking of the unarmed'. In the end, the Irish rally for the army, but under the green flag, reform the square, and die bravely.

The Sudan theme continues in that collection with 'The Three Correspondents', which was published in *The Windsor Magazine* in October 1896. In this, three journalists defend themselves from Mahdist attack, Doyle commenting, 'The law-abiding Briton is so imbued with the idea of the sanctity of human life that it was hard for the young pressman to realise that these men had every intention of killing him, and that he was at perfect liberty to do as much for them'. Getting the news to the public from the war zone is presented as heroic in a powerful tribute to war correspondents. Doyle's portrayal of the Irish in 'The Green Flag' corresponded to that of his letter in *The Irish Times* on 3 October 1900, which had closed with an attack on intolerance in Irish politics: 'By such an attitude they alienate from themselves the sympathy of many men, who like myself care nothing for the bolstering up of any sect or of any narrow party, but who are whole-souled in one desire that Ireland should become prosperous, happy, and reconciled to that great empire which has been so largely built up by Irish valour and Irish intellect'.

Doyle was far from alone. Sudan was to the fore for many writers. A. E. W. Mason's *The Four Feathers*, a successful novel of 1902, was a presentation of British operations in Sudan as a definition of manliness and heroism. Mason (1865–1948) also wrote detective stories and short stories, introducing the French detective Inspector Hanaud in *At The Villa Rose* (1910). He was elected for Parliament as a Liberal in 1906, sitting for only one term, and served in the army and in naval intelligence in World War One. Hanaud is a stout professional policeman who relies on psychology.

Sudan also appeared in the adventure stories for boys by the war correspondent George Alfred Henty. These included *The Dash for Khartoum: A Tale of the Nile Expedition* (1891), two on the Boer War – *With Buller in Natal* (1900) and *With Roberts to Pretoria* (1901) – and *With Kitchener in the Soudan* (1902). Henty presented the conquest of Sudan as a 'stupendous achievement', the preface declaring 'Thus a land that had been turned into a desert by the terrible tyranny of the Mahdi and his successor, was wrested from barbarism and restored to civilization; and the stain upon British honour, caused by the desertion of Gordon by the British ministry of the day, was wiped out', the last a reference to the events of 1885.

As with so many stories of the period, including the Holmes stories and Mason's *Four Feathers*, there was a mystery as part of the narrative of *With Kitchener in the Soudan*, in this case the protagonist's background. The story finally reveals that he is heir to the title and estates of the Marquis of Langdale. A different form of heroism was offered by Churchill in *The River War: An*

Historical Account of the Reconquest of the Soudan (1899). This provided a useful and thoughtful account of the British defeat of the Mahdists: 'They lived by the sword. Why should they not perish by the magazine rifle? A state of society which, even if it were tolerable to those whom it comprised, was an annoyance to civilised nations has been swept aside. . . . The Government was a cruel despotism';[10] which, indeed, was the case.

The very positive image of the army seen in these works by Doyle and others was linked to a more general feeling that manliness was best developed and shown through military training and action, with appropriate ethos displayed accordingly. British character and values were to be moulded by fighting for Britain, and manliness thereby protected. In addition to the depiction of war in newspapers as well as Baden-Powell's Boy Scouts, this feeling was reflected in the reorganisation and modernisation of the militia and volunteers into a Special Reserve and the Territorial Force, later the Territorial Army.[11]

While some acquisitions such as Uganda were made with reluctance on the part of government, much British imperial expansion, especially in 1880–1914, arose directly from the response to the real or apparent plans of other powers, particularly France and Russia. However, the search for markets for British industry was also important. Thus, both economic and political security were at stake and, as a result, the imperialist surge of activity at the close of the century has been seen as marking the beginning of a long decline from the zenith of British power, and of imperial position starting to fray under pressure at the same time that it continued to expand and, thereby, encounter additional problems.

The nature of the Empire also changed. Sovereignty and territorial control became crucial goals. They replaced the pursuit of influence and of island and port possessions which had been the characteristic features of much, although by no means all, British expansion earlier in the nineteenth century. Suspicion of Russian designs on the Turkish empire, and of French schemes in North Africa, led the British to move into Cyprus (1878) and Egypt (1882); concern about French ambitions in South-East Asia resulted in the conquest of Mandalay (1885) and the annexation of Upper Burma (1886); while Russia's advance across Central Asia led to attempts to strengthen and move forward the 'North-West Frontier' of British India and also to the development of British influence in southern Iran and the Persian Gulf, through which the British routed the telegraph to India. French and German expansion in Africa led Britain to take counter measures in Gambia, Sierra Leone, the Gold Coast (Ghana), Nigeria and Uganda, all moves in the 'Scramble for Africa' by the European powers. Doyle was far more interested in southern Africa and Sudan, and clearly saw them as more noble tasks than expansion in West Africa. Britain's opponents in both were certainly stronger and had earlier been successful, the Boers in 1881 in the First Boer War, and the Mahdists in 1885. Each remained formidable opponents and were not overcome until 1900–1902 and 1898–99 respectively.

Specific clashes over colonial influence with other European powers increasingly interacted from the late 1870s with a more general sense of imperial insecurity as confidence was put under pressure by the growing strength of other states. More clearly, in the 1880s, there was public and governmental concern about naval vulnerability and, in 1889, this concern led to the Naval Defence Act, which sought a two-power standard: superiority over the next two largest naval powers combined. The importance of naval dominance was taken for granted. It was a prerequisite of an ideal of national self-sufficiency that peaked in the late nineteenth century.

Empire Day was launched in 1896 on 24 May, Victoria's birthday. While having defeated France in 1871, Wilhelm I, King of Prussia, became Emperor of Germany; Victoria, five years later, as a result of the Royal Titles Act, became Empress of India – an empire that was to last until the subcontinent was granted independence in 1947, with the title being inherited by her four successors. Streets, towns, geographical features and whole tracts of land were named or renamed in her honour, including the Australian state of Victoria, the city of Victoria on Vancouver Island in

Canada, Victoria Falls on the Zambezi and Lake Victoria in East Africa. So also with the naming of places after other members of the royal family and after British politicians, for example Salisbury in Southern Rhodesia, now Harare in Zimbabwe.

Imperial status was also part of the re-creation of Victoria in the late 1870s. She was coaxed from reclusive widowhood to a new public role by Disraeli, who, as prime minister, combined imperial policies with social reform and who sought, in doing so, to foster a sense of national unity and continuity. He realised that monarchy was a potent way to lead the public and control the consequences of the spread of the franchise, a view gently mocked in Gilbert and Sullivan's comic operetta, the *Pirates of Penzance* (1879), in which the pirates, victorious over the maladroit police, rapidly surrender at the close when summoned to do so in the name of the Queen.

At once an opportunistic and skilful political tactician and also an acute and imaginative thinker, Disraeli was able to create a political culture around the themes of national identity, national pride and social cohesion. He was able to focus popular support for the Conservatives on these themes as an alternative to the Liberal moral certainty in which Gladstone flourished. Disraeli carefully manipulated Victoria into accepting his view and playing the role he had allocated her.

The government of Victoria's empire was extremely varied. In some colonies, notably in much of Africa, there was straightforward imperial rule by representatives of the British state, whereas in India there was a careful attempt to incorporate existing hierarchies, interests and rituals. There, the princely dynasties were wooed, from the 1870s, by the creation of an anglicised princely hierarchy that gave them roles and honours, such as the orders of the Star of India and the Indian Empire, in accordance with British models and interests – a process which was also to be followed in Malaya and in parts of Africa. This process led to a stress on status, not race, that is easy to criticise, not least because the resulting emphasis on inherited privilege served as a brake on inculcating values of economic, social and political development. This policy was also a response to the large amount of India that had been left under princely rule. Nevertheless, in practice, the search for support in India and elsewhere was not restricted to the social élite. Instead, the search was a multi-layered one, extending to the co-optation or creation of professional and administrative groups, able to meet local as well as imperial needs. Moreover, princes were downgraded to knights in these orders, a subtle demotion that suited British interests.

In the long-established colonies of white settlement, as aspects of the Greater Britain that Doyle favoured,[12] self-government was extended from the mid-nineteenth century, with the growth of what was called 'responsible government'. This meant that, in a major measure of liberalisation, colonial governors were to be politically responsible to locally elected legislatures, rather than to London, a process that reflected the comparable parliamentary arrangement in Victorian Britain. The counterpart of 'responsible government' was the psychological and physical self-reliance Doyle gives his colonials visiting Britain and meeting Holmes.

Dominion status, self-government under the Crown, took this process further, offering a peaceful, evolutionary route to independence. Canada became a Dominion in 1867, Australia in 1901, and New Zealand in 1907. Although the Colonial Laws Validity Act of 1865 had declared invalid any colonial legislation that clashed with that from Westminster, the Act was only rarely invoked. This was a federalism that worked. Meetings of prime ministers from 1887 helped give the Dominions a voice in imperial policy and also offered a means of coherence. During the Boer War, the Empire, particularly Australia, Canada, Cape Colony and New Zealand, sent troops to help the British forces, actions which helped foster Dominion nationalism within the Empire, rather than having this nationalism act as a separatist element.

Imperial subjects in Britain in the Doyle stories were generally white, but Daulat Ras, the Indian at St Luke's, an imaginary Oxford college, is one of 'The Three Students', a story set in 1895 that was published in *The Strand Magazine* in June 1904. Daulat Ras is described as a 'quiet, inscrutable fellow, as most of those Indians are. He is well up in his work, though his Greek is his weak subject. He is steady and methodical'. Holmes defends Daulat Ras from Watson's unfounded suspicions and the misdirection they represent. 'That Indian was a sly fellow also. Why should he be pacing his room all the time?' Watson counters, 'There is nothing in that. Many men do it when they are trying to learn anything by heart.' Holmes replies, 'He looked at us in a queer way'. Holmes settles the matter. 'So would you if a flock of strangers came in to you when you were preparing for an examination next day, and every moment was of value. No, I see nothing in that'.

The guilty party in the theft of the question paper in fact is Gilchrist, a prominent athlete and 'fine, manly fellow', in other words the standard hero. Gilchrist then decides, in a *Four Feathers* fashion, to seek redemption in Empire: 'I have determined not to go in for the examination. I have been offered a commission in the Rhodesian Police, and I am going out to South Africa at once'. This is the frontier of Empire, and Holmes concludes the story by telling him: 'I trust that a bright future awaits you in Rhodesia. For once you have fallen low. Let us see in the future how high you can rise'. Formed in 1889 as mounted infantrymen, the British South Africa Police operated in Rhodesia and took a major role in the Matabele wars of 1893–97. In 1909, it merged with the Southern Rhodesia Constabulary, which was the police force for the cities of Salisbury and Bulawayo.

Aside from the fictional Daulat Ras, Doyle himself was concerned about the miscarriage of justice suffered by George Edalji (1876–1953), the son of a vicar of Parsee descent from India married to an Englishwoman. George became a lawyer and was unjustly convicted in 1903 of animal maiming. Racial prejudice played a role in the conviction, which was a serious miscarriage of justice. Doyle's involvement in the case helped make it more prominent. He played a major role in seeking to have the conviction overturned, and in 1907 Edalji was granted a pardon. Doyle was a great supporter of the British Empire and a very fair man,[13] and not inherently harsh to non-whites at a time when Empire was very frequently seen at least in part in racial terms.[14]

In contrast to Daulat Ras, in *The Sign of Four*, Lal Rao, the butler at Pondicherry Lodge, a British house named after an Indian city, is a confederate of Jonathan Small. Mrs Bernstone gives Lal Rao 'far from a good character'. In 'The Three Gables' (1926), there is a hostile and derogatory account of Steve Dixie that is unremitting in its nastiness. It is unclear whether Dixie is an American or a West Indian:

> If I had said that a mad bull had arrived, it would give a clearer impression of what occurred. The door had flown open and a huge negro had burst into the room. He would have been a comic figure if he had not been terrific, for he was dressed in a very loud grey check suit with a flowing salmon-coloured tie . . . broad face and flattened nose . . . sullen dark eyes, with a smouldering gleam of malice in them . . . the savage . . . hideous mouth.

Holmes adds to Watson's account: 'the smell of you . . . his woolly head . . . he is really rather a harmless fellow, a great muscular, foolish, blistering baby, and easily cowed'.

Outside the Holmes corpus of mysteries, and while Holmes had apparently been disposed of in the Reichenbach Falls, Doyle added the mystery 'The Black Doctor', which was printed in *The Strand Magazine* in August 1898. This presented Aloysius Lana, an effective doctor trained in Glasgow and working in a village ten miles southwest from Liverpool:

> he came undoubtedly of a tropical race, and was so dark that he might almost have had a strain of the Indian in his composition. His predominant features were, however, European, and he possessed a stately courtesy and carriage which suggested a Spanish extraction. A swarthy skin, raven-black hair, and dark, sparkling eyes under a pair of heavily-tufted brows made a strange contrast to the flaxen or chestnut rustics of England, and the newcomer was soon known as 'The Black Doctor of Bishop's Crossing'. At first it was a term of ridicule and reproach; as the years went on it became a title of honour which

> was familiar to the whole country-side, and extended far beyond the narrow confines of the village.

Lana is not in fact black, but the key element is not his colour. It is his medical skill and personal behaviour that leads to his integration into rural society:

> A remarkable surgical cure in the case of the Hon. James Lowry, the second son of Lord Belton, was the means of introducing him to county society, where he became a favourite through the charm of his conversation and the elegance of his manners. An absence of antecedents and of relatives is sometimes an aid rather than an impediment to social advancement, and the distinguished individuality of the handsome doctor was its own recommendation.

At a garden party, Lana meets Frances Morton of Leigh Hall, the daughter of a local squire, and the story ends with the news of their marriage, which is even more one of integration as Aloysius, a Catholic, has married in the local Anglican Church. Argentina was part of the 'informal empires' of British influence, and this story captured the possibility for entry into the élite by those who could fit into its parameters. As the cases of both Benjamin Disraeli and Rosebery's wife Hannah Rothschild amply showed, this integration was not only a matter of fiction.

Separately, the Empire was more integrated as a result of the development of more-frequent steamer services, services that brought the characters in Doyle stories to England. In 'The Abbey Grange' (1904), two shipping lines connect Adelaide and Southampton, and there is a reference to the *Rock of Gibraltar*, the largest and best boat of the major line then being south of the Suez Canal. That year, the Channel Squadron of the British fleet visited Gibraltar, while Emperor Wilhelm II arrived at the same time on a German liner escorted by a German cruiser.

Yet, alongside expansion as well as changes designed both to mould and to benefit from the situation of flux in the Empire, cracks were appearing in the imperial edifice. Due, in part, to the diffusion within it of British notions of community, identity and political action, there was a measure of opposition to imperial control, with the Indian National Congress formed in 1885 and the Egyptian National Party in 1897.

The most immediate challenge to Empire during Doyle's adult life prior to World War One was the Boer War. It was waged with the Afrikaner (Boer – whites of Dutch descent) republics of the Orange Free State and the Transvaal in Southern Africa. Regional hegemony was a key issue. British leaders found it difficult to accept Boer views and were willing to risk war in order to achieve a transfer of some power in southern Africa. The Boer War is often seen as a classic instance of 'capitalist-driven' empire building. However, Alfred Milner, the aggressive governor of Cape Colony, was essentially driven by political considerations, his own ambition, and his strong sense of imperial mission on behalf of a British race.[15] The British ministers were greatly influenced by the fear that if, given the gold and diamond discoveries, the Boers became the most powerful force in Southern Africa, it might not be long before they were working with Britain's imperial rivals, especially the Germans in South-West Africa, and threatening its strategic interests at the Cape. The prime minister, Salisbury, remarked that Britain had to be supreme. South African gold features in several Holmes stories. Thus, Baron Gruner in 'The Illustrious Client' (1924) set in 1902, lives in an imposingly large (but ugly) house 'built by a South African gold king in the days of the great boom'. Ministers in London thought (wrongly) that the Boers were bluffing and would not put up much of a fight if war followed, while the failure of the British to send sufficient reinforcements persuaded the Boers to think it was the British who were bluffing. The Boer republics declared war after Britain had isolated them internationally and had done everything possible to provoke them.[16]

Initially, the outnumbered and poorly led British were outfought by the Boers' effective combination of the strategic offensive and a successful use of defensive positions, as well as by the Boers' superior marksmanship with smokeless, long-range Mauser magazine rifles. Boer capabilities revealed serious deficiencies in British tactics and training, not least a continued preference for frontal attacks and volley firing, a lack of emphasis on the use of cover and of understanding of the consequences of smokeless powder, and, more generally, a lack of appreciation of enhanced defensive firepower. In 'Black Week', in December 1899, British forces suffered heavy casualties in a series of battles, including Magersfontein and Colenso, foolishly preferring frontal attacks to the uncertainties of flank movement.

More effective generalship by Roberts and Kitchener transformed the situation in 1900. Moreover, the army proved adaptable, both tactically and organisationally, as when, responding to Boer tactics, mounted infantry was extensively deployed. Britain's larger force was applied methodically with the overrunning of the Boer heartland in the Transvaal: its capital, Pretoria, was captured on 5 June 1900. The British then turned to the more difficult task of countering Boer raiders. Boer guerrilla operations proved a formidable, but ultimately unsuccessful, challenge, not least because of the British combination of methodical force with flexible mobility.

The ability of Britain to allocate about £200 million and to deploy four hundred thousand troops was a testimony to the strength of its economic and imperial systems. Yet, income tax had to be doubled to pay for the war, which also greatly pushed up government borrowing. The Conservative policy of low taxation with financial retrenchment had to be abandoned under the pressure of imperial expansion.

Doyle's role, as both doctor and writer, in defence of British interests during the War led to his being awarded a knighthood, one that was bestowed by Edward VII in person in October 1902; whereas Holmes is described in 'The Three Garridebs' as having refused one. The king had given a clear sign of public approval by attending at the Lyceum Theatre on 30 January 1902 the play *Sherlock Holmes*, with the American William Gillette in the title role. Also in 1902, Doyle was made a deputy lieutenant of Surrey, which very much affirmed his role in county society.

The accidents of timing and age ensured that the personal references in the Holmes/Watson stories were to the Second Anglo-Afghan War and notably the battle of Maiwand, where Watson had nearly been killed. In *A Study in Scarlet*, Watson comments: 'I ought to be more case-hardened after my Afghan experiences. I saw my own comrades hacked to pieces at Maiwand without losing my nerve'. In 'The Illustrious Client', set in 1902, General de Merville is referred to as 'De Merville of Khyber fame', but now, due to insinuating Baron Gruner 'he has lost the nerve which never failed him on the battlefield and has become a weak, doddering old man'. Holmes's job is to save the former war hero.

There is not the comparable engagement with the Boer War in the Holmes stories. Indeed, alongside the grounding in the present, and looking to the future, of the Holmes stories, there is a strong sense of a past defining both. The Indian Mutiny of 1857–59 provided part of this legacy as it provided a narrative about the British presence in India. In contrast, Arthur Raffles, a successful short-story creation in 1898 of Doyle's brother-in-law, Ernest Hornung, is killed in 1900 in the Boer War at the very close of the 'The Knees of the Gods'. His companion, Bunny Manders, has already been wounded in that story. Empire was more widely a background for detective stories set in Britain, as in Godfrey Benson's *Tracks in the Snow* (1906).[17]

Doyle, nevertheless, was writing against the background of an apparently continuously expanding Empire. In 1901, Asante was annexed, while an expeditionary force was sent to the interior of British Somaliland in order to confront the rising by Sayyid Muhammad 'Abdille Hassan, who in 1899 had declared holy war on Christians. By 1905, the British had forced a peace on their opponents. In 1903, the army of the Emirate of Sokoto was smashed at Burmi in northern Nigeria. The following year, a force advanced from India to Lhasa, the capital of Tibet, in order to thwart alleged Russian influence and dictate terms. In Kenya in 1905, tribal opposition was overcome. And so on. There was a strong degree of force underlying imperial expansion and consolidation.

Moreover, opposition to British control or influence in the colonies and in the informal empire was still limited in scope, certainly in comparison to the situation after World War One; and there was also a considerable measure of compliance with British rule. In Ireland, the preferred option was Home Rule under the Crown, not republican independence, which, at the time, was the preference of only a minority. Meanwhile, Scots benefited greatly from the Empire, while the degree to which they retained considerable independence within the United Kingdom – including their own established church and legal and educational systems – also militated against political nationalism.

Without Empire, its people, wealth, impact and mysteries, the Holmes stories would have been far less interesting. His essential loyalty is displayed in his lodgings rented from Mrs Hudson, where, as recorded in 'The Musgrave Ritual' (1893), he would 'proceed to adorn the opposite wall with a patriotic V. R. [Victoria Regina] done in bullet-pocks'.

7

HOLMES AND THE AMERICAS

> The savage man, and the savage beast, hunger, thirst, fatigue, and disease – every impediment which Nature could place in the way – had all been overcome with Anglo-Saxon tenacity.
>
> – *A Study in Scarlet*

Dickens's career and commercial success had already shown the significance of America to British popular writers. So also with Doyle, whose stories enjoyed major sales in the United States, which, indeed, was the principal foreign market for British authors. Doyle's pieces were serialised there as well as in Britain.

The British attitude towards America was ambivalent and vice versa. Many Victorians wrote about the United States, for example Dickens, Doyle, Anthony Trollope and James Bryce, all of whom were popular there and taken by its energy and drive, yet often shocked by its 'vulgar' (populist) politics. A standard means of criticising a politician was to accuse him of the 'Americanisation' of British politics, and Gladstone and Joseph Chamberlain both suffered accordingly.

On the one hand, there was also much downright hostility between the two countries: over the Crimean War (1853–54), when the British, being very short of troops by 1855, tried to recruit American mercenaries; the American Civil War (1861–65), when the British were considered favourable to the South; and in disputes over clashing imperial interests in the New World and the Pacific, for example involving Venezuela in the 1890s, although Britain had accepted America's Monroe Doctrine of 1823 with its demand for non-intervention in the Americas. The Civil War divided British public opinion fairly widely. The South sought to win diplomatic recognition, a step that would have legitimated secession. The Foreign Secretary, Lord John Russell, and, even more, the Chancellor of the Exchequer, Gladstone, were sympathetic, but fears that recognition would lead to war with the Union prevented the step. It was not only power politics that led to hostility. There were also cultural and economic rivalries, for example over copyright law in the 1850s, an issue that greatly concerned Dickens and the resolution of which benefited Doyle.

On the other hand, despite disagreements over the Maine frontier and, more seriously, tension over the fate of modern British Columbia, the British and the Americans managed to agree to the course of the long Canadian border without war. Similarly, cross-border raids on Canada by the Fenians, American-based Irish terrorists, did not trouble relations for long. There was massive British investment in America, particularly in railways, the transfer of British technology, again in railways, and important cultural and social links. A number of American women married peers or their heirs in 1870–1914, some bringing great wealth, as when Consuelo Vanderbilt married Charles, 9th Duke of Marlborough, in 1895.

Doyle's attitudes reflected this ambivalence. He can be readily seen as part of a current of Anglo-Saxonism on both sides of the Atlantic, one that, eased by the settlement of differences with the Treaty of Washington in 1871,[1] was particularly strong at the turn of the century. The crushing American defeat of Spain in 1898 was widely applauded in Britain and regarded as a triumph over Mediterranean Catholic culture. Moreover, the British deployed a naval squadron to help ensure that America, and not Germany, gained the Philippines from Spain, its former imperial ruler. The subsequent American subjugation of the Philippines was seen in terms of an extension of Western influence comparable to that by Britain. The resistance in the Philippines was most strong among Muslims and could be counterpointed by that to Britain in Sudan.

Britain managed its disputes with the United States in the New World and the Pacific skilfully. American hegemony in the Western Hemisphere was accepted, in part by being more conciliatory over the Canadian frontier than the Canadians would have preferred. American expansion in the Pacific was also accepted, even if, as with the gain of Hawaii, it led to the overthrow of British interests. In 1908, the Committee of Imperial Defence and the Foreign Office concluded that the possibility of war with the United States was remote. This Anglo-American current was subsequently greatly strengthened by the United States becoming an ally in World War One, and if tensions revived thereafter they were limited, and Britain aligned with America and not Japan in the 1920s.

Some of the Anglo-Americanism in the Holmes works is particularly notable. At the close of 'The Noble Bachelor', after the hostile and repressed Lord St Simon has departed, Holmes enjoys himself in the very different company of Frank Moulton, a brave man who had been taken prisoner in an Apache attack on a New Mexico miners' camp, only to escape. In this story, published in April 1892, Holmes is clear:

> 'It is always a joy to me to meet an American, Mr. Moulton, for I am one of those who believe that the folly of a monarch and the blundering of a Minister in fargone years will not prevent our children from being some day citizens of the same world-wide country under a flag which shall be a quartering of the Union Jack with the Stars and Stripes'.

At the level of criminals, the reality offered in the stories is repeatedly more troubling. America is frequently the source of crime in Britain, and notably so in two of the novels. *A Study in Scarlet* presents the quote offered at the start of this chapter, but then offers a savage indictment of the Mormons during the early settlement period. That might seem distant history, but, in 1890,

Utah had joined the Union, and Doyle is suggesting that Mormon politics and violence are still present, not least with the reference to the secessionism of some Mormons. A large minority of Mormons were British, and Mormon missionaries in Britain were taking people across the Atlantic to Utah.

Somewhat differently, in *The Valley of Fear* (1914–15), an American in the person of Birdy Edwards of Pinkerton's is the hero of the story, and Edwards finds Captain Marvin of the Coal and Iron Police a worthy supporter. But the villains in an account which was based, as Doyle noted in 1929, on his reading of the 'Molly Maguire outrages in the coalfields of Pennsylvania', from 1867 to 1876, are Americans, and the account of Councillor McGinty is of a takeover of government by a murderous conspiracy:

> 'Besides those secret powers which it was universally believed that he exercises in so pitiless a fashion, he was a high public official, a municipal councillor, and a commissioner for roads, elected to the office through the votes of the ruffians who in turn expected to receive favours at his hands. Rates and taxes were enormous, the public works were notoriously neglected, the accounts were slurred over by bribed auditors, and the decent citizen was terrorised into paying public blackmail, and holding his tongue lest some worse thing befall him'.

This is a critique as much of corrupt Irishmen as of Americans. Moreover, as part of a globalisation of crime, the Scowrers, who are based on the Molly Maguires, become even more menacing as they take Professor Moriarty into partnership. The Scowrers have a long range, including the attempted killing of John Douglas at Birlstone in Sussex. This is with a sawn-off shotgun that blows a dead man's head almost to pieces: it is Pennsylvania-made, and the detective White Mason notes reading that such a shotgun is a weapon used in some parts of America. Moriarty's agents are able to have Birdy Edwards killed on a ship in the Atlantic.

The non-Holmes 'The Man with the Watches' (1898) includes the comment that an individual was probably American, as carrying guns was, according to a letter in the *Daily Gazette* from a 'well-known criminal investigator', 'an unusual thing in England'. Possibly the investigator was Holmes, but the story makes no specific identification.

In 'The Five Orange Pips' (1891), the Confederate/KKK background of one of the victims is a major stain on his character and an indicator of his personality. The story relates first to the fate of Elias Openshaw, who emigrated from Britain when young, becoming a planter in Florida, where he did very well. In the Civil War, Openshaw rises to be a colonel in the Confederate army, going back to his plantation with the peace. He returns to England and, as so often with Doyle, to Sussex. His nephew, John, recalls Elias's 'aversion to the negroes, and his dislike of the Republican policy in extending the franchise to them'. Opposed to the carpetbaggers of Reconstruction, Elias Openshaw is presented as unpleasant, quick-tempered, foul-mouthed and unsociable, as well as being a heavy drinker and smoker. First, he is murdered, and then, in pursuit of the papers he had, his brother is murdered, followed by John.

Doyle, who was clearly interested in such organisations, gives Holmes the opportunity to describe the KKK in terms of a secret society of sinister power and method, thus matching his presentation of America in the two novellas:

> 'Ku Klux Klan. . . . This terrible secret society was formed by some ex-Confederate soldiers. . . . Its power was used for political purposes, principally for the terrorising of the negro voters and the murdering or driving from the country of those who were opposed to its views. . . . So perfect was the organisation of the society, and so systematic its methods, that there is hardly a case upon record where any man succeeded in braving it with impunity, or in which any of its outrages were traced home to the perpetrators . . . the sudden breaking up of the

> society was coincident with the disappearance of Openshaw from America with their papers'.

Holmes's account depicts the Confederate cause in the Civil War in a negative light, and is that of a liberal rather than a conservative, contrasting, for example with the view of Salisbury. Indeed, as with 'The Yellow Face' (1893), Holmes's approach is the very opposite of racism. The KKK killers are further contextualised by the identification with Captain James Calhoun of the Savannah ship *Lone Star*, which is named after Texas. The ship sinks, with all hands lost, in an equinoctial gale on a voyage from London to Savannah; but the role of the Atlantic as bringing together the two countries is apparent. So also with Holmes having cabled the police in Savannah about Calhoun and the two American mates on the *Lone Star*. The transatlantic underwater cable, which, after earlier efforts in 1858 and 1865, was finally permanent in 1866, was one of the achievements of the Victorian age. The Irish link in the name Calhoun is also an echo of a once-prominent Southern politician John C. Calhoun (1782–1850), a South Carolinian defender of slavery and states' rights and vice president, whose grandfather, Patrick, had emigrated from County Donegal, Ireland, in 1733. There is also a clearly anti-Irish dimension to *The Valley of Fear*, with James Stanger of the *Herald* linking McGinty's murderous existence to refugees from Europe.

In 'The Adventure of the Cardboard Box' (1893), Watson has a portrait of Henry Ward Beecher which he considers placing to correspond with General George Gordon's newly framed portrait. Gordon had died two years before Beecher. Holmes reflects on Watson's response:

> 'You were recalling the incidents of Beecher's career . . . you could not do this without thinking of the mission which he undertook on behalf of the North at the time of the Civil War, for I remember your expressing your passionate indignation at the way in which he was received by the more turbulent of our

> people. You felt so strongly about it, that I knew you could not think of Beecher without thinking of that also'.

Beecher (1813–87), was an American Congregationalist cleric who was a prominent Abolitionist, raising funds to send rifles to Abolitionists fighting slavery in Kansas in the 1850s, and he had toured Europe in 1863 during the Civil War (1861–65), speaking at public meetings in favour of the Union. Beecher was also a prominent supporter of women's rights, temperance, and Darwinian evolution, and a critic of strikers. He was also controversial. Tried for adultery in 1875, Beecher was not convicted, but was widely believed to be guilty. He made another lecture tour of England in 1886.[2] This was certainly an arresting choice by Doyle, both with respect to Beecher and as a counterpart to Gordon, another noted, but very different, Christian figure. Holmes pressed on in that conversation with Watson to reflect on the latter's views of the Civil War:

> 'I was positive that you were indeed thinking of the gallantry which was shown by both sides in that desperate struggle. But then, again, your face grew sadder. . . . You were dwelling upon the sadness and horror and useless waste of life . . . the ridiculous side of this method of settling international questions had forced itself upon your mind. . . . I agreed with you that it was preposterous'.

'The Adventure of the Cardboard Box', to a degree, reflected a sympathy for moves against war that were increasingly common in the 1890s and 1900s, leading to arms-limitations conferences at The Hague in 1899 and 1907, in part as a reaction to fears about the greater destruction that would result from industrial capacity and technological advance. This was a case of war between Western powers and not with weaker non-Western counterparts. Doyle, however, was not offering, here or elsewhere, a course in systematic thought. This 1893 view could be seen as an aspect of the reconciliation of the post-Reconstruction period, a reconciliation essentially of whites, that was also an aspect of a broader

Anglo-American current. Yet, although Doyle's targets in his two American novellas were not Southerners, but, instead, Mormons and Molly Maguires, this reflection did not mean that Doyle welcomed the Southern Cause in the Civil War. Nor was he a pacifist.

There are also less-violent accounts of American links. In 'The Yellow Face', there is a very positive account of interracial marriage:

> 'That is John Hebron, of Atlanta', said the lady, 'and a nobler man never walked the earth. I cut myself off from my race in order to wed him; but never once while he lived did I for one instant regret it'.

In the event, Grant Munro is happy to accept Lucy as his stepdaughter, and emerges with great credit accordingly. This is very different to the hostile portrayal of Steve Dixie, the 'huge negro . . . bruiser' in 'The Three Gables'.

America as a source of wealth emerges in 'The Stockbroker's Clerk', in which Beddington steals from Mawson and Williams's in London nearly £100,000 worth of American railway bonds. An American case was presumably what is referred to in 'Vanderbilt and the Yeggman', an item in Holmes's index that is not explained. A yeggman was a safebreaker. The theme of American wealth as ill-gotten was seen with Sigsbee Manderson, the ruthless American millionaire murdered in E. C. Bentley's wonderfully ironic *Trent's Last Case* (1913).

A sense of America as a crime-ridden frontier is repeatedly present in the Holmes stories. In 'The Dancing Men' (1903), the root of the problem is a Chicago gang from which Elsie Cubitt seeks to escape. America as violent is captured in 'The Three Garridebs', which is set in 1902, although published in 1925. The American lawyer John Garrideb is identified by Holmes as Chicago-born 'Killer' Evans, who murdered three men in America before escaping from prison 'through political influence', an echo of McGinty's influence in *The Valley of Fear*. Coming to London in 1895, he kills Rodger Prescott, a Chicago forger, in Waterloo Road that year. Thus, American gangsters fight each other in London, where Prescott threatened the country by printing forged banknotes. This story very much drew on the interest in the 1920s in American criminals.

In the non-Holmes 'The Man with the Watches' (1898), Sparrow MacCoy, the villainous New York card sharp, links up with Edward, the bad son of an English family who had emigrated to America in the early 1850s, running a large dry goods store in Rochester, New York. They travel to London, which is presented as 'the effete Old Country, where law and order run, and Tammany had no pull. Gaol and the gallows wait for violence and murder'. In contrast, in this story, 'in the days before the Lexow Commission', the New York police are presented as corrupt. That commission of the New York State Senate sat in 1894–95 and helped lead to the defeat of Tammany Hall in the 1894 election. There is a subplot here about Irish Catholic corruption, and thus linked to *The Valley of Fear*.

Returning to Holmes, there are also problems with Latin America. In 'Thor Bridge' (1922), Neil Gibson, an American gold-mining magnate and onetime senator, who looks like Abraham Lincoln, settles in an attractive English estate. That story sees an attitude taken to Latin America that is a counterpart to British views of Mediterranean Europe. Gibson's wife, a Brazilian, is presented as a child of passion, 'tropical by birth and tropical by nature', very different both from the American women he had known, and from Grace Dunbar, the governess. Her 'tropical nature' is reiterated and, disguising it as murder, she commits suicide in order to do down Dunbar, whom she sees as her rival for Gibson's love.

In 'The Sussex Vampire' (1924), the 'tropical nature' comes rather from a Peruvian wife. Her merchant husband, Robert Ferguson, had met her in connection with the import of nitrates, which was a major British import from that area. She is very beautiful, 'but the fact of her foreign birth and of her alien religion' caused a separation of interests and feelings between husband and wife: 'she is very jealous – jealous with all the strength of her fiery tropical love'. In 'The Second Stain' (1904), Madame Fournaye is presented as extremely excitable and jealous due to her 'Creole origin'. Yet, in 'The Sussex Vampire', it is not the Peruvian wife that is the would-be murderer. Instead, she is being framed by the use of South American weapons. Similarly, in *The Hound of the Baskervilles*, Stapleton's Costa Rican wife Beryl Garcia rejects his murderous scheme.

At the political level, the Latin American situation is far more troubling, in 'Wisteria Lodge', with High Gables, 'a famous old Jacobean grange' in Surrey in 1892, becoming the refuge of Don Murillo, the Tiger of San Pedro, 'the most lewd and bloodthirsty tyrant that had ever governed any country with a pretence to civilisation'. Terrorising his Central American country from 1874 or 1876 to 1886, he was overthrown in a 'universal rising', but escaped. To underline the exotic difference, 'The Sussex Vampire' sees Holmes present reports of vampirism as rubbish, but in 'Wisteria Lodge', Murillo's 'hideous . . . yellowish' mulatto cook is a voodoo-worshipper and makes sacrifices accordingly. The parallel is with *The Hound of the Baskervilles*. Murillo's papers are referred to subsequently in 'The Norwood Builder'. The very toxic South American arrow poison in *A Study in Scarlet* contributes to its sense of menace, which is more disturbing than that of the United States. Agatha Christie makes fun of this poison in the Poirot adventure *Death in the Clouds* (1935).

Less fatally, the Venezuelan loan is responsible for the City firm of Coxon and Woodhouse going bankrupt in 'The Stockbroker's Clerk' (1893). Venezuela indeed had hit major problems in its international debts, and these caused serious disputes in the 1890s. In 1902–3, American intervention led Britain, Germany and Italy to end their blockade of Venezuela in pursuit of unpaid debts. Argentina had defaulted on Sovereign debt in 1890, creating a financial crisis that nearly led to the bankruptcy of the House of Baring, a major London investment bank. In turn, the crisis affected other Latin American debtors.[3] In Doyle's 'The Black Doctor' (1898), Aloysius Lana tells the court that he was from Argentina and that his 'father, who came of the best blood of old

Spain, filled all the highest offices of the State, and would have been President but for his death in the riots of San Juan'. Indeed, Don Alfredo had risen to be Foreign Minister. Aloysius's identical twin Ernest, however, is a villain.

On the whole, the British exports to the New World are not as bad as the countervailing immigrants. Nevertheless, in 'The Abbey Grange', the Randall gang from Kent are arrested in New York. In *The Hound of the Baskervilles*, Selden, the convict who has escaped from Dartmoor Prison, is en route to South America, while Rodger Baskerville, the black sheep of the family, had fled to Central America, dying there of yellow fever in 1876. In *The Sign of Four*, Jonathan Small is trying to leave London 'for the Brazils'. In 'The Resident Patient', the three murderers are lost with all hands in the ill-fated steamer *Norah Creina* off Portugal, which was the standard route to South America. In 'The Musgrave Ritual', Rachel Howells, one of the maids, is assumed to have fled with 'the memory of her crime, to some land beyond the seas'. In the non-Holmes 'The Brazilian Cat', the sadistic, malevolent Everard King makes his fortune in Brazilian coffee plantations, before settling in Suffolk with his Brazilian wife, who seeks to warn of the evil intentions focused on his deadly puma-like killer-cat. In Edward Benson's *The Blotting Book* (1908), the corrupt solicitors, having wrongly risked the inheritance of a trustee in South African mines, have to consider fleeing to Argentina.

Conversely, in 'The Red Circle', the impressive Leverton of Pinkerton's is on the track of Giuseppe Gorgiano, who 'is at the bottom of fifty murders'. Earlier, Gorgiano had become 'red to the elbow in murder' in Naples where the Red Circle was 'allied to the old Carbonari', a radical organisation. In turn, Gorgiano moves on to London, where he is killed by a Gennaro Lucca, an Italian he is intimidating. The story underlines the extent to which countries are envelopes within which many national types are present. So also with Empire and with Europe.

Meanwhile Britain and the United States became closer as Atlantic crossings became quicker and more predictable. In 1914, it took only a week to cross compared to six in the 1850s. Safety was generally provided, and the *Titanic*, which sank in 1912, showed in its passenger list an Anglo-American élite that shared much in experiences and values. The Holmes stories were not for this élite alone but rather for the mass readerships of both countries.

8

HOLMES AND EUROPE

It is my business to follow the details of Continental crime.

– Holmes to Colonel Sir James Damery, 'The Illustrious Client', set in 1902

Holmes was nearly thrown to his death in Switzerland, the apparent culmination of a journey from Dieppe via Brussels, Strasbourg (then Strasburg as part of the German empire after the Franco-Prussian War of 1870–71) and Geneva. As revealed in 'The Adventure of the Empty House' (1903), which is set in 1894, Holmes then spent several months in research in a laboratory in Montpellier in his subsequent travels, returning thence to London. Holmes, indeed, was familiar with Europe, even if he was not as well-travelled there as Poirot (who was born in Belgium) was to be once established in London.

Educated Victorians were acutely aware of what they shared with other European peoples as a result of a common culture based upon Christianity and the legacy of Greece and Rome. Gladstone published three books on the Classical Greek writer Homer and edited Bishop Joseph Butler's sermons. The growing number of public schools made the Classics the centre of their teaching. Those who could afford to do so performed and listened to German music, read French novels and visited the art galleries of Italy. The British were involved, intellectually and at times materially, in European politics. This was obviously the case with the Napoleonic and Crimean wars in which Britain participated, but, in addition, the *Risorgimento* (Italian unification) aroused enormous interest, and more so than many of the British minor colonial wars and acquisitions of colonial territory. The manner in which the Italian hero Giuseppe Garibaldi was mobbed by working-class crowds when he visited England in 1864 testified to the way in which Victorians of all social classes were able to relate many of the events taking place on the Continent to their own struggles and aspirations: the logbooks of Southampton's schools show massive truancy when he landed in the city. In 1876, moreover, Gladstone was able to embarrass Disraeli's ministry seriously over the massacre of Bulgarians by the Turks, agitation to which Doyle refers in 'Crabbe's Practice' (1884). Continental news remained very important in the British press, although more attention was devoted to imperial questions from the 1870s. Furthermore, most Britons by 1901 saw their 'family of nations' in the Dominions and Empire.

A major difference between Britain and Continental countries was that Britain traded abroad far more than they did, and far more widely. Continental economies were more self-sufficient; what foreign trade they did was mainly with other European countries. In Doyle's 'The Stockbroker's Clerk' (1893), there is a major enterprise, 'the Franco-Midland Hardware Company', which is to 'pour a flood of English crockery into the shops of one hundred and thirty-four agents in France', but this enterprise proves a fraudulent delusion. Holmes, however, suggests in *The Valley of Fear* (1914–15) that Moriarty has accounts in Deutsche Bank or the Crédit Lyonnais.

Britain was more dependent on foreign trade, and on the wider world outside Europe, than other European states. From this followed many aspects of Britain's difference from the Continent: Britain's outward-looking perspective and internationalism; its interest in peace, which was believed to create the best conditions for trade, and which determined its relatively limited diplomatic engagement with the Continent between 1815 and 1914 (except during the Crimean War of 1854–56) – to avoid being dragged into European wars; and its opposition to a large and expensive army. The British also saw their police and judiciary as better than their Continental counterparts. Thus, in 'The Dancing Men' (1903), when Abe Slaney, an American, is about to tell the truth, Inspector Martin intervenes: '"It is my duty to warn you that it will be used against you", cried the Inspector, with the magnificent fair-play of the British criminal law'.

France was the traditional national and imperial foe, and colonial rivalries provided fresh fuel to keep fear and animosity alive, with the two powers coming close to war over Sudan in 1898 in the Fashoda Crisis as each sought to establish a position on the Upper Nile. Yet, Britain and France went to war as allies against Germany in 1914. Chance played a central role in this: a major European war broke out at a moment very different to those of heightened Anglo-French and Anglo-Russian colonial tension in the late nineteenth century. Indeed, in 'The Naval Treaty', which was published in *The Strand Magazine* in October–November 1893, Holmes is called in to help discover what has happened to the secret Anglo-Italian treaty:

> 'The French or Russian embassy would pay an immense sum to learn the contents of these papers . . . it defined the position of Great Britain towards the Triple Alliance, and foreshadowed the policy which this country would pursue in the event of the French fleet gaining a complete ascendancy over that of Italy in the Mediterranean. The questions treated in it were purely naval'.

At this point, the developing relationship between France and Russia, a treaty in 1892 and a military convention in 1894, was a matter of considerable concern both to Britain and to Italy as it threatened their positions in the Mediterranean. The opening of the Suez Canal in 1869 had made the Mediterranean the route to India and, therefore, part of the key axis of British power. France was hostile both to this and to Britain's developing presence in Egypt, while Russia challenged Britain's interests from the Turkish Empire to the land approaches to India. Thus, Britain wanted better relations with Italy. Both powers were also involved in a naval race with France and Russia. The Holmes story was very much relevant to the context, one in which navalism was to the fore as a measure of naval strength. Secret treaties were certainly a major part of the diplomacy of the period, as with that of 1898 between Britain and Germany over Portugal's African colonies.

Well before the naval race with Germany that began in 1906, the British public was sensitive to naval vulnerability. On 4 July 1885, 'Fresh Paint', a cartoon in *Punch*, presented Britannia, depicted as the figurehead of a warship, but holding only an olive branch. A carpenter resembling Salisbury noted that there was no time to modernise the warship before she must go to sea. His helper, resembling Lord Randolph Churchill, recommends a cosmetic paint job to provide an appearance of power. Churchill was secretary of state for India and father of Winston Churchill.

The exchange of naval visits at Toulon and Kronstadt in 1891 and 1893 provided a clear demonstration of the threat latent in the Franco-Russian alliance. In 1894, Rosebery, as prime minister, informed the Austrian foreign minister, Count Gustav Kalnoky, that a British fleet could no longer, as in 1878, be deployed to defend Constantinople (Istanbul) against a Russian attack, for fear of what the French navy would then do in support of Russia in the western and central Mediterranean, severing the route to the Suez Canal. Two years later, the director of naval intelligence conceded that the Dardanelles could not be held by the Royal Navy and that, therefore, the Russian Black Sea fleet would be able to sortie into the eastern Mediterranean and thus threaten the Suez Canal.[1] In the Fashoda Crisis of 1898 over competing interests in Sudan, a French military expedition was faced down at Fashoda in a confrontation with a more powerful British force under General Kitchener. French lobbies pressing for a robust imperialism, in particular, from the early 1890s, the *parti colonial* in the *Chambre des Deputés* played a key role.[2]

In the crisis, the British sent the Channel fleet to Gibraltar in order to put pressure on the French position in the Mediterranean. Abandoned by Russia and conscious, not least as a result of the very impressive 1897 Diamond Jubilee Fleet Review, of being weaker at sea, France gave way in 1898. The British had benefited from the Naval Defence Act of 1889, an expensive but popular measure which ensured a major expansion of the navy and which Gladstone failed to limit in 1893.[3] Held at Spithead on 26 June 1897, the review saw the presence of twenty-one battleships and fifty-six cruisers.

In August 1898, Doyle published the non-Holmes 'The Story of the Lost Special' in *The Strand Magazine*. Supposedly based on a confession that year by a Marseilles criminal awaiting execution, this story allegedly relates to 1890, and takes French political corruption for granted:

> 'There was a famous trial in Paris, in the year 1890, in connection with a monstrous scandal in politics and finance. How monstrous that scandal was can never be known save by such confidential agents as myself. The honour and careers of many of the chief men in France were at stake'.

As a result, they have the Latin American figure who can bring them down murdered in Britain en route to Paris. Yet there is no equivalent in Holmes to Monsieur Grabeau, the frequent foreign villain in Bodkin's Paul Beck stories.

Instead of war with France, fear of German intentions, reflected in Doyle's 'The Adventure of the Second Stain' published in December 1904, and particularly of her naval ambitions, encouraged closer British relations with France from 1904. The Anglo-French *entente* of 1904 led to military talks in part because defeat in the Russo-Japanese war of 1904–5 weakened Russia (France's ally) as a balancing element within Europe, thereby exposing France to German diplomatic pressure, and both creating and increasing British alarm about German intentions, as in the First Moroccan Crisis of 1905–6. This crisis, provoked by Germany, was followed by Anglo-French staff talks aimed at dealing with a German threat. In 1907, British military manoeuvres were conducted for the first time on the basis that Germany, not France, was the enemy, while, also that year, fears of Germany contributed to an Anglo-Russian *entente* which eased tensions between the two powers, notably competing ambitions and contrasting anxieties in South Asia. Germany, with its great economic strength, and its questing search for a transoceanic 'Place in the Sun', was increasingly seen in Britain as the principal threat.

The economic statistics were all too present to British commentators, not least because they enabled Germany to pursue a 'naval race' for battleship strength with Britain from 1906.[4] The annual average output of coal and lignite in million metric tons in 1870–74 was 123 for Britain and 41 for Germany, but, by 1910–14, the figures were 274 to 247. For pig-iron, the annual figures changed from 7.9 and 2.7 in 1880 to 10.2 and 14.8 in 1910; for steel from 3.6 and 2.2 in 1890, to 6.5 and 13.7 in 1910. In 1900, the German population was 56.4 million, but that of Britain excluding Ireland only 37 million and including it still only 41.5 million. Britain was still a leading economy, but its position in manufacturing suffered a relative decline.

In December 1899, the rising journalist James Garvin, recently appointed a leader-writer on the *Daily Telegraph*, decided that Germany and not, as he had previously thought, France and Russia, was the greatest threat to Britain. Rejecting the view of Joseph Chamberlain, secretary of state for the Colonies, that Britain and Germany were natural allies, their peoples of a similar racial 'character', Garvin saw 'the Anglo-Saxons' as the obstacle to Germany's naval and commercial policy. Anglo-Americanism, and British imperial federalism in the Dominion system, were widely seen as opposed not only to France, but also to Germany.

British resources and political will were subsequently tested in a major naval race between the two powers, in which the British, in 1906, launched HMS *Dreadnought*, the first of a new class of battleships and one that reflected the vitality of British industry, at least in shipbuilding. Imaginative literature reflected the sense of crisis and contributed to it. A projected German invasion was central to *The Riddle of the Sands* (1903), a novel by Erskine Childers which was first planned in 1897,[5] when, indeed, the Germans discussed such a project. It includes a reference to Holmes, who provides a standard of understanding. There was also a more general sense of international flux and, therefore, crisis.[6] This was politicised, notably in 1909–10 when the Conservatives pressed the government hard to spend more on defence, the Conservative press, particularly the *Daily Telegraph*, playing a major role. This issue helped the Conservatives in the two 1910 elections.[7]

The Holmes stories frequently related to the Continent even if the link was generally a matter of Continentals resident in, or visiting, Britain; most prominently 'The Illustrious Client' and 'A Scandal in Bohemia'. The rivalries of European politics and the nature of European policing wind up in rural England in 'The Golden Pince-Nez', a story published in *The Strand Magazine* in July 1904 that provides an account of Russian revolutionaries, but from a relatively sympathetic perspective. At that point, Russia was not an ally of Britain, so that the revolutionaries were not a threat to Britain's position, as was crucially the case in 1917–18. Anna, Professor Coram's wife, tells Holmes:

> 'We were reformers – revolutionists – Nihilists, you understand . . . there came a time of trouble, a police officer was killed, many were arrested, evidence was wanted, and in order to save his own life and to earn a great reward my husband betrayed his own wife and his companions'.

She is trying to find evidence to lead to the release of Alexis, an unfairly imprisoned former member of the Brotherhood, now held as a prisoner in a Siberian salt mine. This is an account primarily of personal tension, but Anna, who commits suicide, is very much foreign. She is presented as having a bold and honest character, but as not being attractive: 'She has a remarkably thick nose, with eyes which are set close upon either side of it. She has a puckered forehead, a peering expression, and probably rounded shoulders . . . a long and obstinate chin'. In the non-Holmes 'The Man with the Watches', a story published in 1898 and set in 1892, press discussion of a murdered man on a London-to-Manchester train leads to foolish speculations about anarchists:

> It was surmised, by some, that he was concealed under the seat, and that, being discovered, he was for some reason, possibly because he had overheard their guilty secrets, put to death by his fellow-passengers. When coupled with generalities as to the ferocity and cunning of anarchical and other secret societies, this theory sounded as plausible as any. The fact that he should be without a ticket would be consistent with the idea of concealment, and it was well known that women played a prominent part in the Nihilistic propaganda.

This hysteria is shown to be totally mistaken.

On the whole, Doyle met many of the cultural suppositions of the period, although, just possibly because he was Scottish, he was less class-obsessed than many contemporaries and indeed also than some of the characters he held up for criticism in the Holmes stories, notably the Duke of Holdernesse in 'The Priory School'. Doyle certainly offered some standard tropes of nationality. Thus, as in 'The Six Napoleons', Italians were volatile. So also with their willingness to kill. In that story, Lestrade tells Holmes that the police have Inspector Hill,

> 'who makes a speciality of Saffron Hill and the Italian quarter. Well, this dead man had some Catholic emblem round his neck, and that, along with his colour, made me think he was from the South. . . . His name is Pietro Venucci, from Naples, and he is one of the greatest cut-throats in London. He is connected with the Mafia, which, as you know, is a secret political society, enforcing its decrees by murder'.

A Sicilian gang is involved in Baroness Orczy's 'The Irish-Tweed Coat', one of the Lady Molly adventures.

In a classically liberal tone, the memory of successful past immigration is offered by Doyle in 'The Naval Treaty', with reference to Charles Gorot, a Foreign Office clerk:

> 'The suspicions of the police then rested upon young Gorot. . . . His remaining behind and his French name were really the only two points which could suggest suspicion; but . . . I did not begin until he had gone, and his people are of Huguenot extraction, but as English in sympathy and tradition as you and I are. Nothing was found to implicate him in any way'.

Anti-Semitism is far less to the fore than with other writers of the period, and indeed Oscar Slater, for whose innocence Doyle campaigned, was a German Jewish immigrant. Irene Adler was probably Jewish as Adler was a common Jewish name, and the Chief Rabbi of the British Empire from 1844 until his death in 1890 was Nathan Adler, his son and successor being Hermann Adler, who held the post until his death in 1911. Moreover, many singers and actresses were Jewish. In the non-Holmes 'The Jew's Breastplate', the narrator and his friend, Ward Mortimer, seek to understand an attack on a 'Jewish relic of great antiquity and sanctity'. The narrator asks:

> 'How about the anti-Semitic movement? Could one conceive that a fanatic of that way of thinking might desecrate – '
>
> 'No, no, no!' cried Mortimer. 'That will never do! Such a man might push his lunacy to the length of destroying a Jewish relic, but why on earth should he nibble round every stone so carefully that he can only do four stones in a night?'

In 'The Stockbroker's Clerk', Hall Pycroft describes Arthur Pinner as 'a middle-sized, dark-haired, dark-eyed black-bearded man, with a touch of the sheeny about his name'. Sheeny was a contemptuous term used to refer to Jews, but, whether he was or not, that is not of consequence to the story. Indeed, many potential links are not in fact developed. Thus Jewish moneylenders play a role in 'Shoscombe Old Place', but to no effect and with no reflection on them. In 'The Cardboard Box', readers are presumably expected to applaud when Holmes tells Watson 'how he had purchased his own Stradivarius [violin], which was worth at least five hundred guineas, at a Jew broker's in Tottenham Court Road for fifty-five shillings'.

In 'The Mazarin Stone', Ikey Sanders refuses to cut up the Crown diamond. Ikey is a diminutive for Isaac. The villain in the story is the half-Italian Count Sylvius, who is described as swarthy. In 'The Norwood Builder', Hyams is Oldacre's tailor, but that is without consequence. In 'The Six Napoleons', Gelder, the proprietor of the Stepney-based producer of the Napoleon busts, might have a Jewish name but is described as 'a big blond German' with 'blue Teutonic eyes'. In 'The Three Gables', the free-living Isadora Klein could be Jewish, but, in fact, is 'pure Spanish', and her name is Klein only because 'she married the aged German sugar king, Klein'. There is no major Jewish or part-Jewish character in the Holmes stories comparable for example to Israel Rank in Roy Horniman's 1907 novel of that name, and Moriarty is certainly not Jewish. The description of 'The Adventure of the Final Problem' is of a very tall, pale individual, not a swarthy one.

Holmes is made very European in his culture. Watson reads Henri Murger's *Vie de Bohème* in *A Study in Scarlet*. Although *A Study in Scarlet* reveals that Holmes has not heard of Thomas Carlyle, that is not the case in *The Sign of Four*, where Holmes praises Carlyle, whom he terms the brook leading 'to the parent lake', in the person of Johann Paul Richter (1763–1825) who, from 1793, wrote under the pen name Jean Paul. Carlyle wrote two essays on Richter. A major Romantic writer, Richter delighted in paradox, as picked up by Holmes: 'He makes one curious but profound remark. It is that the chief proof of man's real greatness lies in his perception of his own smallness. It argues, you see, a power of comparison and of appreciation which is in itself a proof of nobility. There is much food for thought in Richter'. The voluminous writing of the latter included an extensive use of the idea of *Doppelgänger* and a style that was often humorous while also committed to reason. The passage immediately before in *The Sign of Four* is a classic Romantic conceit: 'How small we feel, with our petty ambitions and strivings in the presence of the great elemental forces of Nature'. Doyle himself had spoken to the Portsmouth Literary and Scientific Society on 'Thomas Carlyle and His Works', and he wrote an unfinished work on Carlyle.[8]

Holmes quotes Goethe in *The Sign of Four*, and in *A Study in Scarlet* knows that 'Rache' is the German for revenge. German culture was regarded as important. The Priory School, a preparatory school teaching boys often up to thirteen, might be founded and headed by Dr Huxtable, the author of *Huxtable's Sidelights on Horace*, but, aside from this Classical foundation, it has a German master, the brave Heidegger. Similarly, in James Hilton's affectionate novel *Goodbye, Mr. Chips* (1934), Mr Chipping, a positive figure, announced the death of the former German teacher among the World War One war dead of the fictional Brookfield School where he taught.

Holmes is interested in learning opera and music, as well as owning a Stradivarius violin which he delights in playing. In *The Hound of the Baskervilles* he goes to hear the Reszkes in Meyebeer's *Les Huguenots*. Édouard and Jean de Reszke were notable Polish singers, appearing in *Les Huguenots* at Covent Garden numerous times between 1880 and 1899. In 1869, the march from *Les Huguenots* was adopted as the slow march of the Grenadier Guards. In 'Black Peter' (1904), in an operatic joke, Holmes has just finished 'his famous investigation of the sudden death of Cardinal Tosca', which is a reference to the Puccini opera which had its British premiere in London on 23 July 1900. At the close of 'The Adventure of the Red Circle', Holmes exclaims to Watson 'it is not eight o'clock, and a Wagner night at Covent Garden! If we hurry, we might be in time for the second act'. Holmes hears Pablo de Sarasate in concert in 'The Red Headed League', and, in 'The Mazarin Stone', there is reference to Jacques Offenbach's opera *The Tales of Hoffmann* (1881). Irene Adler sang at La Scala and in the Warsaw Opera before retiring. In 'The Retired Colourman', Holmes wishes to hear Carina sing at the Albert Hall, which had been built in 1867–71. In *A Study in Scarlet*, Holmes wants 'to go to Hallé's concert to hear Norman Neruda this afternoon'.

Music scarcely exhausted Holmes's cosmopolitanism. His knowledge of crime extends across Europe. In *A Study in Scarlet*, he refers to recent murders in Frankfurt and Montpellier (as well as Bradford and New Orleans). In *The Hound of the Baskervilles*, there are references to cases in Grodno and North Carolina, and in *The Sign of Four* to Riga and St Louis. Empire is included, as, in *The Sign of Four*, Holmes refers to 'parallel cases' from India and Senegambia.

Fiction also plays a part. In *A Study in Scarlet*, Holmes refers to Émile Gaboriau's detective Monsieur Lecoq: 'Lecoq was a miserable bungler . . . he had only one thing to recommend him, and that was his energy. . . . It might be made a text-book for detectives to teach them what to avoid'. Employed by the Parisian *Sûreté*, Lecoq appeared in French novels from 1866 and in English translations, while other writers deployed Lecoq, including Ernest Young in *File No. 114* (1886). As with Doyle, Gaboriau published his novels in serial forms, and their detectives proceed by logical reasoning and detection as well as by using surprise. There are also two-part structures in the works of both novelists.[9]

Holmes is also disparaging about Edgar Allan Poe's Auguste Dupin: 'a very inferior fellow. . . . He had some analytical genius, no doubt; but he was by no means such a phenomenon as Poe appeared to imagine'. Dupin appeared in 'The Murders in the Rue Morgue', a short story of 1841, and reappeared in 1842 and 1844. Poe gives Dupin 'ratiocination', a combination of intellect and creative imagination including the ability to understand the thoughts of others. Not a detective, Dupin, like Holmes, makes much use of the press. Doyle followed Poe in having the narrator a personal friend of the detective while keeping the police at a distance.

In turn, Maurice Leblanc had his hero, Arsène Lupin, more successful than Holmes. 'Sherlock Holmès arrive trop tard' [Sherlock Holmes arrives too late] was the title of a short story published in *Je Sais Tout* on 15 June 1906. In response to a complaint by Doyle's lawyers, Holmes became 'Herlock Sholmes' when the publication appeared in book form, as this satisfied copyright constraints. *Arsène Lupin contre Herlock Sholmes* became the title of the collection, published in 1908 and translated into English in 1910 as *Arsène Lupin versus Holmlock Shears*, containing the stories 'The Blonde Lady' and 'The Jewish Lamp' in which the two detectives compete. A film serial of these appeared in French in 1910. In 'The Blonde Lady', Lupin presents his struggle with Holmes as France versus England, indeed as revenge for defeat at Trafalgar in 1805. In the translation, Watson is unimpressive, and Holmlock Shears is described as

> of the sort one meets every day. He is about fifty years of age and looks like a decent City clerk who has spent his life keeping books at a desk. He has nothing to distinguish him from the ordinary respectable Londoner, with his clean-shaven face and his somewhat heavy appearance, nothing except his terribly keen, bright, penetrating eyes.
>
> And then, of course, he is Holmlock Shears, that is to say a sort of miracle of intuition, of insight, of perspicacity, of shrewdness. It is as though nature had amused herself by taking the two most extraordinary types of detective that fiction had invented, Poe's Dupon and Gaboriau's Lecoq, in order to build up one in her own fashion, more extraordinary yet and more unreal. And, upon my word, anyone hearing of the adventures which have made the name of Holmlock Shears famous all over the world must feel inclined to ask if he is not a legendary person, a hero who has stepped straight from the brain of some great novel-writer, of a Conan Doyle, for instance.

A different form of Anglo-French entente was provided by Eugène Valmont, a fictional detective working in London, in short stories of 1904–5 by the Canadian writer Robert Barr.[10]

In the Doyle stories, Holmes is certainly willing to recognise the strengths of Continental policing. In 'Lady Frances Carfax' (1911), he tells Watson that it is unlikely that she ever reached

London 'as, with their system of registration, it is not easy for foreigners to play tricks with the Continental police'.

The most chilling Continental in the Holmes stories is Baron Adelbert Gruner, in 'The Illustrious Client'. It was published in 1924, but the story dates from the reign of Edward VII (1901–10). A past murderer, 'poisonous as a cobra', is described by Watson in terms of a sinister appeal but also with a clear warning: 'His straight, thin-lipped mouth. If ever I saw a murderer's mouth it was there – a cruel, hard gash in the face, compressed, inexorable, and terrible. . . . Nature's danger-signal, set as a warning to his victims'. The last is an instructive insight into the idea that the physical outside reveals the mental inside. This, however, does not warn Violet de Merville, who is shown to be readily manipulated by Gruner.

Instead, it is Kitty Winter who is the woman of energy and integrity, a 'flame-like young woman' who had been used by Gruner and brings word of his book detailing his conquests: 'Souls I have ruined'. She it is who brings him to ruin by throwing vitriol into his face. The 'wages of sin', Holmes reflects: 'Sooner or later it will always come'. A horrible man brought low in a fundamentally appropriate fashion in which Edward VII acts an appropriate part, Gruner is the epitome of the cruel, seducing Continental. Rather than a Scandinavian version of Germanic, he is presented as somewhat Mediterranean: 'His face was swarthy, almost Oriental, with large, dark, languorous eyes. . . . His hair and moustache were raven black'. There is a parallel with Wilhelm Gottsreich Sigismond von Ormstein, King of Bohemia, in 'A Scandal in Bohemia', who has a 'thick, hanging lip, and a long straight chin'. That king is one of the many distinguished Continentals, including the Pope, who consult Holmes.

The British Brothers' League, a body opposed to immigration founded in 1901 under the slogan 'England for the English', received a public donation of ten shillings from Doyle during the Germanophobia prior to the start of World War One. In contrast to Germans, Doyle favours Anglo-American integrity, although as most of his characters are found in that vast pool, it is unsurprising that the majority of his villains are Anglo-American as well. However, Doyle's stories would be repurposed for World War One, a titanic struggle which brought the new opponent to the fore.

9

THE LEGACY

> I saw the smoke banks on that October evening swirl slowly up over the Atlantic swell, and rise, and rise, until they had shredded into thinnest air, and lost themselves in the infinite blue of heaven. And with them rose the cloud which had hung over the country; and it also thinned and thinned, until God's own sun of peace and security was shining once more upon us, never more, we hope, to be bedimmed.
>
> – Last sentences of Doyle's novel *Rodney Stone* (1896), referring to the battle of Trafalgar of 1805

Indeed, history as an ongoing process, one of continuity and change, was very much present in the Holmes stories, and, more generally, appealed to Doyle and to his readers. He was keen to write historical novels, though, like those of Dickens, none was set in the distant past. Doyle, moreover, had a strong awareness of the changes of his lifetime, but also presents powerful elements of continuity, including personality and landscape. The theme of change was differently offered with Doyle's interest in science fiction.

With the Holmes stories, there is a sense of a cyclical character in history, as in *The Valley of Fear*, in which Holmes draws the attention of the talented Inspector MacDonald to Jonathan Wild:

> 'A master criminal – 1750 or thereabouts.[1] . . . Everything comes in circles – even Professor Moriarty. Jonathan Wild was the hidden force of the London criminals, to whom he sold his brains and his organisation on a fifteen per cent commission. The old wheel turns and the same spoke comes up. It's all been done before, and will be again'.

Although a man of strong scientific interests with a commitment to new discoveries and their application and use, Holmes is depicted as very interested in the past, both prehistoric and that of recorded annals. Thus, in Cornwall, he studies the remains of prehistoric man, and, more generally, is fascinated with barrows. Landscapes where humans were once more common, notably Dartmoor and, very differently, rural East Anglia, are also of interest in that light. It was a given that, as expressed by Emil Reich in his *New Student's Atlas of British History* (1903), the 'influence of the locality . . . is both spiritual, through its historical traditions, and physiological, through its climatic and other physical factors'.

In *The Hound of the Baskervilles*, Doyle slows the account and lessens the intensity by providing an account of the prehistoric peopling of Dartmoor, which indeed had struck him when visiting in 1901. Watson notes, 'The whole steep slope was covered with grey circular rings of stone, a score of them at least'. Striking a note of continuity, Stapleton explains,

> 'they are the homes of our worthy ancestors. Prehistoric man lived thickly on the moor, and as no one in particular has lived there since, we find all his little arrangements exactly as he left them. These are his wigwams with the roofs off. You can even see his hearth and his couch if you have the curiosity to go inside. . . . He grazed his cattle on these slopes, and he learned to dig for tin when the bronze sword began to supersede the stone axe. Look at the great trench in the opposite hill'.

In turn, and again unnecessarily so, Watson reports to Holmes on this sense of continuity:

> 'The longer one stays here the more does the spirit of the moor sink one's soul, its vastness, and also its grim charm. When you are once out upon its bosom you have left all traces of modern England behind you, but on the other hand you are conscious everywhere of the homes and the work of the prehistoric people. On all sides of you as you walk are the houses of these forgotten folk, with their graves and the huge monoliths which are supposed to have marked their temples. As you look at their grey stone huts against the scarred hillsides you leave your own age behind you, and if you were to see a skin-clad, hairy man crawl out from the low door, fitting a flint-tipped arrow on to the string of his bow, you would feel that his presence there was more natural than your own. The strange thing is that they should have lived so thickly on what must always have been most unfruitful soil. I am no antiquarian, but I could imagine that they were some unwarlike and harried race who were forced to accept that which none other would occupy'.

This is very much Doyle looking towards his novels *The Lost World* (1912) and *The Maracot Deep* (1929). The first, originally published as a serial in *The Strand Magazine*, depicts, alongside dinosaurs, a struggle between a friendly race of natives and a hostile race of ape-men, and the latter offered a sub-marine equivalent. The lost world of Neolithic Devon is presented in a far more vivid fashion than these accounts. All three reflect a fascination with the idea of competing races, and thus with evolution, which seemed to be far from fixed as a process. Hostility to the Irish can be glimpsed in *The Lost World*, but it is far more apparent in the work of Buchan, notably *The Three Hostages*, which was written in the aftermath of Britain's defeat by Irish separatists.[2]

Returning to the West Country, there is a tension between the belief in the supernatural and Holmes's approach. The former had been the basis of the presentation of Egdon Heath as host to pagan spirits in Thomas Hardy's *The Return of the Native* (1878) and also of the Gilbert and Sullivan comic opera *Ruddigore; or, The Witch's Curse* (1887). Moreover, Hardy's *Tess of the d'Urbervilles* (1891) is full of pagan, quasi-Biblical and mythological allusions. Set in Cornwall, *Ruddigore* includes the tale of a wicked ancestor, Sir Rupert Murgatroyd, and a curse on subsequent Baronets of Ruddigore. While willing to admit the existence of evil, Holmes gives it human agency: 'The devil's agents may be of flesh and blood', a theme that is more fully developed in the work of Agatha Christie.

In 'Borrowed Scenes', a non-Holmes short story published in *The Pall Mall Magazine* in September 1913, the narrator brings to his visit to Sussex a strong sense of history:

> As I walked, I entertained myself by recollections of the founders of Sussex, of Cedric that mighty sea-rover, and of Ella his son, said by the bard to be taller by the length of a spear-head than the tallest of his fellows.

There are references to 'half-timbered houses of the early English pattern' and settling differences in 'the old English fashion'. Yet, there is also a clear facetiousness in the treatment, with the locals obviously not interested in the Saxon references. In contrast, there is a much stronger presentation of continuity in 'Black Peter' (1904), which is set in Sussex and provides more than one sense of change:

> We drove for some miles through the remains of widespread woods, which were once part of that great forest which for so long held the Saxon invaders at bay – the impenetrable 'weald', for sixty years the bulwark of Britain. Vast sections of it have been cleared, for this is the seat of the first ironworks of the country, and the trees have been felled to smelt the ore. Now the richer fields of the North have absorbed the trade, and nothing save these ravaged groves and great scars in the earth show the work of the past.

Holmes is presented as doing 'laborious researches in Early English Charters' in 'The Three Students' and 'The Golden Pince-Nez'. As far as more recent history is concerned, Doyle scatters the stories with historical references, expecting that his readers will be able to follow them, or at least be interested, and certainly not be put off. 'The Musgrave Ritual' assumes knowledge of the English Civil War (1642–46) and the Restoration of Charles II (1660). The references include throwaway remarks. In 'The Reigate Squire', a house 'bears the date of Malplaquet upon the lintel of the door'. That was 1709. Readers would have been expected to know the dates of Marlborough's victories. At any rate, the date is not provided.

In 'The Retired Colourman', Holmes describes Josiah Amberley in historical terms: 'He has, to a high degree, the sort of mind which one associates with the medieval Italian nature rather than with the modern Briton'. Napoleon provides a particular source for comparison, notably with 'The Six Napoleons', but also with a reference, in 'The Abbey Grange' (1904), to the key battles of Marengo (1800) and Waterloo (1815). Holmes says of the former: 'this is our Marengo, for it begins in defeat and ends in victory', which was indeed the case for Napoleon in that battle with the Austrians, which was even more prominent to contemporaries for providing the background to the action in Giacomo Puccini's opera *Tosca* (1900). The opera was a total triumph when it opened in London that year, six months after the Rome première.

Doyle's strong sense of change is presented in the opening chapter of his non-Holmes novel *Rodney Stone*, which begins in 1851 and notes the changes with trains and steamboats. The key battle for liberty is seen in this novel as that opposed to Napoleon:

> our weary struggle of two and twenty years with that great and evil man. They can learn how Freedom fled from the whole broad continent, and how Nelson's blood was shed,[3] and Pitt's noble heart was broken [William Pitt the Younger, died 1806] in striving that she should not pass us for ever to take refuge with our brothers across the Atlantic.

The last, ironically, was the point made by Edward Gibbon in his *Decline and Fall of the Roman Empire* when assessing the question of whether Europe would anew fall to 'barbarian' invasion. Rodney Stone comes from a naval family in which the eldest son has taken the name of his father's favourite commander. Thus, Vernon, Hawke, Benbow, Anson, Rodney and Nelson. In Baskerville Hall, the portraits include 'Rear-Admiral Baskerville, who served under Rodney in the West Indies', and 'Sir William Baskerville, who was Chairman of Committees of the House of Commons under Pitt'. Although of course fictional, these heroic and public-spirited figures speak to a glorious past. Navalism is differently presented with 'The Sussex Vampire' in Holmes's recommendation for the errant Jack Ferguson: 'a year at sea would be my prescription'.

As far as British, which for Doyle means English, history is concerned, the interest in old families and historic homes pushes the past to the fore. Indeed, it provides a way to unlock mysteries, as with the ancestral portraits of the Baskervilles or the ability to hide in priest holes. Thus, the sixteenth and seventeenth centuries are very much present. For the Baskervilles, however, this is not a matter of praise, for the mid-seventeenth century Hugo Baskerville is a source of the alleged family curse, and a 1742 document related to this is discussed in the second chapter.

Doyle's depiction of longevity is central to the Baskervilles, albeit a longevity that is dependent on imperial wealth and vigour. It is also seen with 'The Sussex Vampire', in which Holmes and Watson visit Cheeseman's, the ancient Sussex home of Robert Ferguson and his family. The idea of joining of old and new is accompanied by a specificity of place, or, as the French would say, *terroir*:

> It was a large, straggling building, very old in the centre, very nice at the wings, with towering Tudor chimneys and a lichen-spotted, high-pitched roof of Horsham slabs. . . . Within, the ceilings were corrugated with heavy oaken beams. . . . An odour of age and decay pervaded the whole crumbling building . . . a huge old-fashioned fireplace with an iron screen behind it dated 1670. . . . The half-panelled walls may well have

> belonged to the original yeoman farmer of the seventeenth century.

Continuity and accretion were also exemplified by Tuxbury Old Park near Bedford in 'The Blanched Soldier' (1926). The house of Colonel Emsworth, a war hero, is described by James Dodd:

> 'It is a great wandering house, standing in a considerable park. I should judge it was of all sorts of ages and styles, starting on a half-timbered Elizabethan foundation and ending in a Victorian portico. Inside it was all panelling and tapestry and half-effaced old pictures, a house of shadows and mystery'.

In contrast, there was far less favour for eighteenth-century urban buildings and what they suggested of their age. In 'The Second Stain', Holmes visits the eighteenth-century home of Eduardo Lucas in Godolphin Street close to Westminster Abbey: 'a high, dingy, narrow-chested house, prim, formal, and solid, like the century which gave it birth'.

The Abbey Grange near Chislehurst sits in a noble parkland and showed the accretional nature of a great house:

> a low, widespread house, pillared in front after the fashion of Palladio. The central part was evidently of a great age and shrouded in ivy, but the large windows showed that modern changes had been carried out, and one wing of the house appeared to be entirely new.

Birlstone in *The Valley of Fear* has an eleventh-century core, which was burned down in 1543, with a house, built on the castle ruins in the early seventeenth century, subsequently little changed. However, before its current occupants, the house had been untenanted for a while, and there was a risk that it would decline into a picturesque decay. Watson describes Birlstone in terms of continuity:

> two ancient stone pillars, weather-stained. . . . A short walk along the winding drive, with such sward and oaks around it as one only sees in rural England; then a sudden turn, and the long, low, Jacobean house of dingy, liver-coloured brick lay before us, with an old-fashioned garden of cut yews on either side of it. As we approached it there were the wooden drawbridge and the beautiful broad moat, as still and luminous as quicksilver in the cold winter sunshine. Three centuries had flowed past the old Manor House, centuries of births and of homecomings, of country dances and of the meetings of foxhunters. Strange that now in its old age this dark business should have cast its shadow upon the venerable walls.

In 'The Dancing Men', Hilton Cubitt of Ridling Thorpe Manor has a very strong sense of continuity: 'though I'm not a rich man, my people have been at Ridling Thorpe for a matter of five centuries, and there is no better-known family in the county of Norfolk'. In the non-Holmes 'The Beetle-Hunter' (1898), Dr Hamilton visits Delamere Court near Pangbourne, the residence of Sir Thomas Rossiter:

> We had come to two high pillars crowned with heraldic monsters which flanked the opening of a winding avenue. Over the laurel bushes and rhododendrons, I could see a long, many-gabled mansion, girdled with ivy, and toned to the warm, cheery, mellow glow of old brick-work . . . this delightful house.

In 'The Japanned Box' (1899), another non-Holmes story, readers discover Thorpe Place near Evesham,

> that part of the Midlands which is drained by the Avon. It is the most English part of England. Shakespeare, the flower of the whole race, was born right in the middle of it. It is a land of rolling pastures, rising to higher folds to the westward, until they swell into the Malvern Hills. There are no towns, but numerous villages, each with its grey Norman church. You have left the brick of the southern and eastern counties behind you, and everything is stone – stone for the walls, and lichened

> slabs of stone for the roofs. It is all grim and solid and massive, as befits the heart of a great nation. . . . It was a very, very old house, incredibly old – pre-Norman, some of it, and the Bollamores claimed to have lived in that situation since long before the Conquest.[4]

Assumptions about continuity and organic change were long-present in detective fiction, as with John Dickson Carr's *Hag's Nook* (1933):

> There is something spectral about the deep and drowsy beauty of the English countryside; in the lush dark green, the evergreens, the grey church-spire and the meandering white road. To an American, who remembers his own brisk concrete highways clogged with red filling-stations and the fumes of traffic, it is particularly pleasant. It suggests a place where people really can walk without seeming incongruous, even in the middle of the road . . . a feeling which can haunt the traveller only in the British Isles. A feeling that the earth is old and enchanted; a sense of reality in all the flashing images which are conjured up by that one word 'merrie'. For France changes, like a fashion, and seems no older than last season's hat. In Germany even the legends have a bustling clockwork freshness, like a walking toy from Nuremberg. But this English earth seems (incredibly) even older than its ivy-bearded towers. The bells at twilight seem to be bells across the centuries; there is a great stillness, through which ghosts step, and Robin Hood has not strayed from it even yet.[5]

In *An English Murder* (1951), Cyril Hare referred to 'England, where relics of the past are permitted not only to exist but to influence the present'.

Holmes's sense of continuity is to be challenged by a world war that returns the country to the existential threat seen during the French Revolutionary and Napoleonic Wars, the latter of which provides the comparison for Moriarty, 'the Napoleon of crime', who is described in *The Valley of Fear* as 'this Napoleon-gone-wrong'. Such an existential threat was not ignored by British writers, who, indeed, proved very adept at offering tales of challenge, which was very much the case in the two decades before World War One. These years saw invading Martians in Surrey as well as Fu Manchu, a Chinese master criminal based in Limehouse who exceeded Moriarty in the threat he posed, and the persistence of the threat, in part due to his ability to escape death.[6] Arthur Sarsfield Ward, the author, under the pseudonym Sax Rohmer, of the Fu Manchu saga, drew on the Holmes stories with the contrast between the narrator Dr Petrie and his brilliant friend Denis Nayland Smith. Ward (1883–1959) was born in Birmingham to working-class Irish parents, and, like Doyle, did not turn to writing full-time until he finished another career, in his case as a civil servant. Ward's first published works were short stories, the first in 1903, and *The Mystery of Dr Fu-Manchu* was serialised in 1912–13.

The settings of Holmes's adventures could also be those for invasion literature, a process seen with George Chesney's *The Battle of Dorking* (1871), which drew on concerns about a German invasion, concerns encouraged by the German success against France in 1870–71. The book was republished in 1914. Surrey was also the setting of H. G. Wells's Martian invasion, *The War of the Worlds* (1898), which had been serialised the previous year. Popular writers tackling human invasions included William Le Queux offering *The Great War in England in 1897* (1894), a call for conscription in *The Invasion of 1910* (1906) and *Spies of the Kaiser* (1909); Edgar Wallace providing *Private Selby* (1912); Saki predicting German victory in *When William Came: A Story of London Under the Hohenzollerns* (1913); and P. G. Wodehouse managing a comic take in the deliberately ridiculous *The Swoop!, or How Clarence Saved England* (1909), in which the Boy Scouts thwart the nine varied invading powers.

Doyle addressed this anxiety in 'His Last Bow', but, already, in 'The Second Stain', published in December 1904, there is the menace posed, as the prime minister makes clear, by a letter from 'a certain foreign potentate who has been ruffled by some recent colonial developments of this country. It has been written hurriedly and upon his own responsibility entirely'. Holmes has no difficulty in identifying the writer, and readers would have had no doubt that it would have been the bellicose and unpredictable Emperor Wilhelm II of Germany (r. 1888–1918).[7] Readers are assured that any resulting war would be costly in lives and treasure and that Europe is on the brink:

> If you consider the European situation you will have no difficulty in perceiving the motive. The whole of Europe is an armed camp. There is a double league which makes a fair balance of military power. Great Britain holds the scales. If Britain were driven into war with one confederacy, it would assure the supremacy of the other confederacy, whether they joined in the war or not.

Tension mounts for Holmes with 'The Adventure on the Bruce-Partington Plans', published in December 1908. Hugo Oberstein, an agent mentioned in the previous story, and clearly, from his name, German, plays a major role in the theft of the radically new submarine plans through corrupting Colonel Walter, by means of £5,000, and in killing Cadogan West. Mycroft tells Sherlock about the submarine: 'Its importance can hardly be exaggerated. It has been the most jealously guarded of all government secrets. You may take it from me that naval warfare becomes impossible within the radius of a Bruce-Partington operation'. Oberstein is tricked into returning to London, where he is seized and imprisoned.

The sense of naval destiny emphasised by British commentators, such as the academic Sir John Seeley, Regius Professor of Modern History at Cambridge from 1869 to 1895 and author of *The Expansion of England* (1883),[8] made any threats to Britain's naval position particularly important. In *The Sign of Four* (1890), 'the warships of the future' had been one of the topics of Holmes's conversation when he merrily dined with Watson and Athelney Jones on 'oysters and a brace of grouse, with something a little choice in white wines'. By 1908, the submarine was apparently future potential turned into present reality.

The pace of technological change indeed suggested that warfare would change greatly. In 1909, Colonel Frederick Trench, the military attaché in Berlin, reported that the Germans were proposing to introduce power traction vehicles 'of a type suitable for military use' and, in 1910, that they were aiming to build 'large airships of great speed, endurance and gas-retaining capacity'.[9]

Doyle subsequently produced 'Danger!', about the threat of German submarines, which was published in *The Strand Magazine* in July 1914. The article was followed in that issue by 'What Naval Experts Think', which was republished in 1918 when Doyle pronounced: 'It is a matter of history how fully this warning has been justified and how, even down to the smallest details, the prediction had been fulfilled'.[10] In 'Danger!', eight submarines attack British steamers, hitting hard the food supplies for Britain, and raising the price of food such that Britain had to negotiate. As Admiral Sir Compton Domvile correctly pointed out, Doyle had exaggerated the length of time a submarine could stay at sea without supplies. Doyle replied that the story dealt with 'the submarine of the immediate future', but time would tell that his prediction was wrong, and he also neglected the limited number of torpedoes that they could carry. In general, Doyle was strongly thanked for his warning, although, in the *Daily Mail* of 28 October 1914, 'H. B.' criticised him for suggesting a means to German victory. Doyle was also castigated for contributing to the funds of the Committee for the Assistance of Germans, Austrians, and Hungarians in Distress.

In practice, the submarine still faced serious deficiencies as a weapons system, deficiencies Doyle did not address. To move submerged, submarines were dependent on battery motors that had to be recharged on the surface, where submarines were highly vulnerable to attack. In addition, submarines were slow, which lessened their chance of maintaining contact and of hitting a warship moving under full steam. The low silhouette of a submarine limited its surveillance potential. Doyle can be praised for seeing into the more distant future, but, prior to the world war, the emphasis understandably still rested on battleships, which, indeed, with their gunnery had played the decisive role in the Russo-Japanese naval battles of 1904–5, notably Tsushima (1905). In the naval race in 1906–12, Britain launched twenty-nine capital ships and Germany seventeen. Helped by having a much higher earlier basis of naval expenditure as well as the necessary manufacturing capability, Britain could out-produce a Germany that prioritized the necessity of focusing on its army.

A Holmes story with wartime zeal was 'His Last Bow: The War Service of Sherlock Holmes', which was published in *The Strand Magazine* in September 1917. The cover of that issue declared 'Sherlock Holmes Outwits a German Spy', adding 'You can send this Magazine Post Free to the Troops'. Set on 2 August 1914, the story, in which a widespread German spy network, established in 1910, is thwarted, offers not the madcap physical energy of John Buchan's *The Thirty-Nine Steps*, but an almost theatrical mental duel of deception. Baron von Herling, the chief secretary of the German Embassy, at the outset, pays tribute to British character: 'One's first impression is that they are entirely soft. Then one comes suddenly upon something very hard and you know that you have reached the limit, and must adapt yourself to the fact'. He suggests that Britain may leave France and Belgium to German conquest: 'we live in a utilitarian age. Honour is a medieval conception', and notes that Germany has stirred up 'such a devil's brew of Irish civil war, window-breaking Furies, and God knows what to keep her thoughts at home'. The 'Furies' is a reference to the suffragettes, while the Irish republican threat is underlined by Holmes's disguise as a bitterly anti-British American Irishman. Herling also says that Germany will fight Britain at some stage, and that Britain would be wiser to fight then as it would have allies. This is a response to the idea that Britain should not come to the assistance of Belgium and France. The idea of the war as long planned by Germany is given by von Bork's choice of August 1914 for his safe code. There is also a reference back to 'the late lamented Professor Moriarty' in order both to locate Moriarty and to help provide a reference point for the idea that the German espionage system in Britain had 'some strong and secret central force'.

After Holmes's success over von Bork, one that provides the opportunity to demonstrate the arrogance of the Germans, and their crass view of humanity, the story closes with an affirmation of eventual British victory:

> There's an east wind coming all the same, such a wind as never blew on England yet. It will be cold and bitter, Watson, and a good many of us may wither before its blast. But it's God's own wind none the less, and a cleaner, better, stronger land will lie in the sunshine when the storm has cleared.

Echoes were to be offered by later detective novelists.[11] The appearance of 'His Last Bow' in 1917 is instructive because it was a year not only of growing exhaustion in the intractable struggle but also of increased pressure in Britain, France and Russia for a negotiated settlement. Indeed, Arthur Henderson, the Labour leader and a member of the War Cabinet, resigned on 11 August 1917 after the Cabinet rejected his idea for a peace conference to bring the war to a close. In his preface to the collection *His Last Bow*, which gathered stories published from 1908 to 1917, Doyle reported that Holmes had retired to

> a small farm upon the Downs five miles from Eastbourne, where his time is divided between philosophy and agriculture. . . . The approach of the German war caused him, however, to lay his remarkable combination of intellectual and practical activity at the disposal of the Government.

In 1916, Doyle had published a factual work, *The British Campaign in France and Flanders 1914*, and he went on to produce what in total became six volumes of the same series published from 1916 to 1920. They were all based on illustrated articles published in *The Strand Magazine* from April 1916 to February 1919. Doyle had turned down the idea of a history of the war itself, which, instead, was written by his fellow Athenaeum member John Buchan. Earlier, Doyle was one of the twenty-five writers who had attended a meeting at Wellington House on 2 September 1914 that was called by the Liberal MP Charles Masterman, the Chancellor of the Duchy of Lancaster, who had been appointed by Lloyd George to head a secret War Propaganda Bureau. This body encouraged the publication of books and pamphlets, including Buchan's *Nelson's History of the War* and Doyle's books.[12] Other writers present at the meeting included Bennett, Chesterton, Galsworthy, Hardy, Masefield, Newbolt and Wells. The link between writers and the war effort was clear.

In December 1914, Doyle brought out *The German War*, a collection of pieces already published in *The Fortnightly Review* (in March 1913) and *The Daily Chronicle*. He noted that he had been reluctant to credit Germany as a threat until early 1913. In the preface, written in November 1914, Doyle stressed 'the desperate need of national effort' and 'the justice of our cause'. In the first article, which was issued as a recruiting pamphlet in Britain and also used abroad, being published extensively in the United States and translated into Danish and Dutch, the war was very much blamed on Germany, and the struggle was existential: 'The day of God's testing has come'. Doyle's 'Afterthought' to *The German War* (1914) brought up one of his long-standing concerns, manliness, an idea that focused beliefs and anxieties in the prewar era and linked worries about Britain with hopes about Empire. Having reiterated his confidence in a 'virile nation', he added:

> Already those Territorials who were so ignorantly and ungenerously criticised in times of peace are, after nearly three months of camp-life, hardening into soldiers who may safely be trusted in the field. Behind them the greater part of a million men are formed who will also become soldiers in a record time if a desperate earnestness can make them so. It is a glorious spectacle which makes a man thankful that he has been spared to see it. One is more hopeful of our Britain, and more proud of her, now that the German guns can be heard from her eastern shore, than ever in the long monotony of her undisturbed pros-

> perity. Our grandchildren will thrill as they read of the days that we endure.

Doyle had five children but no grandchildren, primarily because of war realities. His wounded eldest son Arthur (known as Kingsley, 1892–1918), died of pneumonia. Doyle wrote of Kingsley that he had 'lived to play a man's part in the Great War' and was 'one of the grandest boys in body and soul that ever a father was blessed with'. The number of men available for marriage was hit hard by the war. Mary, Doyle's elder daughter, did not marry, and Jean, his younger daughter, did not marry until she was past childbearing age. His surviving sons, Denis and Adrian, both married but were childless.

Also in December 1914, Austen Chamberlain, a prominent Conservative, wrote to Francis Dyke Acland, the under-secretary of state for foreign affairs, to press the need for official publications to support the cause, though noting:

> I am deeply impressed by our underserved good fortune in carrying our people so unanimously with us. . . . Now is the time . . . to form an enlightened public opinion which will support the Government through whatever sacrifices are needed in the weary months of war.[13]

Doyle sought to rise to the challenge. The war itself saw the Conservatives re-enter government as part of a patriotic coalition.[14]

Twelve Holmes short stories (but no Holmes novel) were to follow the war in *The Strand Magazine* between October 1921 and April 1927, stories collected in *The Case-Book of Sherlock Holmes* (1927). Although they referred to new developments, such as 'the modern gramophones' in 'The Mazarin Stone', published in *The Strand Magazine* in October 1921, none of these stories were particularly specific to the period, and all could have been set prewar. 'The Mazarin Stone', the first, was very much prewar in its tone and subject, as was 'Thor Bridge' (1922), and the third, the weak 'The Creeping Man' (1923), in which a German, Lowenstein, provided a dangerous drug that made Professor Presbury behave like a monkey. There was, however, no political dimension. 'The Sussex Vampire' and 'The Three Garridebs', both published in late 1924, were again prewar in their setting and style.

The sixth of the sequence, 'The Illustrious Client' (1924), drew on hostility to the Central Powers with its critique of Baron Adelbert Gruner. A French agent, Le Brun, although defeated by Gruner, is mentioned favourably, but the adventure was set prewar and, again, there was no political dimension.

No Holmes story appeared in 1925, but there were four in 1926 and two in 1927, the last 'Shoscombe Old Place'. It relates what turns out to be a benign deception – in marked contrast to the Berkshire Neo-Gothic setting, which triggers the question that Holmes finds very interesting:

> 'What is master doing down at the old church crypt at night? . . . the haunted crypt . . . an old ruined chapel in the park. It's so old that nobody could fix its date. And under it there's a crypt which has a bad name among us. It's a dark, damp, lonely place by day, but there are few in that county that would have the nerve to go near it at night'.

Holmes and Watson surreptitiously come into the park at night, and, in true Neo-Gothic form, enter the chapel:

> It was pitch-dark and without a moon . . . a dark mass loomed up in front of us which proved to be the ancient chapel. We entered the broken gap which was once the porch, and our guide, stumbling among heaps of loose masonry, picked his way to the corner of the building, where a steep stair led down into the crypt. Striking a match, he illuminated the melancholy place – dismal and evil-smelling, with ancient crumbling walls of rough-hewn stone, and piles of coffins, some of lead and some of stone, extending upon one side right up to the arched and groined roof which lost itself in the shadows above our head . . . the gate of Death.

They examine the graves, the oldest of which is apparently Saxon, before coming to a coffin which Holmes jemmies open: 'There was a rending, tearing sound as it gave way, but it had hardly hinged back and partly revealed the contents before'. That is not the end of the drama: 'In the glare of the lantern I saw a body swathed in a sheet from head to foot, with dreadful, witch-like features . . . the dim, glazed eyes staring from a discoloured and crumbling face'.

There was also an eventually benign character to the penultimate story, 'The Veiled Lodger', in which Holmes's intervention in a case of 'terrible human tragedy' leads Mrs Ronder to abandon her plan to commit suicide. Doyle has Holmes deliver a strong moral close: 'The example of patient suffering is in itself the most precious of all lessons to an impatient world'. Such themes were rather different to those of the earlier Holmes.

'The Retired Colourman', which was published in *The Strand Magazine* in January 1927 and in the United States the previous month, began with Holmes being in a melancholic mood: 'Is not all life pathetic and futile? . . . We reach. We grasp. And what is left in our hands at the end? A shadow. Or worse than a shadow – misery'. Technology plays a role. Holmes remarks that 'thanks to the telephone and the help of the Yard, I can usually get my essentials without leaving this room'. This offers an echo of the prewar Holmes, but the detective who did not go far was of less interest in the world of the motorcar and aircraft.

Doyle was bringing out his Holmes stories at the same time as earlier Holmes stories were appearing on screen. Moreover, other detective novelists were producing very different tales. 'Latouche The Apache. Amazing Story of the Paris Underworld' appeared in *The Strand Magazine* of March 1927 that had the last Holmes story. The January 1924 issue, which carried 'The Sussex Vampire', also had pieces by Winston Churchill, P. G. Wodehouse, John Russell, E. Phillips Oppenheim, F. Britten Austin and 'Sapper'.

From 1920, Agatha Christie stories appeared and 1926 saw the most innovative, *The Murder of Roger Ackroyd*. She consciously criticised the Holmes approach by having Hercule Poirot mock the methods employed by Holmes, notably the expertise on the subject of cigar ash and footprints. In practice, there were major similarities between Holmes and Poirot in their emphasis on psychological insight. Holmes also turns up in other Christie stories. Thus, in *The Man in the Brown Suit* (1924), a book that in many respects prefigured *The Murder of Roger Ackroyd*, Sir Eustace Pedler MP refers to the protagonist, Anne Beddingfeld:

> 'The girl's clever, though. All on her own, apparently, she's ferreted out the identity of the woman who was killed in my house. She was a Russian dancer called Nadina. I asked Anne Beddingfeld if she was sure of this. She replied that it was merely a deduction – quite in the Sherlock Holmes manner. However, I gather that she had cabled it home . . . as a proved fact. Women have these intuitions . . . I've no doubt that Anne Beddingfeld is perfectly right in her guess – but to call it a deduction is absurd'.[15]

In Anthony Rolls's *Scarweather* (1934), the narrator notes that he does not 'object to playing the traditional and honourable part of a Watson'.[16]

That the Holmes stories echo back does not mean that they were a failure, conceptually or commercially. Indeed, the idea of the puzzle was one that remained potent. Furthermore, the modern success of backward-looking detective novels does not suggest that Doyle should be castigated on this head. Although not placed in cars or aircraft, Holmes repeatedly uses technology, as in the train, the telegram and the microscope, in fact a seventeenth-century innovation, discussed at the outset of 'Shoscombe Old Place'. Modernising Holmes scarcely seemed necessary while Doyle's other writings were going so boldly into other spheres.

Menace from outside Britain was offered Holmes in 'The Lion's Mane', a story set in 1907 but published in *The Strand Magazine* in December 1926. Holmes kills the large jellyfish and Inspector Stackhurst says, 'I'm born and bred in these parts, but I never saw such a thing. It don't belong to Sussex'. Holmes remarks, 'Just as well for Sussex. It may have been the South-West gale that brought it up'. Holmes then cites John George Wood's *Out of Doors* in which he recounted being stung by one while swimming off Kent: 'He found that the creature radiated almost invisible filaments to the distance of fifty feet'. In fact, the jellyfish, *Cyanea capillata*, which needs cold waters, is common in the English Channel and Irish Sea. As Doyle notes, its sting, though dangerous, is not fatal for those who are healthy. Wood (1827–89), was an Oxford-educated clergyman who lived in Upper Norwood from 1878 and wrote and lectured extensively on natural history. His *The Common Objects of the Country* (1866) was a bestseller that reflected popular interest in the countryside at a time of rapid urbanisation. In his *The Uncivilized Races or Natural History of Man* (1868), Wood provided a form of support for notions of racial superiority.[17]

Doyle's major activity in the 1920s was his Spiritualist work, not least *The Coming of the Fairies* (1922), *The History of Spiritualism* (1926) and his worldwide lecture tours. It was as if Doyle were fulfilling Holmes's prospectus in 'The Final Problem': 'Of late I have been tempted to look into the problems furnished by Nature rather than those more superficial ones for which our artificial state of society is responsible'.

In 'The Leather Funnel', first published in 1902, a non-Holmes story set in Paris in 1882, Lionel Dacre, who is interested in the occult, states the case for strange knowledge as part of the extension and enhancement of humanity:

> 'The charlatan is always the pioneer. From the astrologer came the astronomer, from the alchemist the chemist, from the mesmerist the experimental psychologist. The quack of yesterday is the professor of tomorrow. Even such subtle and elusive things as dreams will in time be reduced to system and order'.

Belief in Spiritualism did not extend to Holmes crediting vampires, and he expresses a more general scepticism in 'The Sussex Vampire':

> 'What have we to do with walking corpses who can only be held in their grave by stakes driven through their hearts? It's pure lunacy'.

Watson counterpoints sensibly:

> 'But surely the vampire was not necessarily a dead man? A living person might have the habit. I have read, for example, of the old sucking the blood of the young in order to retain their youth'.

Holmes responds:

> 'You are right. . . . But are we to give serious attention to such things? This agency stands flat-footed upon the ground, and there it must remain. The world is big enough for us. No ghosts need apply'.

In his fictional writing in the late 1920s, Doyle produced new Doctor Challenger stories: *The Land of Mist* (1926), a somewhat unfocused Spiritualist novel, and the short stories 'When the World Screamed' (1928), which demonstrated that the Earth was a living organism, and 'The Disintegration Machine', published in *The Strand Magazine* in January 1929. Showing anew how Doyle liked to press his imagination, the latter centres on the discovery by Theodore Nemor, a Hampstead-based Latvian, of a machine capable of disintegrating matter and putting it back together. A foreign power has bid most highly for the rights, and could thereby destroy London: 'A gloating smile passed over the man's evil face. . . . I could imagine the whole Thames valley being swept clean, and not one man, woman, or child left of all these teeming millions!' This foreign power is a reflection of contemporary concern about Russia. To stop this, Challenger disintegrates Nemor, killing in order 'to prevent murder'. The detective as puzzle-solver is the role played by Challenger and, like Holmes, he does not always rely on the law or the state.

Also in 1929, *The Maracot Deep*, which had been a *Strand Magazine* series from October 1927 to February 1928, deals with the discovery of Atlantis, where Atlanteans communicate with the explorers through a thought projector. The Atlanteans have slaves descended from their original Greek slaves whom they had captured in war. The villainous Lord of the Dark Face is a supernatural foe who draws on the Devil and Baal. Good battles Evil and wins with a Biblical-style reference to Wanda, a wise Atlantean who had saved some of the Atlanteans when Atlantis is drowned. Maracot, the hero, tells the 'prince of darkness':

> 'Too long have you cursed the world with your presence. . . . The hearts of men will be lighter when you are gone . . . on every plane the good of that plane can be stronger than the evil. The angel will still beat the devil'.

Already, the prospect of new technology was very differently shown in 'The Horror of the Heights', a disturbing non-Holmes story published in *The Strand Magazine* in November 1913. Set in 1912, this brought together the here-and-now with science fiction, and drew on the interest in strange creatures seen in Doyle's *The Lost World* while also providing an echo of the danger outlined in *War of the Worlds* and prefiguring Howard Lovecraft's stories about the vulnerability of humanity in the face of hostile alien forces. The theme is one that Doyle was to offer on other occasions: 'This world of ours appears to be separated by a slight and precarious margin of safety from a most singular and unexpected danger'. Flying a monoplane, the protagonist, Joyce-Armstrong, a daring flying man, sets out to explore the 'jungles of the upper air . . . dressed like an Arctic explorer' and taking a shotgun. This was very much an idea of exploration, and one in which the aviator is the hero:

> The conqueror of Nature. . . . There is surely something divine in man himself that he should rise so superior to the limitations which creation seemed to impose – rise, too, by such unselfish, heroic devotion as this air-conquest has shown. Talk of human degeneration! When has such a story as this been written in the annals of our race?

Joyce-Armstrong rises to 41,300 feet, but then finds himself attacked by giant jellyfish, serpents of the outer air and a patch of vapour with a cruel beak. Escaping, he flies up again to unprecedented heights, only to be killed.

These activities do not bring in Holmes, who, indeed, does not engage greatly with the world of the 1920s. There is, however, at the close of 'The Creeping Man', which was published in *The Strand Magazine* in March 1923, the expression of a eugenicist perspective about the future of humanity. Holmes tells Watson:

> 'The material, the sensual, the worldly would all prolong their worthless lives. The spiritual would not avoid the call to something higher. It would be the survival of the least fit. What sort of cesspool may not our poor world become?'

This is very much a futurist engagement, but Doyle then locates his hero differently: 'Suddenly the dreamer disappeared, and Holmes, the man of action, sprang from his chair'. It was as a thinking man of action that Holmes was stamped on posterity.

10

SEQUELS

> French, pleased with his progress, thought whimsically that if now he only had the great Sherlock's luck, he would find the end of a cigar which would lead him direct to the person who had waited behind the bush. But though he looked everywhere about, he found neither a cigar-end nor anything else.
>
> – Freeman Wills, *The Hog's Back Mystery* (1933)[1]

Doyle was very willing to see Holmes on screen. Indeed, Holmes had already appeared in the feature-length films *A Study in Scarlet* (1914) and *The Valley of Fear* (1916), before, in 1920, Doyle sold the film rights to Sir Oswald Stoll (1866–1942), an Australian-born theatre entrepreneur who moved into films from 1918. The year 1921 saw the first production of fifteen short films, which were entitled *The Adventures of Sherlock Holmes*, and of a feature-length *The Hound of the Baskervilles*. In total, forty-five shorts and two features appeared in 1921–23, and Doyle was delighted by the actor who played Sherlock Holmes, Eille Norwood (1861–1928).[2] In 1923, *The Sign of Four*, the other feature-length film, concluded with a spectacular boat chase down the Thames.

In 1922, meanwhile, John Barrymore, a major actor, starred as Holmes in a film released in America as *Sherlock Holmes* and in Britain as *Moriarty*. Produced by Goldwyn Pictures Corporation, it was based on an 1899 play co-authored by Doyle and the leading American actor-manager William Gillette, who had presented Holmes both frequently on stage (about 1,300 times) and also in a 1916 silent film, *Sherlock Holmes*. Built in 1914–19 and with an addition finished in 1924, in part with the profits, Gillette's 'castle' is a distinctive Gothic-style structure on impressive cliffs over the Connecticut River. With its secret room, secret doors and complex as well as trick locks, the house would have delighted a fan of mysteries. In the 1922 film, Holmes thwarts Moriarty, played by the American-based German actor Gustav von Seyffertitz, and gets to marry the heroine.

It was as a man of action that Holmes appeared on screen, taking forward those portrayals already offered on the stage. This presentation of a man of action in turn affected the parameters within which Holmes could operate. Doyle himself offered a revelatory perspective on his view of what Holmes could do. He appreciated the acting in the early Holmes but criticised the introduction of telephones and motorcars of which 'the Victorian Holmes' never dreamed.[3] This was somewhat surprising as both were Victorian innovations. Moreover, in 'The Illustrious Client', Holmes notes down Sir James Damery's private telephone number.

With Doyle's books and stories published in the United States from the outset, American readers were a key audience. As a consequence, America was important to the profit that came from Holmes. Hollywood sustained this interest, and provided the greatest international impact for Holmes, both outside the British empire and also within it. Yet, Holmes also represented a form of cultural influence or soft power elsewhere. The most important part of the 'informal' British empire in South America was Argentina. There the magazine *PBT* took Holmes to Argentina in 1909, with Julián Bernat's story set on a boat going from Buenos Aires to Asunción in Paraguay. Watson is replaced by John Ranbet, a local journalist, who is both narrator and assistant. Holmes is adapted to the local environment and characters. Two years later, a weekly Spanish-language illustrated magazine, *Sherlock Holmes*, began a two-year run in Buenos Aires. It covered crime in Argentina and more generally, and its reporters supposedly did better than the police.

Aside from translations, Holmes dominated the international as well as the domestic literary discussion of detective fiction, for example in Germany. He was the Great Detective, a global figure already, before the age of talking film and then television series was to take his fame further.[4] Talking films worked much better for Holmes than the silent versions as they were more suitable for the explanation of detection. Such films were frequently made in the 1930s, notably *The Speckled Band* (1931), *Sherlock Holmes* (1932) and the 1931–37 films starring the British actor Arthur Wontner: *The Sleeping Cardinal*, *The Missing Rembrandt*, *The Sign of Four*, *The Triumph of Sherlock Holmes* and *Silver Blaze*. Wontner was not young, but he continued to make films until 1955.

Basil Rathbone, a South African born to British parents who had become a Shakespearean actor and served in World War One, followed in 1939. Already a successful actor, he starred that year in Twentieth-Century Fox's *The Hound of the Baskervilles* and also its *The Adventures of Sherlock Holmes*, fixing the actor as the quintessential Sherlock Holmes in the public eye. Taking forward the 1930–36 American series, also titled *The Adventures of Sherlock Holmes*, the fourteen Rathbone Holmes films saw only the first two with Fox as Universal Studios obtained the rights in 1942, including permission to modernise the films. Rathbone also starred as Holmes from 1939 to 1946 in 220 episodes of a radio series, *The New Adventures of Sherlock Holmes*, an American weekly that continued with other actors playing Holmes until 1950.

The merging of past with present is a hallmark of these films. The second of the Rathbone Universal films, *Sherlock Holmes and the Secret Weapon*, has Moriarty working with the Germans in order to seize a revolutionary bombsight. In *Sherlock Holmes in Washington* (1943), there is a well-placed German espionage network that has to be defeated. *Sherlock Holmes Faces Death* (1943) was more conventional in that Germans are not involved, as is *The Spider Woman* (1944), the Canadian-set *The Scarlet Claw* (1944), *The Pearl of Death* (1944), a very bloody version of 'The Adventure of the Six Napoleons', *The House of Fear* (1945), *The Woman in Green* (1945), *Pursuit to Algiers* (1945), *Terror by Night* (1946) and *Dressed to Kill* (1946).

The films, moreover, had a lasting international following. Thus, in the 1960s and 1970s, the sole Italian TV channel of RAI used to broadcast the series repeatedly. They are memorable but have been superseded by subsequent productions. Moreover, in wandering far from the Holmes plots, even when there are references to them, as in the orange pips in *The House of Fear*, the films detach Holmes from his context. Thus, the adventures include settings on the London-Scotland express, and in Algiers, Scotland, Northumberland and Canada.

Novelists continued to make frequent references to Holmes. In Agatha Christie's *Crooked House* (1949), Josephine Leonides, a well-read twelve-year-old, refers to the narrator, Charles Hayward, as Watson but is not very keen on the Holmes stories: 'It's awfully old-fashioned. They drive about in dog-carts'. In Beverley Nichols's *The Moonflower* (1955), Horatio Green, the middle-aged private detective who is the hero, notes 'there were so very few times when he could pretend to be Sherlock Holmes, and they were so very enjoyable'. Other echoes are less direct, as with the reference to 'the valley of her fear' in George Bellairs's *The Dead Shall Be Raised* (1942).

Sherlock Holmes, a six-part 1951 BBC series aired live starring Alan Wheatley, was the first series of television adaptations of Holmes. The plots of the parts – *The Empty House*, *A Scandal in Bohemia*, *The Dying Detective*, *The Reigate Squires*, *The Red-Headed League* and *The Second Stain* – were based on those by Doyle.[5] A 1954 television series filmed in France and London, with Ronald Howard as Holmes, was the first American television adaptation of Doyle's stories. Thirty-nine episodes were made and were broadcast in 1954–55, although a scheduled second season of an additional thirty-nine episodes did not follow. Some of the 1954 episodes was used for a twenty-four-episode series, 'Sherlock Holmes and Doctor Watson', with Geoffrey Whitehead as Holmes, that was produced in Poland in 1979–80. This low-budget production was not a success: the show was not released in Britain and had scant coverage in America.

The 1950s also saw Peter Cushing as Holmes in *The Hound of the Baskervilles* (1959), the first film adaptation of that novel to be shot in colour, which provided a major opportunity to depict the hound. A femme fatale, Cecile Stapleton, joins the cast of villains.

The BBC followed suit with more television adaptations in 1964–65 and (in colour) 1968. Douglas Wilmer and Cushing were the two Holmeses, and the stories were fairly faithful to the originals. *The Private Life of Sherlock Holmes* (1970), a film directed by Billy Wilder, was innovative, but also ridiculous in the style of the period. It was rather like the *Casino Royale* film of 1967. So also with *The Seven-Per-Cent Solution*, a 1976 film based on the 1974 novel of the same name in which drug addictions and Sigmund Freud play a role.

After the 1983 series *The Baker Street Boys*, based on the Irregulars, the Jeremy Brett Holmes series of forty-one episodes from 1984 to 1994, *The Adventures of Sherlock Holmes*, used a Victorian setting. In what was an impressive portrayal of Holmes's obsessive personality, Brett was very much the star. That Brett had bipolar disorder was part of the drama behind his acting. The series was popular internationally, for example in Japan and Portugal.

Compared to this, *The Adventure of Sherlock Holmes' Smarter Brother* (1975), a Gene Wilder comedy, was a slapstick of singularly little merit other than as an indicator of how Holmes could be used across genres, a point more clearly demonstrated in the 1965 musical *Baker Street*. That musical, which had mixed reviews and did not survive the year, was set in London in 1897, so that Victoria's Diamond Jubilee was a backdrop. The plot drew on 'A Scandal in Bohemia', although with Irene Adler now an associate of Holmes. Another comedy film, *Without a Clue* (1988), was based on the idea that Watson had created Holmes as a character so that he could maintain his medical reputation while solving crimes. He has to hire an actor to play the role, but the latter comes to the fore.[6] Somewhat different was the 1999 album *Sherlock Holmes Meets Dr Who* by the British composer Carey Blyton. I do not recommend it.

Doyle continues to be strongly praised by specialists in the genre, and notably so by P. D. James in 2009.[7] Moreover, Holmes's ability to fascinate the modern age was seen in a major burst of recent commercial commitment and creative energy, especially with the *Sherlock Holmes* films set in the 1890s starring Robert Downey Jr., and the British television series *Sherlock*, of which thirteen episodes appeared in 2010–17. Despite being set in the Holmes era, the films are not the most accurate representations of Doyle's work, but they are popular for their entertaining, tongue-in-cheek portrayal of the sleuth. Downey does mirror Holmes's habit of cloaking his genius until the final denouement, and the pace of the films and energy of the portrayal capture elements of Doyle's style. Set in the present, the imaginative television series starring Benedict Cumberbatch has been widely praised and won a number of prestigious awards. The series was also a major commercial success, being sold widely abroad, for example being successful in France, Germany and Sweden. The co-writer, Mark Gatiss, departed from what he saw as the overly reverential Jeremy Brett approach and, instead, claimed to be inspired by the then-contemporary setting of the Rathbone versions. In practice, the latter had not been as abrupt a departure from the corpus as was *Sherlock* with its use of modern technology, notably the internet. At the same time, there were many references to the originals, offering allusions for enthusiasts. *Sherlock* led to the publication by BBC Books of Holmes stories with introductions by figures linked to the series.

Sherlock worked to create an idea of Holmes for a particular generation and culture, an idea that was very different in content and tone to the Rathbone Holmes. There was a parallel with the Christie television series of the late 2010s as opposed to the earlier one starring David Suchet as Poirot, but also a contrast with the continuity of the visual image and language of James Bond on screen. In large part, this contrast reflects the extent to which copyright over Bond has been retained and, indeed, enhanced as control was obtained over the films to which Eon Productions had lacked the copyright. Moreover, there has not been a television counter or counters to the filmic Bond. With Bond and Connery, it is as if for Holmes the Rathbone version was still canonical albeit with different actors, notably, in his day, Brett. That is not the case, but it is still worth considering the modern resonance of the Rathbone version. This has been enhanced by a process of restoration. Four of the films made by Universal entered the public domain in the 1970s when their copyright was not renewed. In 2006, they were digitally restored and 'colorised' and they are available for purchase. Of the other Universal films, some had deteriorated badly, in part due to a lack of care, but, from 1993, they were restored by means of transfer to polyester film and the restoration of the images. Completed in 2001, this project has made the films newly available. The two Twentieth-Century Fox Rathbone films produced in 1939 have survived in good condition.

Aside from the actual films, the Rathbone impression of Holmes survives through a variety of means, notably stills and posters. Currently, Rathbone, as iconic as he was, appears to be the 'past' visual Holmes, as opposed to the "present' Benedict Cumberbatch and Robert Downey Jr., and it would be easy to accept that interpretation. Whether that discarding of the Rathbone version as past is true at the subliminal level of the Holmes image is less clear. So also is the possible perspective that may be lent by future usage and development. Possibly there is only so much that can be done with the Rathbone films in terms of modern cultural fashions, but the concept of Holmes that may be thus presented may well enjoy a revival in the future: the relationship between past image and present vision is always far from constant.

Sherlock has not been alone. In the United States, *Elementary* (154 episodes from 2012–19) offered a television resetting of Holmes in modern America, with *Sherlok Kholms* following in Russia in 2013. Holmes, played by Jonny Lee Miller, helps the

New York Police Department, and Watson is a woman. In contrast, the eight episodes of *Sherlok Kholms* were set in Victorian London. Guy Ritchie's 2009 film *Sherlock Holmes* starring Robert Downey Jr. made $524 million at the box office on a budget of $90 million, which led to sequels. Set in 1891, the first sequel, *Sherlock Holmes: A Game of Shadows* (2011), made $545.4 million on a budget of $125 million. An invented plot sees Holmes and Moriarty in conflict, with the latter using terrorism in order to gain control of munitions factories and cause a world war. The war is averted, and Holmes survives the plunge into the Reichenbach Falls. As with the first film in the series, there was a linkage with press publicity and with new versions of Holmes novels sold, for example in Argentina. *Sherlock 3* was due for release in December 2021.

Other recent works have included the *Sherlock Gnomes* animation (2018), the *Enola Holmes* (2020) film, in which Sherlock's younger sister plays the key role, and *The Irregulars* (2021), a television series, in which they play the key role while Holmes takes the credit.

So also with fiction. Again, as on screen, there is a range of work that can be cited, and in several languages. Thus, Italian writers produce novels involving Holmes that are sold at newspaper kiosks. In Argentina, *Sherlock Holmes en Buenos Aires* (2015) by Enrique Espina Rawson was based on the idea that Rawson had notebooks belonging to Watson relating to a sensational case investigated by Holmes and Watson in Buenos Aires. Mario Méndez's *Sherlock en Buenos Aires* (2018) covered Holmes's arrival in Buenos Aires in 1905 to help solve the disappearance of the daughter of a British diplomat. The narrator is not Watson, but Manuel Vallejoz, a half-Scottish employee of the embassy, who offers a different perspective to the good doctor, not least being young. There are three Argentinean books for younger readers by Andrea Ferrari: *El Camino de Sherlock* (*On Sherlock's Path*, 2016), *No e fácil ser Watson* (*It's not easy being Watson*, 2016) and *No me digas Bond* (*Don't Call Me Bond*, 2013). Moreover, Holmes is widely referred to across the genre of detective fiction.[8]

Particularly notable works in English focused on Holmes include two by Anthony Horowitz: *The House of Silk* (2011) and *Moriarty* (2014). Set in Victorian London, these were deservedly successful, both as homages to Doyle and as independent stories in their own right. The major difference is that of length. My copy of *The House of Silk* comes with 'The Adventure of the Bruce-Partington Plans' which Horowitz, in a thoughtful introduction, explains he has chosen as a sequel. The short story also shows Doyle's brilliance, notably his economy of writing, an almost shockingly sharp style in which he gets so much done in so few words. It is to be hoped that more of the sequel originators will return to this brilliance in, and of, brevity. The master-detective still has many crimes to solve, both in the England of his original appearance and in the present day.

SELECTED FURTHER READING

There is no shortage of excellent studies of Doyle, Holmes and their worlds. Focus on the Holmes stories, including *The Uncollected Sherlock Holmes* (1983) compiled by Richard Lancelyn Green, but explore the other works of Doyle as well, both fictional and factual. A brief selection of secondary works should begin with Andrew Lycett's *The Man Who Created Sherlock Holmes: The Life and Times of Sir Arthur Conan Doyle* (2007) and Martin Booth's *The Doctor, the Detective and Arthur Conan Doyle* (1997). For Holmes, there are valuable resources on the web, primarily Sherlockian.net at https://www.sherlockian.net. Other interesting sites include Sherlocktron and the online version of Ronald De Waal's *The Universal Sherlock Holmes* at https://special.lib.umn.edu/rare/ush/ush.html. For historical background, read Joseph Kestner, *The Edwardian Detective, 1901–1915* (reissued, Abingdon, 2018).

For England in the Holmes years, there are the massed ranks of scholarly tomes, among which Geoffrey Searle's *A New England? Peace and War 1886–1918* (2004) and Philip Waller's *Town, City, and Nation: England 1850–1914* (2006) are particularly worthy of note; but it might be more interesting to gauge the social timbre of the age through novelists such as Arnold Bennett and John Galsworthy. Reading newspapers of the period can be illuminating and fun. Remember to include provincial ones as well as their London counterparts. For the world of print, see Philip Waller, *Writers, Readers, and Reputations: Literary Life in Britain 1870–1918* (2008). On London, Andrew Saint, *London 1870–1914: A City at Its Zenith* (2022).

NOTES

1. INTRODUCTION

1. Richard Dalby, 'Arthur Conan Doyle and the Paranormal', *Book and Magazine Collector* 168 (March 1998).

2. Dorothy L. Sayers, 'Holmes' College Career', in *Baker-Street Studies*, ed. H. W. Bell (London: Constable, 1934); Richard Chorley, *Sherlock Holmes at Sidney Sussex College, 1871–1873: An Imaginative Reconstruction* (Cambridge: printed by Chorley, 1997).

3. *Daily Mail*, 23 January 1912, and *The Times*, 9 February 1914.

4. Richard Dalby, 'The Historical Fiction of Sir Arthur Conan Doyle', *Book and Magazine Collector* 131 (February 1995).

5. Howard Cox and Simon Mowatt, *Revolutions from Grub Street: A History of Magazine Publishing in Britain* (Oxford: Oxford University Press, 2014).

6. Richard Altick, *The English Common Reader: A Social History of the Mass Reading Public, 1800–1900* (Chicago: University of Chicago Press, 1957).

7. William Robinson, *Muckraker. The Scandalous Life and Times of W.T. Stead, Britain's First Investigative Journalist* (London: Robson Press, 2012); R. Luckhurst, L. Brake, E. King and J. Mussell (eds.), *William T. Stead: Newspaper Revolutionary* (London: British Library, 2012).

8. George Orwell, 'The Decline of the English Murder', *Tribune*, 15 February 1946. This can be readily read in any collection of Orwell's essays, for example the Penguin edition published in 1984 and reprinted in 2000: 346.

9. Joel Weiner, *Papers for the Millions: The New Journalism in Britain, 1850s to 1914* (New York: Greenwood Press, 1988).

10. Linda Stratmann, *The Illustrated Police News. The Shocks, Scandals and Sensations of the Week, 1864–1938* (London: British Library Publications, 2019).

11. Andrew Griffiths, *The New Journalism, the New Imperialism and the Fiction of Empire, 1870–1900* (Basingstoke: Palgrave, 2015).

12. Matthew Rubery, *The Novelty of Newspapers: Victorian Fiction and the Invention of the News* (Oxford: Oxford University Press, 2009).

13. Judith Walkowitz, *City of Dreadful Delight: Narratives of Sexual Danger in Late-Victorian London* (Chicago: University of Chicago Press, 1992); Robin Odell, *Ripperology: A Study of the World's First Serial Killer and Literary Phenomenon* (Kent, OH: Kent State University Press, 2006).

2. THE SITE FOR HOLMES

1. Jonathan Schneer, *London 1900. The Imperial Metropolis* (New Haven, CT: Yale University Press, 1999).

2. Charles Booth, *Life and Labour of the People I* (London: Macmillan, 1889).

3. Ross Forman, 'A Cockney Chinatown: The Literature of Limehouse, London', in *China and the Victorian Imagination: Empires Entwined* (Cambridge: Cambridge University Press, 2013), 193–223.

4. Diane Rappaport, *Shopping for Pleasure: Women in the Making of London's West End* (Princeton, NJ: Princeton University Press, 2000).

5. Amy Milne-Smith, *London Clubman: A Cultural History of Gender and Class in Late Victorian Britain* (Basingstoke: Palgrave, 2011).

6. Michael Wheeler, *The Athenaeum* (New Haven, CT: Yale University Press, 2020), 181–82.

7. Andrew Lycett, *The Man Who Created Sherlock Holmes: The Life and Times of Sir Arthur Conan Doyle* (London: Weidenfeld & Nicolson, 2007), 241.

8. Patricia Malcolmson, 'Getting a Living in the Slums of Victorian Kensington', *London Journal* 1 (1975): 28–55.

9. Anne Witchard, 'Thomas Burke, the "Laureate of Limehouse": A New Biographical Outline', *English Literature in Transition, 1880–1920* 48 (2005): 164–87, and *Thomas Burke's Dark Chinoiserie* (Farnham: Ashgate, 2009).

10. Christopher Breward, *The Hidden Consumer: Masculinities, Fashion, and City Life, 1860–1914* (Manchester: Manchester University Press, 1999).

11. John Barry, 'The Streets and Traffic of London', *Journal of the Royal Society of Arts* 47 (1898–99): 9.

12. Larry Witherell, *Rebel on the Right: Henry Page Croft and the Crisis of British Conservatism, 1903–1914* (Newark, DE: University of Delaware Press, 1997).

3. HOLMES'S FORAYS

1. Herbrand, 11th Duke of Bedford, *The Story of a Great Agricultural Estate* (London: John Murray, 1897).

2. Mark Freeman, *Social Investigation and Rural England, 1870–1914* (Woodbridge: Boydell & Brewer, 2003).

3. *Daily News*, 3 November 1888.

4. Clarence Glacken, *Traces on the Rhodian Shore: Nature and Culture in Western Thought from Ancient Times to the End of the Eighteenth Century* (Berkeley: University of California Press, 1967).

5. Halford Mackinder, 'On the Scope and Methods of Geography', *Proceedings of the Royal Geographical Society and Monthly Record of Geography* 9, no. 3 (March 1887): 141–74; Richard Peet, 'The Social Origins of Environmental Determinism', *Annals of the Association of American Geographers* 75 (1985): 309–33.

6. Robin Butlin, 'Historical Geographies of the British Empire, c. 1887–1925', in *Geography and Imperialism, 1820–1940*, ed. Morag Bell, Robin Butlin and Michael Hefferman (Manchester: Manchester University Press, 1995): 169–72.

7. Jan Marsh, *Back to the Land: The Pastoral Impulse in Victorian England, from 1880 to 1914* (London: Faber, 1982).

8. Stephen Badsey, 'Great Britain', in *1914–1918 Online International Encyclopaedia of the First World War*, https://encyclopedia.1914-1918-online.net/themes.

4. SOCIETY

1. Published in 1901 though set in 1889.

2. John Tosh, *A Man's Place: Masculinity and the Middle-Class Home in Victorian England* (New Haven, CT: Yale University Press, 1999).

3. Arthur Silverstein and Christine Ruggere, 'Dr Arthur Conan Doyle and the Case of Congenital Syphilis', *Perspectives in Biology and Medicine* 49, no 2 (Spring 2006): 209–19; see, more generally, Magdolna Zajácz, 'Medical History Curiosities in the Life and Work of Arthur Conan Doyle', translated by Zsófia Marincsák, accessed 21 April 2021, https://sherlockian-sherlock.com/conan-doyle-medical-history-study.php.

4. Martin Weiner, *Men of Blood: Violence, Manliness, and Criminal Justice in Victorian England* (Cambridge: Cambridge University Press, 2004).

5. Martin Pugh, *The March of the Women: A Revisionist Analysis of the Campaign for Women's Suffrage, 1866–1914* (Oxford: Oxford University Press, 2000).

6. Patricia Hollis, *Ladies Elect: Women in English Local Government 1865–1914* (Oxford: Oxford University Press, 1987).

7. Patrick McDevitt, *May the Best Man Win: Sport, Masculinity, and Nationalism in Great Britain and the Empire, 1880–1935* (Basingstoke: Palgrave, 2004).

8. For violent ruffians attacking racegoers at race meetings, see *The Times*, 5 April 1921.

9. Richard Green, 'Conan Doyle and His Cricket', in *The Victorian Cricket Match* (London: Sherlock Holmes Society of London, 2001), 34–36.

10. Eric Hopkins, *Childhood Transformed: Working-Class Children in Nineteenth-Century England* (Manchester: Manchester University Press, 1994).

11. Jose Harris, *Private Lives, Public Spirit: A Social History of Britain, 1870–1914* (Oxford: Oxford University Press, 1993).

12. First published under the title 'Burger's Secret'.

13. Gregory Phillips, *The Diehards: Aristocratic Society and Politics in Edwardian England* (Cambridge, MA: Harvard University Press, 1979).

5. POLITICS

1. Later republished as *The Mayfair Mystery*.

2. Jon Agar, *The Government Machine: A Revolutionary History of the Computer* (Cambridge, MA: MIT Press, 2003).

3. That was £5,000.

4. Thomas Otte and Paul Readman, 'Introduction', in *By-Elections in British Politics, 1832–1914* (Woodbridge: Boydell and Brewer, 2013), 16–17.

5. Ian Cawood, 'The 1892 General Election and the Eclipse of the Liberal Unionists', *Parliamentary History* 29 (2010): 331–57; Naomi Lloyd-Jones, 'The 1892 General Election in England: Home Rule, the Newcastle Programme and Positive Unionism', *Historical Research* 93 (2020): 73–104.

6. Andrew Roberts, *Salisbury: Victorian Titan* (London: Allen Lane, 1999).

7. Arthur Ponsonby, *Democracy and Diplomacy: A Plea for Popular Control of Foreign Policy* (London: Routledge, 1915), 61–67.

8. Jason Tomes, *Balfour and Foreign Policy: The International Thought of a Conservative Statesman* (Cambridge: Cambridge University Press, 1997).

9. Paul Readman, 'The Conservative Party, Patriotism, and British Politics: The Case of the General Election of 1900', *Journal of British Studies* 40 (2001): 107–45.

10. Peter Marsh, *Joseph Chamberlain: Entrepreneur in Politics* (New Haven, CT: Yale University Press, 1994).

11. Frans Coetzee, *For Party or Country: Nationalism and the Dilemmas of Popular Conservatism in Edwardian England* (Oxford: Oxford University Press, 1990).

12. Alfred Gollin, 'England's No Longer an Island: The Phantom Airship Scare of 1909', *Albion* 13 (1981): 43–57.

13. Halford Mackinder, 'The Geographical Pivot of History', *Geographical Journal* 23, no. 4 (April 1904): 441.

14. For the background, Charles Townshend, *The Partition: Ireland Divided, 1885–1925* (London: Allen Lane, 2021).

15. Alex Windscheffel, *Popular Conservatism in Imperial London, 1868–1906* (London: Royal Historical Society, 2007).

16. Henry Pelling, *Social Geography of British Elections, 1885–1910* (London: Macmillan, 1967), 56–58.

17. Nick Draper, "'Across the Bridges': Representations of Victorian South London', *London Journal* 29 (2004): 36.

18. For the background, Clive Emsley, *The Great British Bobby: A History of British Policing from the 18th Century to the Present* (London: Quercus, 2009).

6. HOLMES AND EMPIRE

1. Brian Blouet, *Halford Mackinder: A Biography* (College Station: Texas A & M Press, 1987). Brian Blouet has kindly told me that he is unaware of links between the two men. Daniel Deudney, 'Greater Britain or Greater Synthesis? Seeley, Mackinder, and Wells on Britain in the Global Industrial Era,' *Review of International Studies* 27 (2001): 187–208.

2. Jacqueline S. Bratton, Richard Allen Cave, Michael Pickering, Breandan Gregory and Heidi J. Holder, *Acts of Supremacy: The British Empire and the Stage, 1790–1903* (Manchester: Manchester University Press, 1991); Peter Hoffenberg, *An Empire on Display: English, Indian, and Australian Exhibitions from the Crystal Palace to the Great War* (Berkeley: University of California Press, 2001).

3. *Julian Browning Autographs and Manuscripts*, catalogue 24 (London, 2001), 7, item 55.

4. Tim Jeal, *Baden-Powell* (New Haven, CT: Yale University Press, 1989).

5. W. S. Hamer, *The British Army: Civil-Military Relations, 1885–1905* (Oxford: Oxford University Press, 1970).

6. For the BBC changing the presentation of Doyle's *The Lost World* (1912): 'BBC Will Strip Conan Doyle of Racial Overtones', *Daily Telegraph*, 12 November 2000.

7. Barbara English, 'The Kanpur Massacres in India in the Revolt of 1857', *Past and Present* 142, no. 1 (1994): 169–78.

8. Brian Robson (ed.), 'The Kandahar Letters of the Reverend Alfred Cane', *Journal of the Society for Army Historical Research* 69 (1991): 215.

9. A reference to Hell.

10. Richard Toye, *Churchill's Empire: The World that Made Him and the World He Made* (Oxford: Oxford University Press, 2010).

11. Glenn Wilkinson, *Depictions and Images of War in Edwardian Newspapers, 1899–1914* (Basingstoke: Palgrave, 2003); Peter Donaldson, *Remembering the South African War: Britain and the Memory of the Anglo-Boer War, from 1899 to the Present* (Liverpool: Liverpool University Press, 2013).

12. Duncan Bell, *The Idea of Great Britain: Empire and the Future of World Order, 1860–1900* (Princeton, NJ: Princeton University Press, 2007).

13. Julian Barnes, *Arthur and George* (London: Vintage, 2005); Shrabani Basu, *The Mystery of the Parsee Lawyer: Arthur Conan Doyle, George Edalji and the Case of the Foreigner in the English Village* (London: Bloomsbury, 2021).

14. Marilyn Lake and Henry Reynolds, *Drawing the Global Colour Line: White Men's Countries and the International Challenge of Racial Equality* (Cambridge: Cambridge University Press, 2008).

15. J. Lee Thompson, *Forgotten Patriot: A Life of Alfred, Viscount Milner of St James's and Cape Town, 1854–1925* (Madison, NJ: Fairleigh Dickinson University Press).

16. Iain Smith, *The Origins of the South African War, 1899–1902* (Harlow: Longman, 1996).

17. Joseph Kestner, *The Edwardian Detective 1901–15* (Farnham: Ashgate, 2000).

7. HOLMES AND THE AMERICAS

1. Duncan Campbell, *Unlikely Allies: Britain, America and the Origin of the Special Relationship* (London: Bloomsbury, 2007).

2. Debby Applegate, *The Most Famous Man in America: The Biography of Henry Ward Beecher* (New York: Doubleday, 2006).

3. Kris Mitchener and Marc Weidenmier, 'The Baring Crisis and the Great Latin American Meltdown of the 1890s', *Journal of Economic History* 68 (2008): 462–500.

8. HOLMES AND EUROPE

1. Arthur Marder, *The Anatomy of British Sea Power: A History of British Naval Policy in the Pre-Dreadnought Era, 1880–1905* (New York: Alfred Knopf, 1940), 578–80; Jon Sumida, *In Defence of Naval Supremacy: Finance, Technology and British Naval Policy, 1889–1914* (Annapolis, MD: Naval Institute Press, 1990); Roger Parkinson, *The Late Victorian Navy: The Pre-Dreadnought Era and the Origins of the First World War* (Woodbridge: Boydell and Brewer, 2008).

2. L. Abrams and D. J. Miller, 'Who Were the French Colonialists? A Reassessment of the *Parti Colonial*, 1890–1914,' *Historical Journal* 19 (1976): 685–725.

3. Thomas Otte, 'From "War-in-Sight" to Nearly War: Anglo-French Relations in the Age of High Imperialism, 1875–1898', *Diplomacy and Statecraft* 17 (2006): 693–714.

4. Rolf Hobson, *Imperialism at Sea: Naval Strategic Thought, the Ideology of Sea Power, and the Tirpitz Plan, 1875–1914* (Boston: Brill, 2002).

5. Maldwin Drummond, *The Riddle of the Sands* (London: Nautical Books, 1985).

6. Jon Hendrickson, *Crisis in the Mediterranean: Naval Competition and Great Power Politics, 1904–1914* (Annapolis, MD: Naval Institute Press, 2014).

7. Rhodri Williams, *Defending the Empire: The Conservative Party and British Defence Policy, 1899–1915* (New Haven, CT: Yale University Press, 1991).

8. Owen Dudley Edwards, 'Conan Doyle on Carlyle: A New Edinburgh Manuscript', *Carlyle Newsletter* 5 (Spring 1984): 28–35.

9. R. Bonnoit, *Émile Gaboriau ou la Naissance du Roman Policier* (Paris: Librairie Philosophique J. Vrin, 1985).

10. Robert Barr, *The Triumphs of Eugène Valmont* (New York: D. Appleton and Company, 1906).

9. THE LEGACY

1. In fact, 1683–1725.

2. Lisa Hopkins, 'Passing: The Irish and the Germans in the Fiction of John Buchan and Erskine Childers', *Irish Studies Review* 9 (2001): 69–80.

3. Trafalgar, 1805.

4. A reference to the Norman Conquest of 1066.

5. John Dickson Carr, *Hag's Nook* (London: Hamish Hamilton, 1933), 5. For the earlier developments and social broadening of 'Englishness', Robert Colls and Philip Dodd (eds.), *Englishness: Politics and Culture, 1880–1920* (London: Bloomsbury, 1986).

6. Christopher Frayling, *The Yellow Peril: Dr Fu Manchu and the Rise of Chinaphobia* (London: Thames and Hudson, 2014); R. Mayer, *Serial Fu Manchu: The Chinese Supervillain and the Spread of Yellow Peril Ideology* (Philadelphia: Temple University Press, 2013) and 'Machinic Fu Manchu: Popular Seriality and the Logic of Spread', *Journal of Narrative Theory* 43, no. 2 (Summer 2013): 186–217.

7. Roderick McLean, *Royalty and Diplomacy in Europe, 1890–1914* (Cambridge: Cambridge University Press, 2001).

8. Deborah Wormell, *Sir John Seeley and the Uses of History* (Cambridge: Cambridge University Press, 1980).

9. Matthew Seligmann, 'A View from Berlin: Colonel Frederick Trench and the Development of British Perceptions of German Aggressive Intent, 1906–1910', *Journal of Strategic Studies* 23 (2000): 131.

10. Arthur Conan Doyle, *Danger! and Other Stories* (London: John Murray, 1918), v.

11. Anthony Rolls, *Scarweather* (London: Geoffrey Bles, 1934), 109.

12. M. L. Sanders, 'Wellington House and British Propaganda During the First World War', *Historical Journal* 18 (1975): 119–46.

13. Keith Wilson, 'In Pursuit of the Editorship of British Documents *On the Origins of the War, 1898–1914*: J. W. Headlam-Morley before Gooch and Temperley', *Archives* 22 (1995): 83.

14. Nigel Keohane, *The Party of Patriotism: The Conservative Party and the First World War* (Farnham: Ashgate, 2010).

15. Agatha Christie, *The Man in the Brown Suit* (London: Bodley Head, 1924; 1953 edition), 117.

16. Rolls, *Scarweather*, 15.

17. Richard Whittington-Egan, *The Natural History Man: A Life of the Reverend J. G. Wood* (Malvern: Cappella Archive, 2014).

10. SEQUELS

1. Freeman Wills Croft, *The Hog's Back Mystery* (1933; London: British Library, 2015), 184–85.
2. Alan Barnes, *Sherlock Holmes on Screen: The Complete Film and TV History* (London: Titan Books, 2002).
3. Vincent Starrett, *The Private Life of Sherlock Holmes* (new edition, New York: Ottom Panzler Books, 2011), 156.
4. Julia Karolle-Berg, 'The Case of the Missing Literary Tradition: Reassessing Four Assumptions of Crime and Detective Novels in the German-Speaking World, 1900–1933', *Classical and Modern Languages and Literatures* 6 (2015), accessed 28 March 2021, https://collected.jcu.edu/cmll-facpub/6.
5. Peter Haining, *The Television Sherlock Holmes*, 2nd ed. (London: Virgin Books, 1991).
6. Sabine Vanacker and Catherine Wynne (eds.), *Sherlock Holmes and Conan Doyle: Multi-Media Afterlives* (Basingstoke: Palgrave, 2013).
7. P. D. (Phyllis Dorothy) James, *Talking about Detective Fiction* (Oxford: Oxford University Press, 2009), 31–41.
8. See, for example, Lynne Truss, *Murder by Milk Bottle* (London: Raven Books, 2020), 23.

INDEX